T0280990

JavaScript Recipes

A Problem-Solution Approach

Russ Ferguson
Keith Cirkel

Apress®

JavaScript Recipes: A Problem-Solution Approach

Russ Ferguson
Ocean, New Jersey, USA

Keith Cirkel
London, United Kingdom

ISBN-13 (pbk): 978-1-4302-6106-3
DOI 10.1007/978-1-4302-6107-0

ISBN-13 (electronic): 978-1-4302-6107-0

Library of Congress Control Number: 2016960744

Managing Director: Welmoed Spahr
Acquisitions Editor: Louise Corrigan
Technical Reviewer: Luca Mezzalira
Editorial Board: Steve Anglin, Pramila Balan, Laura Berendson, Aaron Black, Louise Corrigan, Jonathan Gennick, Todd Green, Robert Hutchinson, Celestin Suresh John, Nikhil Karkal, James Markham, Susan McDermott, Matthew Moodie, Natalie Pao, Gwenan Spearing
Coordinating Editor: Nancy Chen
Copy Editor: Kezia Endsley
Compositor: SPi Global
Indexer: SPi Global
Artist: SPi Global

Distributed to the book trade worldwide by Springer Science+Business Media New York, 233 Spring Street, 6th Floor, New York, NY 10013. Phone 1-800-SPRINGER, fax (201) 348-4505, e-mail orders-ny@springer-sbm.com, or visit www.springer.com. Apress Media, LLC is a California LLC and the sole member (owner) is Springer Science + Business Media Finance Inc (SSBM Finance Inc). SSBM Finance Inc is a **Delaware** corporation.

For information on translations, please e-mail rights@apress.com, or visit www.apress.com.

Apress and friends of ED books may be purchased in bulk for academic, corporate, or promotional use. eBook versions and licenses are also available for most titles. For more information, reference our Special Bulk Sales–eBook Licensing web page at www.apress.com/bulk-sales.

Any source code or other supplementary materials referenced by the author in this text are available to readers at www.apress.com. For detailed information about how to locate your book's source code, go to www.apress.com/source-code/. Readers can also access source code at SpringerLink in the Supplementary Material section for each chapter.

Printed on acid-free paper

This space is always reserved for my brother Rodd and my Dad.
You guys are severely missed.

—Russ

Contents at a Glance

Contents

About the Authors

Russ Ferguson is a freelance developer and instructor in the New York City area. His interest in computers goes back to Atari Basic, CompuServe, and BBS systems in the mid-1980s. For over 10 years, he has been fortunate to teach at Pratt Institute, where the subjects have been as diverse as the student body. Working in New York has given him the opportunity to work with a diverse group of companies whose projects ranged from developing real-time chat/video applications for startups to developing and managing content management systems for established Media and Advertising agencies like MTV and DC Comics.

Keith Cirkel is a JavaScript Consultant from London, United Kingdom, specializing in writing open source JavaScript libraries and literature. To find out more about his work, visit http://keithcirkel.co.uk, reach him via GitHub at github.com/keithamus, or via Twitter at twitter.com/keithamus.

About the Technical Reviewer

Luca Mezzalira is an Italian solutions architect with 13 years of experience, a Google developer expert on web technologies, and the manager of London JavaScript community (`www.londonjs.uk`). He has worked on cutting-edge projects for mobile (iOS, Android, and Blackberry), desktop, web, TVs, set-top boxes, and embedded devices.

He believes the best way to use any programming language is to master its models. He spends much of his time studying and researching topics like OOP, functional programming, and reactive programming. With these skills, he's able to swap easily between different programming languages, applying the best practices learned and driving any team to success.

In his spare time, he writes for national and international technical magazines. He has also tech reviewed for Packt Publishing, Pragmatic Bookshelf, and O'Reilly.

He was a speaker at O'Reilly media webinars, O'Reilly Solutions Architect (San Francisco), O'Reilly Oscon (London), Voxxed Days (Belgrad), JSDay (Verona), CybercomDev (Łódź), Jazoon Conference (Bern), JDays (Göteborg), Codemotion (Milan), FullStack Conference (London), React London UG (London), Node London UG (London), Scrum Gathering (Prague), Agile Cymru (Cardiff), Scotch on the rocks (Edinburgh and London), 360Max (San Francisco), PyCon (Florence), Lean Kanban Conference (London), Flash Camp (Milan), Adobe Creative Suite CS 5.5 - Launch event (Milan), HFWAA (Milan, Turin, Padua, Bari, and Florence), and Mobile World Congress (Barcelona).

Acknowledgments

There are always a lot of people to thank. Thanks to Keith for letting me help with this project. Thanks to the nice people at Apress, Nancy Chen and Louise Corrigan, who showed a great amount of patience and understanding while this was being made.

Thanks to Luca Mezzalira and James Markham, for looking this over and giving good advice.

I really do appreciate it.

CHAPTER 1

Working with JavaScript Datatypes

Assigning Variables with the var Statement

Problem

When programming (just like in algebra), you need to be able to assign a variable piece of data to a keyword that you can reference in your code, for example x = 5.

Solution

With JavaScript, variable assignment needs to be declared using a keyword, which helps to determine the behavior of a variable. The most common way to do this is with the var statement. When defining a variable, one must use the var statement to tell JavaScript you are about to declare one or more variables.

The Code

Listing 1-1. Assigning Variables with the var Statement

```
var a; // The variable "a" has been declared
var a, b; // Both the variable "a" and the variable "b" have been declared.
var a, b, c, d; // The 4 variables; "a", "b", "c" and "d" have all been declared.
var a = 1, b; // The variables "a" and "b" have been declared, and variable "a" has been
assigned the number 1 and "b" is undefined.
var a = 1, b = 2; // The variables "a" and "b" have been declared, variable "a" is assigned
to the number 1, and "b" is assigned to the number 2
```

How It Works

The JavaScript interpreter will see the var keyword, followed by a set of variable names, with optionally assigned values. It knows this is a VariableDeclaration statement, and it will declare those variables, then assign them. You can now continue to use the variable names and do not have to use their values. This is very similar to how algebra works; for example, you may say a = 5, b = a/2. You're assigning a to 5 and assigning b to half of a, which is half of 5, so b becomes 2.5. You would do this almost identically in JavaScript, but simply add the var keyword and end with a semicolon: var a = 5, b = a/2;

Electronic supplementary material The online version of this chapter (doi:10.1007/978-1-4302-6107-0_1) contains supplementary material, which is available to authorized users.

R. Ferguson and K. Cirkel, *JavaScript Recipes*, DOI 10.1007/978-1-4302-6107-0_1

Solving Errors with Variable Names

Problem

You attempted to declare a variable, but during runtime your code throws an Error, not letting you assign that variable name. You are presented with one of the following errors:

```
SyntaxError: Unexpected token <name>
SyntaxError: Unexpected number
SyntaxError: Unexpected string
SyntaxError: Unexpected reserved word
SyntaxError: missing variable name
SyntaxError: <name> is a reserved identifier
SyntaxError: Use of reserved word '<name>'
SyntaxError: Expected an identifier but found '<name>' instead
SyntaxError: The use of a keyword for an identifier is invalid
SyntaxError: Expected identifier
SyntaxError: Expected string '<name>'
SyntaxError: Expected number '<name>'
SyntaxError: Expected an identifier but found '<name>' instead
```

Solution

Variable names have a strict set of rules. You must **not** pick a variable name that is a keyword (these are words already used in the language) or a reserved word (these are words which are reserved for future use), or literal values (the value of a literal, such as true or null). The full list of reserved words is shown in Table 1-1.

Table 1-1. *Reserved Keywords in JavaScript*

break	case	catch	class	const	continue
debugger	default	delete	do	else	enum
export	extends	false	finally	for	function
if	implements	import	in	Infinity	instanceof
interface	let	NaN	new	null	package
private	protected	public	return	static	super
switch	this	throw	true	try	typeof
undefined	var	void	while	with	yield

In addition to having a set of reserved words, JavaScript has some other rules around variable naming. They can include numbers, but cannot start with a number (this would confuse them with number literals, discussed later in this chapter in longer detail in Chapter 4), they also cannot contain any spaces. Generally speaking though, the names of JavaScript variables are quite flexible—perhaps too flexible, for example you could use "ಠ_ಠ" as a variable name (but please don't). As a good rule of thumb, it is recommended you name your variables using the English Alphabet (A-Z), avoid the use of numbers, and use camelCasing for multiple word variables.

camelCasing is where each word is given a capital letter, except for the first word. The rest of the letters are lowercase. For example if you had a variable called Number of Days, in camelCase that would be numberOfDays. As another example, a variable called Cache Control would be cacheControl. Examples of camelCasing in the real world are brands like *iPhone* or *eBay*.

While you should use camelCasing for variable names, there are a few exceptions to this best practice rule. One is with *constructors* (functions that create new objects with the new keyword), which should use TitleCase (camelCase but with a capital first letter). Another is constants, which should be UPPERCASE_WITH_UNDERSCORES. Of course, all of these are best practices, and so can be disobeyed, but it is strongly recommended to use them.

It is very important to note that JavaScript variable names are case sensitive, that is byteLength is a different variable than ByteLength, which is a different variable than BYTE_LENGTH and so on. This is why it is vitally important to stick to a good naming convention for your variables. It can be very easy to get caught by inconsistent naming schemes, and spend hours debugging code only to find your variable was missing an uppercase character.

The Code

Listing 1-2. Rules for Variable Names

```
var break = 3; // Raises a `SyntaxError: Unexpected token break`
var brake = 3; // This is fine, because "brake" is not a Reserved Keyword
var π = 3.1415926; // This works, but can be irritating to use
var ಠ_ಠ = eval; // This works, but can be irritating to use
var numberOfDays = 3; // This is an ideal, readable camelCase variable name that isn't a
reserved word!
```

How It Works

JavaScript needs to impose limits on variable names, otherwise you could accidentally override language features and functions. Some other languages, such as PHP, get around this by forcing you to prefix every variable name with a $ sign; however, this becomes very limiting, so most languages including JavaScript simply disallow a small subset of variable names. Some reserved words are not used in the language today, such as enum, but are intended to be included in the future and so become reserved as placeholders, to prevent use.

Solving Reference Errors When Declaring Variables Inside a Function's Scope

Problem

You have attempted to declare a variable inside a function's scope, but during runtime your code throws a ReferenceError, not letting you use that variable, or if you're not using strict mode, your variables are *undefined*. Alternatively you've tried to assign a variable without using the var keyword. You have been presented with one of the following errors:

```
ReferenceError: <name> is not defined
ReferenceError: assignment to undeclared variable <name>
ReferenceError: Can't find variable: <name>
```

Solution

JavaScript features something called "variable scopes." Every time a variable is declared, it is given a "scope." Variables declared with the var keyword can only be used in the function containing them—that is to say, they are given the scope of that function. There is an additional global scope, which contains all variables that aren't contained in functions. Variables cannot be used outside of their scope. The solution is to move them to a higher scope, i.e., out of the function. Look closely at the following examples.

The Code

Listing 1-3. Global Variables and the Notion of Scope

```
function foo() { // This is a Function, which var a is wrapped in
    var a = 3; // declare variable `a` inside foo()s scope.
}
console.log(a); // Raises `ReferenceError: a is not defined` (in strict mode, returns
undefined otherwise)
foo();
console.log(a); // Raises `ReferenceError: a is not defined` (in strict mode, returns
undefined otherwise)

var a = 3; // declare variable `a` in the global scope
function foo() {
    a = 4; // reference the variable `a` from the global scope
}
console.log(a); // logs 3, because the variable `a` was declared in the global scope,
outside of any function scopes
foo();
console.log(a); // logs 4, because the function foo(); took the globally scoped `a` and
changed it to 4

var a = 3; // declare variable `a` in the global scope
function foo() {
    var a = 4; // declare variable `a` in foo()s scope, without touching the globally scoped `a`
}
console.log(a); // logs 3, because the variable `a` was declared in the global scope,
outside of any function scopes
foo();
console.log(a); // logs 3, because foo() declared its own `a` variable inside its own scope,
and so modified the variable belonging to foo, not the global one
```

How It Works

Each function is given a "scope" or "sandbox," so that it can manage its own variables without overriding or leaking its own variables into the global scope. Variables inside of a function's scope cannot be used outside of the function, or in other functions; this is very useful because it avoids conflicting variable names. If my function has a variable named length and so does yours, we don't want to override each others variables with different values, so they are scoped for protection.

Function scoped variables also have an important use—they only live as long as the function runs, meaning they are cleaned from memory as soon as the function finishes. This is a very useful trick but can trip a lot of beginners up, so be careful and think hard about where you use your variables. The basic principle of scoping is similar to a "tree." It begins with the root scope, and with each new function, a new "function scope" branch is created, functions inside functions are branches of branches, and the whole thing goes on indefinitely. Consider the code in Listing 1-4.

Listing 1-4. A "Functional Scope" Example

```
function foo() {
    var a = 1;
    function bar() {
        var b = 2;
        function baz() {
            console.log(a, b);
        }
    }
}

function bing() {
    var a = 1;
    function boo() {
        console.log(a);
    }
}
```

This code can be expressed as a tree of scopes (see Figure 1-1).

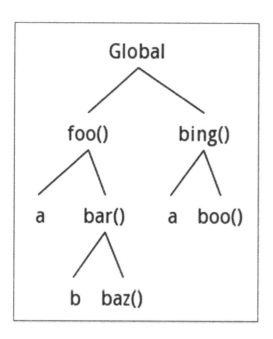

Figure 1-1. *A "functional scope" tree of Listing 1-4*

From the Figure 1-1, you can see the global scope holds the two functions: foo() and bing(). foo() has its own scope, which holds the a variable and the bar() function. bar() has its own scope, containing b and baz(). bing() has its own scope, containing a and boo().

It is important to note that the scope has an upwards chain, meaning baz() can access its sibling, b, as well as its parents bar(), a, and foo(). Similarly, boo() can access its sibling a and its parent bing(). However, this chain does not flow in the opposite direction, so foo() cannot access bar()'s scope of b and baz() (it can, of course, access its own scope of a and bar()). This is a pretty contrived example, but real-world codebases can have much larger and more complex scope chains than this.

Assigning Variables with the Let Statement

░ **Caution**   The let statement is an ECMAScript 6 (ES6, the new standard of JavaScript) feature. Older browsers still in use, such as Internet Explorer 10 and below or Safari 7 and below, do not support this feature (they work with the older ECMAScript 5 or ES5 standard).

Problem

When using a variable, you want its life to be shorter than the functional scope. For example, you'd like the variables life to exist within an if statement.

Solution

Not only does JavaScript have a "functional scope," it also has another level of scope, called "block scope." Block scoped variables offer the same semantics as function scoped variables, in that they are locked to a block, they cannot be accessed outside of a block, and they are removed from memory as soon as the block finishes executing. A block is delimited by braces ({...}), and each new set of braces is a new block scope.

The Code

Listing 1-5. Assigning Variables with the Let Statement

```
let a = 4; // The variable "a" has been declared and assigned to `4`
{
    let b = 2; // The variable "b" has been declared and assigned to `2`
    console.log(b); // Logs 2
}
if (a === 4) { // For more on the Strict Equality Operator (`===`), see Chapter 2-10
    let a = 1; // The variable "a" has been redeclared in this block scope (the braces)
    console.log(a); // Logs 1
}
console.log(b); // Raises a ReferenceError in strict mode, or logs undefined
console.log(a); // Logs 4, the `let a = 1` in the block scope above was only associated with
that block scope
```

How It Works

The JavaScript interpreter will see the let keyword, followed by a set of variable names, with optionally assigned values. It then creates each of these keywords as a variable, for the life of the "block scope." It follows the same semantics as var, with the exception that it is tied to the block scope, not the function scope. Let variables also have another trick up their sleeve. When used in an if statement, or a for or while loop, the let variable is bound to the attached block, even though it is not inside the block itself. Take, for example, the code in Listing 1-6.

Listing 1-6. Letting Variables Block

```
for (let i = 0, i < 4; ++i) {
    console.log(i); // Logs 0, 1, 2, and 3
}
console.log(i); // Raises a ReferenceError in strict mode, or logs undefined

// Swap two variables:
var a = 1, b = 2;
{
    let temp = a;
    a = b;
    b = temp;
}
console.log(a, b, typeof temp); // logs '2, 1, undefined'
```

This is useful because it provides another scoping layer for variables. Variables using the var keyword are accessible to the whole function's scope. For temporary variables, such as the i in a loop (which get thrown away as soon as the loop is done) the variable would normally hang around until the end of the function's life, which can be a nuisance. With a let variable this is very effectively solved, as the let variable only exists for the life of the loop, and is then nicely cleaned up. You can also apply this by using blocks to encapsulate temporary variables, such as the second example in Listing 1-6.

Assigning Constants with the Const Statement

■ **Caution** The const statement is an ECMAScript 6 (ES6, the new standard of JavaScript) feature. Older browsers still in use, such as Internet Explorer 10 and below, Safari 7 and below, and Firefox 13 and below do not support this feature (they work to the older ECMAScript 5, or ES5 standard).

Problem

You want to use a variable, but you want to ensure that it is not overridden by a new value later on in the code.

Solution

The var and let statements certainly have their uses, but both are vulnerable to being unexpectedly overridden in the life of running code. Luckily, the const statement provides you with a way of declaring a variable that is immutable; that is, it will always be assigned to its initial value, and cannot be changed, cannot be "mutated". It is a constant. One of the things to keep in mind is that objects can be updated. Constants only work with primitive values.

The Code

Listing 1-7. Assigning Constants with the Const Statement

```
var A = 3;
let B = 3;
const C = 3;
A = 4; B = 4; C = 4;
console.log(A, B, C); // Logs 4, 4, 3. `C`s value doesn't change, as it is a `const`.
```

How It Works

The JavaScript interpreter will see the const keyword, followed by a set of constant names, with assigned values, and set those values to the constants as read-only (immutable). It follows the same semantics as let, including using block scoping just like let, with the exceptions that it can never be reassigned to a new value (it is immutable), and that it must be initially assigned to a value.

It is important to note that constants can never be declared without a value; this will cause a SyntaxError. Constants must always have a value assigned to them upon declaration.

Listing 1-8. Attempting to Declare Constants Without Assigning Them

```
const a; // Raises a SyntaxError (some browsers which have misinterpreted the ES6 spec may
not raise this)
const a = 3; // Works as expected
```

The spec is somewhat unclear about what precisely to do when a const is declared but not assigned, as a result, some browsers will not raise the SyntaxError, and the constant is permanently set to undefined, which is obviously pretty useless.

Creating and Using Literals

▓ **Caution**   Template string literals are an ECMAScript 6 (ES6, the new standard of JavaScript) feature. Older browsers still in use, such as Internet Explorer 11 and below, Safari 7 and below do not support this feature (they work to the older ECMAScript 5, or ES5 standard). In fact, at the time of writing only the Taceur Compiler tool could support template string literals. Check http://kangax.github.io/es5-compat-table/es6/ for the current compatibility charts.

Problem

You want to create literal values of different types in JavaScript; for example, you want to create a piece of text (string), or perhaps a number, or even a list of items (an array).

Solution

Literals are types of data that can be defined without explicitly creating some kind of object or instance. A literal can be a string (i.e., a piece of text), a decimal (base-10, 0-9), binary (base-2, 0-1), hexadecimal (base-16, 0-F), or octal (base-8, 0-7) number, a Boolean (true or false), an array (a list of other literals), an object (a named list of other literals), a regular expression (a complex text matching function), a function (a piece of code that can be repeatedly called), a template string (similar to a string, but replaces variable names with their values), as well as some standalone "primitive" values such as null and undefined. Each literal has a unique piece of syntax to denote its type, with perhaps the exception of decimal numbers.

The Code

Listing 1-9. Literals

```
'this is a string'; // A String literal (using Single Quotes)
"this is another string"; // A String literal (using Double Quotes)
true; // A Boolean literal
false; // A Boolean literal
3; // A Number literal
3.1415926; // Another Number literal
0b0101; // A Binary Number literal
0xFFF; // A Hexadecimal Number literal
0o888; // An Octal Number literal
[]; // An (empty) Array literal
[ 1, 2, 3, ]; // An Array literal populated with 3 Number literals
[ 'hello', 'world']; // An Array literal populated with 2 String literals
{}; // An (empty) Object literal
{ first: 1, second: 2 }; // An Object literal populated with 2 Number literals, named
"first" and "second"
/abc/; // A Regular Expression literal
/^\w{3,4}$/g; // A more complex Regular Expression literal
function () {}; // A Function literal
function foo() {}; // A named Function literal
null; // The null literal
undefined; // The undefined literal
`this is a template string`; // A Template String literal
`Hello #{name}
How are you?`; // A more complex Template String literal
```

How It Works

The JavaScript interpreter will see each piece of unique syntax at the start of a literal; for example, a single/double quote for a string. It understands the specific rules around these and essentially creates that value as a literal instance of that type. The literals also borrow all properties from their "prototypes," for example everything you can do with new String('hello') you can also do with hello. Each of these literals can be assigned to a variable, or put inside an array or object. Each one has its own properties and attributes—you need to deal with each one in a different way. Chapters 3-15 guide you through how to utilize each of these types properly.

Creating Types Using Their Constructors

Problem

You want to be able to create literals more programmatically.

Solution

Some literals can also be created as instances from their constructor functions, with the new keyword. These instances allow for finer control of how they are created; however, it should be noted that some of these instances have very subtle differences to their literal counterparts. More about this later.

The Code

Listing 1-10. Literals versus Their Constructors

```
'hello'; // A String literal (using Single Quotes)
new String('hello'); // A String created from its constructor

[ 1, 2, 3 ]; // An Array literal with 3 Number literal values
new Array(1,2,3); // An Array created from its constructor
new Array(5); // An Array populated with 5 undefined values

/abc/; // A Regular Expression literal
new RegExp('abc'); // A Regular Expression created from its constructor
/^\w{3,4}$/g; // A more complex Regular Expression literal
new RegExp('^\\w{3,4}$', 'g'); // A more complex Regular Expression literal created from its
constructor

function () { return 1 }; // A Function literal
new Function('return 1'); // A Function created from its constructor

{}; // An empty Object literal
new Object(); // An empty Object created from its constructor
```

How It Works

JavaScript contains constructor functions, which relate to each literal. Some of these allow you to invoke them manually, which can be useful for creating these objects programmatically, especially arrays and regular expressions. You should be aware that there are subtle differences between creating instances from the constructor functions and their literal counterparts, and you should always use the literal notation over constructors, unless you have a very specific reason for using the constructors. Constructors with the `new` keyword will actually create objects of that particular datatype, which is different than how literals work. This means, for example, `typeof new String("hi")` is equal to `object`, while `typeof "hi"` is equal to `"string"`. While the `Boolean(0)` or `Boolean("")` will equal `false`, `Boolean(new Number(0))` or `Boolean(new String(""))` will equal `true`. More details about the differences between these are featured in the later chapters for each datatype.

Determine If a Variable Has Been Defined Using an Equality Operator

Problem

You want to determine if the variable you have created is defined.

Solution

A variable is `undefined` when it has been declared but has not been assigned a value, or the assigned value is the `undefined` literal. Just imagine that when you are declaring variables that you're making an entry in a dictionary. Every word (variable) that you use in JavaScript is `undefined` until you assign it a definition or value. The same holds true for function return values: if a function has no `return` statement, or if the `return` statement is used without specifying a value (i.e., `return;`), then the `return` value has not been defined and will therefore be the `undefined` literal.

The Code

Listing 1-11. Determining if a Variable Has Been Defined Using an Equality Operator

```
var a; // The Variable "a" has been declared but it
       // hasn't been assigned a definition.

var b = 5; // The variable "b" has been declared and
           // assigned the number 5 as it's definition.

if (a === undefined) { // For more on the Strict Equality Operator (`===`), see Chapter 2-10
  console.log("Variable 'a' is undefined");
} else {
  console.log("Variable 'a' is defined");
}
```

```
if (b === undefined) { // For more on the Strict Equality Operator (`===`), see Chapter 2-10
   console.log("Variable 'b' is undefined");
} else {
   console.log("Variable 'b' is defined");
}
```

The output is:

```
Variable 'a' is undefined
Variable 'b' is defined
```

How It Works

Variable a has been declared but has not been assigned a value (a definition). A variable that has not been assigned a value is automatically assigned the undefined literal. Variable b has been declared and is defined as the numeric value 5. The first if statement compares variable a to the undefined primitive value. Because variable a has not been defined, the comparison is true and the message Variable 'a' is undefined is displayed. On the other hand, variable b was defined so the same comparison to the undefined primitive value fails and the message Variable 'b' is defined is displayed.

Determining If a Variable Has Been Declared Using typeof( )

Problem

You test a variable to see if it is undefined using an equality operator and your script throws an exception because the variable has never been declared.

Solution

The typeof operator can be used to determine if a type is undefined. It returns a string indicating the type of the operand, but does not throw an error if the variable has never been declared.

The Code

Listing 1-12. Determining If a Variable Has Been Declared Using typeof

```
// The declaration for variable a is commented out,
// therefore a has not been declared.

var a, b = 4;

if (typeof a === 'undefined') { // For more on the Strict Equality Operator (`===`), see
Chapter 2-10
         console.log("Variable 'a' is undefined");
}
```

```
if (typeof b === 'undefined') { // For more on the Strict Equality Operator (`===`), see
Chapter 2-10
        console.log("Variable 'b' is undefined");
}
```

The output is:

```
Variable 'a' is undefined
```

How It Works

Using the typeof operator is useful if a variable's declaration status is not known, or for checking its value if it has been declared. By asserting if a variable is undefined using typeof variable === 'undefined', you can safely see if a variable has a value, without causing a ReferenceError.

Determining If a Function Defines and Returns a Value

Problem

You are using a function to perform a task and need to determine if the return value has been defined, once the operation is complete.

Solution

All functions return a value whether the original developer intended it or not. If a value was defined and passed back to the function caller, it can be assigned to a variable or used directly. A function returns undefined if a value was not returned, or the return statement inside a function is empty.

The Code

Listing 1-13. Determining If a Function Defines and Returns a Value

```
// A function with an empty return-statement
// returns undefined
function function1() {
        return;
}

// A function with no return-statement
// returns undefined
function function2() {
}

function function3() {
        return 2 + 2;
}
```

```
function function4() {
        return true;
}

function function5() {
        return {};
}

var fn1 = function1();
console.log("Function1 returns: " + fn1);        // undefined

var fn2 = function2();
console.log("Function2 returns: " + fn2);        // undefined

var fn3 = function3();
console.log("Function3 returns: " + fn3);        // 4

var fn4 = function4();
console.log("Function4 returns: " + fn4);        // true

var fn5 = function5();
console.log("Function5 returns: " + fn5);        // Object{}

// Test the return value of function1
if ( function1() === undefined ) { // For more on the Strict Equality Operator (`===`), see
Chapter 2-10
        console.log( "Function 1 returns undefined." );
}
else {
        console.log( "Function 1 returns a value other than undefined." );
}

// Test the return value of function2
if ( function2() === undefined ) { // For more on the Strict Equality Operator (`===`), see
Chapter 2-10
        console.log( "Function 2 returns undefined." );
}
else {
        console.log( "Function 2 returns a value other than undefined." );
}

// Test the return value of function3
if ( function3() === undefined ) { // For more on the Strict Equality Operator (`===`), see
Chapter 2-10
        console.log( "Function 3 returns undefined." );
}
else {
        console.log( "Function 3 returns a value other than undefined." );
}
```

```
// Test the return value of function4
if ( function4() === undefined ) { // For more on the Strict Equality Operator (`===`), see
Chapter 2-10
        console.log( "Function 4 returns undefined." );
}
else {
        console.log( "Function 4 returns a value other than undefined." );
}

// Test the return value of function5
if ( function5() === undefined ) { // For more on the Strict Equality Operator (`===`), see
Chapter 2-10
        console.log( "Function 5 returns undefined." );
}
else {
        console.log( "Function 5 returns a value other than undefined." );
}
```

The output is:

```
Function1 returns: undefined
Function2 returns: undefined
Function3 returns: 4
Function4 returns: true
Function5 returns: [object Object]
Function 1 returns undefined.
Function 2 returns undefined.
Function 3 returns a value other than undefined.
Function 4 returns a value other than undefined.
Function 5 returns a value other than undefined.
```

How It Works

Five functions are defined; the first two return undefined. Function 1 explicitly returns undefined by using an empty return statement. Function 2 returns undefined implicitly by not using the return statement at all. Just as we can test the value of a variable, we can test the return value of a function using an equality operator. In many cases, functions' return values can be treated like variables. A function's return value can be printed to the console or used otherwise. Note that because a function is already declared, its return value is implicitly declared too—so checking the return value of a function will never raise ReferenceError, unlike variables, which may if they're undeclared.

Determining If a Defined Variable Has a Value Using Equality Operators

Problem

You know a variable has been previously defined but aren't certain if its value is null or if it has another value.

Solution

You can use the equality operators to test for null values just like you test for undefined variables. null is an object and has only one value in JavaScript, null. A variable that is assigned null contains no valid data of the types Array, Boolean, String, Number, Date, Template String, or Object. When you want to declare a variable and initialize it, but do not want to give it value, just assign it the value null. This is useful if you need to declare a variable now but must wait for an operation to complete before assigning a value to the variable. Such cases may include number crunching or waiting for a response from a server. If the operation fails, the variable will remain null and this failure can be detected with code.

The Code

Listing 1-14. Determining If a Defined Variable Has a Value Using Equality Operators

```
// myvar is undefined
var myvar = undefined;
if ( myvar === undefined) { // For more on the Strict Equality Operator (`===`), see Chapter
2-10
        console.log("myvar is undefined");
}
if ( myvar === null) { // For more on the Strict Equality Operator (`===`), see Chapter 2-10
        console.log("myvar is null");
}

// myvar is null
var myvar = null;
if ( myvar === undefined) { // For more on the Strict Equality Operator (`===`), see Chapter 2-10
        console.log("myvar is undefined");
}
if ( myvar === null) { // For more on the Strict Equality Operator (`===`), see Chapter 2-10
        console.log("myvar is null");
}

var myvar = null;

// Determine if myvar is null using the bang (!) operator
if ( !myvar ) {
        console.log("The variable myvar is null or undefined");
} else {
        console.log("The variable myvar is not null or undefined");
}
```

The output is:

```
myvar is undefined
myvar is null
The variable myvar is null or undefined
```

How It Works

Because null is *falsey* (it is equivalent to false when coerced to a Boolean), we can determine if a variable is null by using the bang operator (!) to perform a logical NOT operation. In other words, we're asking if the variable myvar is "not false," meaning true. This is the simplest (shortest code) technique for determining if a variable is null.

Performing Operations If a Defined Variable Has a Value

Problem

You need to perform different operations based on the value of a variable. You may need to test that a variable is strictly equal, simply equivalent, or strictly not equal to a value.

Solution

As we have done in previous sections, we will use comparison operators to detect the value of a variable and then branch to specific code blocks based on the value of the if statements.

The Code

Listing 1-15. Performing Operations If a Defined Variable Has a Value

```
var myNumber = 10;

// Determine if myNumber is equivalent to the number 10
if ( myNumber === 10 ) { // For more on the Strict Equality Operator (`===`), see Chapter 2-10
        console.log( "myNumber equals 10");
}
else {
        console.log( "myNumber is not equal to 10");
}

// Determine if myNumber is less than the number 10
if ( myNumber < 10 ) {
        console.log( "myNumber is less than 10");
}
else {
        console.log( "myNumber is equal to or greater than 10");
}

// Determine if myNumber is less than or equal to the number 10
if ( myNumber <= 10 ) {
        console.log( "myNumber is less than or equal to 10");
}
else {
        console.log( "myNumber is greater than 10");
}
```

```
// Determine if myNumber is greater than the number 10
if ( myNumber > 10 ) {
        console.log( "myNumber is greater than 10");
}
else {
        console.log( "myNumber is less than or equal to 10");
}

// Determine if myNumber is greater than or equal to the number 10
if ( myNumber >= 10 ) {
        console.log( "myNumber is greater than or equal to 10");
}
else {
        console.log( "myNumber is less than 10");
}
```

The output is:

```
myNumber equals 10
myNumber is equal to or greater than 10
myNumber is less than or equal to 10
myNumber is greater than or equal to 10
```

How It Works

Flow control of a script is very important to all programmers. Most scripts except the simplest of examples will have flow control of some kind. This example uses if statements to compare a variable to a fixed numeric value. If the comparison is true, the first code block below the comparison is executed. If the comparison is false, that block is not executed, and the next block is compared. else blocks are executed if no other blocks in the whole if statement were true. We will take an in-depth look at expressions in Chapter 2.

What's the Difference Between Null and Undefined?

Problem

When working with an unfamiliar variable, you are uncertain if the variable is null or undefined and don't know how to test the variable before working with it.

Solution

A variable is undefined only when the variable is declared but not assigned a value, or the variable has been explicitly assigned the undefined value. A variable is null only when it has been assigned the null value. This being the case, we can easily detect undefined and null variables as shown in the example. This makes null useful for explicitly representing a no-value variable, rather than a not-yet-defined variable, for example, in a function's return statement.

The Code

Listing 1-16. The Difference Between Null and Undefined

```
var a;
var b = null;

if ( typeof a === 'undefined' ) { // For more on the Strict Equality Operator (`===`), see Chapter 2-10
        console.log( "Variable a is undefined" );
}

if ( a === null ) { // For more on the Strict Equality Operator (`===`), see Chapter 2-10
        console.log( "Variable a is null" );
}

if ( typeof b === 'undefined' ) { // For more on the Strict Equality Operator (`===`), see Chapter 2-10
        console.log( "Variable b is undefined" );
}

if ( b === null ) { // For more on the Strict Equality Operator (`===`), see Chapter 2-10
        console.log( "Variable b is null" );
}
```

The output is:

```
Variable a is undefined
Variable b is null
```

How It Works

The typeof operator is used again as a more error-proof method of determining the type of a variable. The typeof operator returns a string label for the variable type. The operator will return the string undefined for any variable that is truly undefined.

Coercing a Boolean Variable Using the Boolean Constructor

Problem

There are many cases where you will need to coerce an existing value into a Boolean true or false value for use in an if statement or other condition statements.

Solution

Strings, numeric types, arrays, and objects can have an unlimited number of values, but the Boolean datatype can only have two: either true or false. A Boolean value indicates whether a condition, like those in an if statement, is true or not. The Boolean constructor can be used to convert any values passed into it to their Boolean equivalent.

The example in Listing 1-17 demonstrates coercion from various types into Boolean. Notice that we are not invoking a new Boolean—new Boolean()—we are instead using the Boolean constructor as a function—Boolean()—to coerce the given value into a Boolean primitive.

The Code

Listing 1-17. Coercing a Boolean Variable Using a Boolean Constructor

```
console.log( Boolean(-0) ); // logs false
console.log( Boolean(0) ); // logs false
console.log( Boolean(new Number(0)) ); // logs true
console.log( Boolean(1) ); // logs true
console.log( Boolean(NaN) ); // logs false
console.log( Boolean(-1) ); // logs true

console.log( Boolean(false) ); // logs false
console.log( Boolean(true) ); // logs true

console.log( Boolean(undefined) ); // logs false
console.log( Boolean(null) ); // logs false

console.log( Boolean(new String()) ); // logs true
console.log( Boolean("") ); // logs false
console.log( Boolean('a string') ); // logs true
console.log( Boolean("true") ); // logs true
console.log( Boolean("false") ); // logs true

console.log( Boolean(function () {}) ); // logs true
console.log( Boolean({}) ); // logs true
console.log( Boolean([]) ); // logs true
```

How It Works

The Boolean constructor can take a single parameter and will convert it to a Boolean value internally based on the ToBoolean internal function, as part of the ECMAScript spec (specifically, section 7.1.2 of the ES6 spec, or 9.2 of the ES5 spec). If the value is 0, -0, null, false, NaN, undefined, or an empty string (''), the ToBoolean internal function will convert these to a value of false. The Boolean constructor, when used without new will simply reuse the underlying ToBoolean internal logic, as does the bang operator (!) and other logical operators, such as AND (&&) and OR (||).

Determining If a Boolean Variable Is Initialized

Problem

You need to test a variable to determine if it is a Boolean or other datatype and determine if the Boolean variable has been initialized.

Solution

Using the typeof operator, we can determine the datatype of a variable. If the variable is a Boolean value, typeof will return the string 'boolean'.

The Code

Listing 1-18. Determining If a Boolean Variable Is Initialized

```
var a = Boolean(true);
var b = false;
var c = "";
var d = new Date();

if ( typeof a === 'boolean' ) { // For more on the Strict Equality Operator (`===`), see Chapter 2-10
        console.log("a is a Boolean");
} else {
        console.log("a is not a Boolean");
}

if ( typeof b === 'boolean' ) { // For more on the Strict Equality Operator (`===`), see Chapter 2-10
        console.log("b is a Boolean");
} else {
        console.log("b is not a Boolean");
}

if ( typeof c === 'boolean' ) { // For more on the Strict Equality Operator (`===`), see Chapter 2-10
        console.log("c is a Boolean");
} else {
        console.log("c is not a Boolean");
}

if ( typeof d === 'boolean' ) { // For more on the Strict Equality Operator (`===`), see
Chapter 2-10
        console.log("d is a Boolean");
} else {
        console.log("d is not a Boolean");
}
```

The output is:

```
a is a Boolean
b is a Boolean
c is not a Boolean
d is not a Boolean
```

How It Works

The typeof operator returns the string value Boolean for Boolean objects. To determine if a variable is a Boolean, all we need to do is strictly compare the return value of the typeof operator to the string 'boolean'. Other datatypes, such as strings and numbers, return different strings that represent them.

Valid Representations of the False and True Values

Problem

You need to make a Boolean decision based on the value of a variable that is neither true nor false.

Solution

There are only two Boolean values: true and false. However, many different types such as numbers, strings, null, and undefined can be coerced to Boolean. if statements, switch statements, for statements, and while statements all coerce their given values to Booleans.

The Code

Listing 1-19. Valid Representations of the False and True Values

```
// If statements internally convert the given condition or value into Boolean values.
if (0) {
    console.log( "0 is true");
} else {
        console.log("0 is false");
}

if (-0) {
    console.log( "-0 is true" );
} else {
        console.log("-0 is false");
}

if (null) {
    console.log( "null is true" );
} else {
        console.log("null is false");
}

if (false) {
    console.log( "false is true" );
} else {
        console.log("false is false");
}

if (NaN) {
    console.log( "NaN is true" );
} else {
```

```
        console.log("NaN is false");
}

if (undefined) {
    console.log( "undefined is true" );
} else {
        console.log("undefined is false");
}
if ("") {
    console.log( "Empty String is true" );
} else {
        console.log("Empty String is false");
}
// Variable b holds the outcome of the comparison
// between Variable 'a' and the number 1.
var a = 1;
b = (a === 1);    // true
if ( b ) {
    console.log("Variable b is true");
} else {
    console.log("Variable b is false");
}

// Examples of conditional or comparative expressions
var c = 1 + 2;
var d = null;
var e = a - 3;
var f = undefined;

if (c) {
        console.log("Variable c is true");
} else {
        console.log("Variable c is false");
}

if (d) {
        console.log("Variable d is true");
} else {
        console.log("Variable d is false");
}

if (e) {
        console.log("Variable e is true");
} else {
        console.log("Variable e is false");
}

if (f) {
        console.log("Variable f is true");
} else {
        console.log("Variable f is false");
}
```

The output is:

```
0 is false
-0 is false
null is false
false is false
NaN is false
undefined is false
Empty String is false
Variable b is true
Variable c is true
Variable d is false
Variable e is true
Variable f is false
```

How It Works

Every statement that expects a condition (if, switch, for, and while) will automatically coerce the given value into a Boolean (using the internal ToBoolean method described in Listing 1-14). If the Boolean value returned is false, the condition fails and the statement (if, switch, for, and while) is skipped. If the value is true then the block inside the statement is executed.

Coercing a String Using the String Constructor

Problem

You want to create a string representation of another value.

Solution

The string constructor takes a single parameter and will automatically convert that value into a string literal.

The Code

Listing 1-20. Coercing a String Using the String Constructor

```
String("hello world"); // The String "hello world"
String(1); // The String "1"
String(false); // The String "false"
String(true); // The String "true"
String({}); // The String "[object Object]"
String([1,2,3]); // The String "1,2,3"
String(function foo() {}); // The String "function foo() {}"String(0b0101); // The String "5"
String(/abc/); // The String "/abc/"
String(undefined); // The String "undefined"
String(null); // The String "null"
// String casting can be overridden by providing the toString() method
String({ toString: function () { return 'hi!'; } }); // The String "hi!"
String({ toString: function () { return false; } }); // The String "false"
```

How It Works

Similarly to the Boolean constructor, the string constructor can also coerce values into its literal type. The ECMAScript spec contains an internal ToString function (ES6 section 7.1.12, ES5 section 9.8), which is used by the string constructor. It converts undefined to "undefined", null to "null", true to "true", false to "false" and number values to the string version of that number.

For other values, it checks to see if there is a toString method attached to the value. If there is one, it will use the resulting value, coerced as a string, meaning the string constructor will always return a string. Arrays have a toString function on their prototype which simply calls Array.prototype.join(',')—this is explained in Chapter 6. Using the toString method is a powerful feature of JavaScript, as it allows you to create your own objects, which can coerce to a string in a customized way.

Determining If a Variable Is a String

Problem

You need to test a variable to determine if it is a string or other datatype.

Solution

Using the typeof operator, we can determine the datatype of a variable. If the variable is a string value, typeof will return the string "string".

The Code

Listing 1-21. Determining If a Variable Is a String

```
var a = String("I'm a String Object");
var b = "I'm a string literal";
var c = 7;
var d = new Date();

if ( typeof a === 'string' ) {
        console.log("a is a String");
} else {
        console.log("a is not a String");
}

if ( typeof b === 'string' ) {
        console.log("b is a String");
} else {
        console.log("b is not a String");
}

if ( typeof c === 'string' ) {
        console.log("c is a String");
} else {
        console.log("c is not a String");
}
```

```
if ( typeof d === 'string' ) {
        console.log("d is a String");
} else {
        console.log("d is not a String");
}
```

The output is:

```
a is a String
b is a String
c is not a String
d is not a String
```

How It Works

The typeof operator returns the value "string" for string objects and literals. To determine if a variable is a string, all you need to do is compare the return value of the typeof operator to "string". Other datatypes such as objects and numbers return different strings that represent them.

Coercing a Numeric Value Using the Number Constructor

Problem

Sometimes you have numbers being represented as strings in your application. How can you convert these strings into actual number literals so you can use them effectively?

Solution

The number constructor takes a single parameter and will automatically convert a string parameter into a number.

The Code

Listing 1-22. Coercing a Numeric Value Using the Number Constructor

```
var strNumber = "3.14159265";
var myNumber = Number(strNumber);

console.log("mynumber = " + myNumber);
console.log("mynumber type is " + typeof myNumber);
console.log("2 * mynumber = " + (2 * myNumber));
```

The output is:

```
mynumber = 3.14159265
mynumber type is number
2 * mynumber = 6.2831853
```

How It Works

The number constructor will attempt to convert its only parameter into a numeric value. If that is not possible, the number object will be initialized to NaN (Not a Number).

Creating a Numeric Value Using Number Literals

■ **Caution** Binary and octal notation are ECMAScript 6 (ES6) features. Older browsers still in use, such as Internet Explorer 11 and below and Safari 7 and below, do not support this feature (they work to the ECMAScript 5, or ES5 spec).

Problem

Not all numeric values in your application will come from your user or external data. In many cases you will need to use literal or hard-coded mathematical expressions in your script.

Solution

JavaScript represents numbers using the double-precision 64-bit IEEE 754 floating-point standard. The JavaScript Number object represents all numbers as floating-point values, meaning there is no internal difference between Integers (whole numbers) and floating-point numbers.

Floating-point numbers contain a decimal portion and may be expressed in scientific notation. Also known as "E notation," this represents "times ten raised to the power of". For example, 1.02e3 means "1.02 times 10 raised to the power of 3," or 1020.

Numbers can be written in decimal, hexadecimal, binary, and octal. Hexadecimal and octal numbers can have negative values. Binary, hexadecimal, and octal numbers can only represent integer values; they cannot be written in E notation. When the JavaScript runtime finds one of these number literals, it will automatically convert it to the decimal, or base-10 representation (with no decimal places, of course).

Hexadecimal integers (referred to as base-16 numbers) are notated by prefixing them with a 0x. They can contain digits 0 through 9, and letters A through F only. The letters A through F represent 10 through 15 in decimal (Base-10). Using letters other than A through F will raise a SyntaxError.

Octal integers (referred to as Base-8 numbers) are notated by prefixing them with a 0o. They can contain digits 0 through 7 only. Using numbers outside of 0 through 7 will raise a SyntaxError.

Binary integers (referred to as Base-2 numbers) are notated by prefixing them with 0b. They can only contain digits 0 and 1. Using numbers outside of 0 and 1 with a binary integer will raise a SyntaxError.

Hexadecimal, binary, and octal are the most commonly used numeral systems, next to decimals, in computing. This is why they come built into the language. Examples of other popular numeral systems that you may encounter in computing, but aren't built into JavaScript, are Base-32 (Duotrigesimal) and Base-64 (Tetrasexagesimal). Refer to Table 1-2 for a handy guide on how each of the built-in JavaScript numerals convert.

Table 1-2. *Decimal, Hexadecimal, Octal, and Binary Conversion Chart*

Decimal (Base-10)	Hexadecimal (Base-16)	Octal (Base-8)	Binary (Base-2)
0	0	0	0
1	1	1	1
2	2	2	10*
3	3	3	11*
4	4	4	100*
5	5	5	101*
6	6	6	110*
7	7	7	111*
8	8	10*	1000*
9	9	11*	1001*
10	A	12*	1010*
11	B	13*	1011*
12	C	14*	1100*
13	D	15*	1101*
14	E	16*	1110*
15	F	17*	1111*

* *These numbers don't exist as single numerals, and so have to be created from multiple numerals.*

The Code

Listing 1-23. Creating a Numeric Value Using Number Literals

```
// Basic arithmetic
var a = 1 + 1;
console.log( typeof a );                        // number
console.log( "1 + 1 = " + a );                  // 1 + 1 = 2
console.log(10 - 5.52 );                        // 4.48
console.log(3.49 / .52 );                       // 6.711538461538462
console.log(95.78 * 627 );                      / 60054.06

// Comparing integer and floating-point values
console.log( 1 === 1.000 );                     // true
console.log( typeof 1 === typeof 1.000 );       // true

// Scientific Notation
console.log( 1e1 );                             // 10
console.log( 1e3 );                             // 1000
console.log(1.51e-6 );                          // 0.00000151
console.log( 1.7985e19 );                       // 17985000000000000000
```

```
// Hexadecimal Notation
console.log( 0x01 );                                    // 1
console.log( 0x1a );                                    // 26
console.log( 0xbc );                                    // 188
console.log( 0xff );                                    // 255

// Octal Notation
console.log( 0o1 );                                     // 1
console.log( 0o32 );                                    // 26
console.log( 0o274 );                                   // 188
console.log( 0o377 );                                   // 255

// Octal Notation
console.log( 0b1 );                                     // 1
console.log( 0b11010 );                                 // 26
console.log( 0o10111100 );                              // 2134592
console.log( 0o11111111 );                              // 2396745
```

How It Works

This simple overview is an introduction to the basics of numeric representation and manipulation. To get the most out of number literals and the number object, make sure you read Chapter 4 to get an in-depth look at what JavaScript mathematics can really do. You will learn how to perform trigonometric, algebraic, calculus operations, and more.

Determining If a Defined Variable Is a Number

Problem

You need to test a variable to determine if it is a numeric value or another datatype.

Solution

Using the typeof operator, you can determine the datatype of a variable. If the variable is a Number value, typeof will return the string "number".

The Code

Listing 1-24. Determining If a Defined Variable Is a Number

```
var a = Number(5.912);
var b = 4.7;
var c = "";
var d = new Date();
```

```
if ( typeof a === 'number' ) { // For more on the Strict Equality Operator (`===`), see Chapter 2-10
        console.log("a is a Number");
} else {
        console.log("a is not a Number");
}

if ( typeof b === 'number' ) { // For more on the Strict Equality Operator (`===`), see Chapter 2-10
        console.log("b is a Number");
} else {
        console.log("b is not a Number");
}

if ( typeof c === 'number' ) { // For more on the Strict Equality Operator (`===`), see Chapter 2-10
        console.log("c is a Number");
} else {
        console.log("c is not a Number");
}

if ( typeof d === 'number' ) { // For more on the Strict Equality Operator (`===`), see Chapter 2-10
        console.log("d is a Number");
} else {
        console.log("d is not a Number");
}
```

The output is:

```
a is a Number
b is a Number
c is not a Number
d is not a Number
```

How It Works

The typeof operator returns the string value "number" for number objects. To determine if a variable is a number, all you need to do is compare the return value of the typeof operator to the string "number". Other datatypes such as strings and objects return different strings that represent them.

Dealing with NaN and Infinity

■ **Caution** Number.isNaN() and Number.isFinite() are ES6 features. Older browsers still in use, such as Internet Explorer 11 and below and Safari 7 and below do not support this feature. However, they are supported on the global object, so for these browsers, you can use isNaN() or isFinite() (without the Number. prefix).

Problem

Sometimes you may encounter the literals `NaN` (Not a Number) and ±Infinity (`Infinity` or `-Infinity`). All of these values are the typeof number, and need extra checks to ensure the number you want is a finite number.

Solution

The number constructor has two static methods (functions attached directly to the number constructor), Number.isNaN and Number.isFinite. Both return Booleans determining if the passed parameter is NaN or ±Infinity, respectively.

The Code

Listing 1-25. Dealing with NaN and Infinity

```
var a = NaN;
var b = Infinity;
var c = -Infinity;
var d = 3;

if ( Number.isNaN(a) ) {
        console.log("a is a NaN (not a number)");
} else {
        console.log("a is a real Number, not NaN");
}

if ( Number.isFinite(b) ) {
        console.log("b is a finite Number");
} else {
        console.log("b is not a finite Number, it is either +Infinity or -Infinity");
}

if ( Number.isFinite(c) ) {
        console.log("c is a finite Number");
} else {
        console.log("c is not a finite Number, it is either +Infinity or -Infinity");
}

if ( Number.isNaN(d) ) {
        console.log("d is a NaN (not a number)");
} else {
        console.log("d is a real Number, not NaN");
}

if ( Number.isFinite(d) ) {
        console.log("d is a finite Number");
} else {
        console.log("d is not a finite Number, it is either +Infinity or -Infinity");
}
```

The output is:

```
a is a NaN (not a number)
b is not a finite Number, it is either +Infinity or -Infinity
c is not a finite Number, it is either +Infinity or -Infinity
d is a real Number, not NaN
d is a finite Number
```

How It Works

NaN and ±Infinity are Number objects, which makes dealing with them difficult to detect; however, the two methods Number.isNaN() and Number.isFinite() are specifically built to detect these two edge cases. They are also available on the global object, meaning one can write, for example window.isNaN() or more simply isNaN(). It is especially important when taking user input as numbers, to check if the number is NaN.

Generating a Date Using the Date Object

Problem

You need to generate a date or timestamp for your application. You may need to pass this value back to the server or simply use it client-side.

Solution

It's easy to create a timestamp with the date constructor; all you need to do is create an instance of the Date object without any parameters and assign it to a variable. The date constructor is also useful for recording timespans such as the length of time required for an operation to complete.

The Code

Listing 1-26. Generating a Date Using the Date Object

```
// The current date and time
// Wed Apr 10 2013 15:01:06 GMT-0400 (Eastern Daylight Time)
var today = new Date();
console.log(today);

// Thu Mar 14 2013 03:14:15 GMT-0400 (Eastern Daylight Time)
var dateOne = new Date("March 14, 2013 03:14:15");
console.log(dateOne);

// Wed Apr 10 2013 00:00:00 GMT-0400 (Eastern Daylight Time)
var dateTwo = new Date(2013,03,10);
console.log(dateTwo);

// Thu Mar 14 2013 03:14:15 GMT-0400 (Eastern Daylight Time)
var dateThree = new Date(2013,02,14,3,14,15);
console.log(dateThree);

// Working with Date components
var date = today.getDate();          // 13
var month = today.getMonth();        // 3
var year = today.getFullYear();      // 2013
console.log(date + "/" + month + "/" + year);
```

```
// Determine the duration of an event
var start = Date.now();
alert("Wait a few seconds then click OK");
var time = Date.now() - start;
console.log( "The operation took " + time + " milliseconds" );
```

The output is:

```
Sun Dec 15 2013 23:46:08 GMT+0000 (GMT) // (this output may be different based on your timezone!)
Thu Mar 14 2013 03:14:15 GMT+0000 (GMT)
Wed Apr 10 2013 00:00:00 GMT+0100 (BST) // (this output may be different based on your timezone!)
Thu Mar 14 2013 03:14:15 GMT+0000 (GMT)
15/11/2013 // (this output may be different based on your locale!)
The operation took 1326 milliseconds
```

How It Works

The JavaScript Date object offers many powerful functions such as measuring a timespan, converting times from one time zone to another, adding and subtracting moments in time, and more. Be sure to read Chapter 6 about dates and time, where the topic is covered in much more detail.

Generating a Date with a Date String

Problem

You have been given a date string from a server, client-side database or possibly generated from user input and need to manipulate it by using Date object methods.

Solution

The Date object constructor can accept a string that's RFC 2822 (for example "Fri, 24 Jan 2014 21:18:23 +0000"), or RFC 3339 compliant (for example, "2014-01-24T21:18:23+00:00"). We'll pass the date string into the date constructor to create a Date object instance.

The Code

Listing 1-27. Generating a Date with a Date String

```
var myDateString = "January 16, 1975 17:07:00";

var myDate = new Date(myDateString);
console.log(myDate);

myDate.setMonth(2);
console.log(myDate);
```

```
myDate.setHours(10);
console.log(myDate);

myDate.setMinutes(51);
console.log(myDate);
myDate.setSeconds(59);
console.log(myDate);

var myDateString = "1985-04-12T23:20:50.52Z";

var myDate = new Date(myDateString);
console.log(myDate);

myDate.setMonth(2);
console.log(myDate);

myDate.setHours(10);
console.log(myDate);

myDate.setMinutes(51);
console.log(myDate);
myDate.setSeconds(59);
console.log(myDate);
```

The output is:

```
Thu Jan 16 1975 17:07:00 GMT+0000 (GMT)
Sun Mar 16 1975 17:07:00 GMT+0100 (GMT)
Sun Mar 16 1975 10:07:00 GMT+0100 (GMT)
Sun Mar 16 1975 10:51:00 GMT+0100 (GMT)
Sun Mar 16 1975 10:51:59 GMT+0100 (GMT)
Sat Apr 13 1985 00:20:50 GMT+0100 (BST)
Wed Mar 13 1985 00:20:50 GMT+0000 (GMT)
Wed Mar 13 1985 10:20:50 GMT+0000 (GMT)
Wed Mar 13 1985 10:51:50 GMT+0000 (GMT)
Wed Mar 13 1985 10:51:59 GMT+0000 (GMT)
```

How It Works

The JavaScript Date object will attempt to parse many types of date strings, most notably RFC 3339 and RFC 2822 formatted date strings. This can be very useful as a tool for receiving dates from the server side. RFC 3339 strings are the recommended format for receiving and sending dates from the server side.

Determining If a Defined Variable Is a Date

Problem

You need to test a variable to determine if it is a Date object or another datatype.

Solution

We can't use the typeof operator to return the variable's type because typeof will return the string "object" for a Date instance (as it is not a literal). Instead we'll use the instanceof operator to determine if a variable is an *instance* of the Date object.

The Code

Listing 1-28. Determining If a Defined Variable Is a Date

```
var a = new Date();
var b = 3.14;
var c = "I'm a string";

if (a instanceof Date) {
        console.log("a is a Date");
} else {
        console.log("a is not a Date");
}

if (b instanceof Date) {
        console.log("b is a Date");
} else {
        console.log("b is not a Date");
}

if (c instanceof Date) {
        console.log("c is a Date");
}
else {
        console.log("c is not a Date");
}
```

The output is:

```
a is a Date
b is not a Date
c is not a Date
```

How It Works

The instanceof operator determines if a variable is an instance of an object. In this example, various variables are tested to see if they are instances of the Date object. If a variable is an instance of the Date object, the instanceof operator returns true, otherwise false.

Creating an Object and Assigning Properties

Problem

You are required to create an object and give it some properties to use object-oriented practices in your code base.

Solution

Objects are collections of methods and properties. A method is a function in an object. A property is one or more values or objects in an object. JavaScript supports its own internal objects, objects that you create, and host objects.

To create your own objects, you first create an object literal, and then populate it with properties and methods using the well-known dot notation.

The Code

Listing 1-29. Creating an Object and Assigning Properties

```
// Create a House object
var House = {};
House.address = "123 Main Street, Podunkville, NC 28328";
House.area = 2800;
House.constructionDate = new Date(1991,0,16);

// The Architecture object contains structural information about the House
House.architecture = {};
House.architecture.floorPlan =
            "http://upload.wikimedia.org/wikipedia/commons/b/b8/HouseFlrPlan.svg";
House.architecture.style = "American FourSquare";
House.architecture.doorsExternal = ["Living Room","Kitchen","Foyer"];
House.architecture.rooms = ["Kitchen","Living Room","Bathroom", "Guest Bedroom",
"Secondary Bedroom", "Master Bedroom", "Master Bathroom"];
House.architecture.windows = ["Kitchen (2)","Living Room (2)","Bathroom (1)", "Guest Bedroom
(1)", "Secondary Bedroom (1)", "Master Bedroom (1)", "Master Bathroom (1)"];

// House owner object
House.owner = {};
House.owner.name = "Matthew Stephen Skipper";
House.owner.phone = "123-456-7890";

// Display basic house data
console.log( "House at: " + House.address );
console.log( "Built on: " + House.constructionDate );
console.log( "Area: " + House.area + " square feet" );

// Display house owner data
console.log( "\nHouse Owner" );
console.log( "Name: " + House.owner.name );
console.log( "Phone: " + House.owner.phone );
```

```
// Display house architecture data
console.log( "\nHouse Architecture" );
console.log( "Area: " + House.area + " square feet" );
console.log( "Floor Plan URL: " + House.architecture.floorPlan );
console.log( "Style: " + House.architecture.style );
console.log( "External Doors: " + House.architecture.doorsExternal );
console.log( "Rooms: " + House.architecture.rooms );
console.log( "Windows: " + House.architecture.windows );
```

The output is:

```
House at: 123 Main Street, Podunkville, NC 28328
Built on: Wed Jan 16 1991 00:00:00 GMT-0500 (Eastern Standard Time)
Area: 2800 square feet
House Owner
Name: Matthew Stephen Skipper
Phone: 123-456-7890
House Architecture
Area: 2800 square feet
Floor Plan URL: http://upload.wikimedia.org/wikipedia/commons/b/b8/HouseFlrPlan.svg
Style: American FourSquare
External Doors: Living Room,Kitchen,Foyer
Rooms: Kitchen,Living Room,Bathroom,Guest Bedroom,Secondary Bedroom,Master Bedroom,Master Bathroom
Windows: Kitchen (2),Living Room (2),Bathroom (1),Guest Bedroom (1),Secondary Bedroom (1),
Master Bedroom (1),Master Bathroom (1)
```

How It Works

The object created is a very simple representation of a house, its owner, and architecture. The house object contains five properties: address, area, constructionDate, architecture, and owner. The architecture property is another custom object with various properties about the house. The owner property is a third custom object containing data about the owner.

This house object is very simple and has no methods. However, it does show the basics of object creation and JavaScript object-oriented programming (OOP). Objects and object-oriented programming are discussed in much more detail in Chapter 9.

Determining If a Defined Variable Is an Object

Problem

You need to test a variable to determine if it is an object or another datatype.

Solution

Using the typeof operator, we can determine the datatype of a variable. If the variable is an object, typeof will return the string "object".

The Code

Listing 1-30. Determining If a Defined Variable Is an Object

```
var a = {};
var b = "I'm a string";
var c = 7;

if ( typeof a === 'object' ) {
        console.log("a is an Object");
} else {
        console.log("a is not an Object");
}

if ( typeof b === 'object' ) {
        console.log("b is an Object");
} else {
            console.log("b is not an Object");
}

if ( typeof c === 'object' ) {
        console.log("c is an Object");
} else {
        console.log("c is not an Object");
}
```

The output is:

```
a is an Object
b is not an Object
c is not an Object
```

How It Works

The typeof operator returns the string "object" for all objects derived from the built-in "object" object. Other datatypes such as strings and numbers return a string that represents them.

Determining If an Object Is an Instance

Problem

You need to determine if an object, such as a Date object, is an instance of a constructor, or an instance of the Object constructor; however, typeof returns the "object" value for all of these.

Solution

If you have an object, such as a Date object, and using typeof returns "object", but you still want to assert that the object is an instance of a constructor you can use the instanceof keyword.

The Code

Listing 1-31. Differences Between Objects and Instances

```javascript
var date = new Date();
var error = new Error();
var blob =  new Blob();
var object = new Object();

typeof date; // Returns "object"
typeof error; // Returns "object"
typeof blob; // Returns "object"

if ( date instanceof Date ) {
        console.log("date is a Date instance");
} else if ( date instanceof Error ) {
        console.log("date is an Error instance");
} else if ( date instanceof Blob ) {
        console.log("date is a Blob instance");
} else {
        console.log("date is an unknown instance");
}

if ( error instanceof Date ) {
        console.log("error is a Date instance");
} else if ( error instanceof Error ) {
        console.log("error is an Error instance");
} else if ( error instanceof Blob ) {
        console.log("error is a Blob instance");
} else {
        console.log("error is an unknown instance");
}

if ( blob instanceof Date ) {
        console.log("blob is a Date instance");
} else if ( blob instanceof Error ) {
        console.log("blob is an Error instance");
} else if ( blob instanceof Blob ) {
        console.log("blob is a Blob instance");
} else {
        console.log("blob is an unknown instance");
}

if ( object instanceof Date ) {
        console.log("object is a Date instance");
} else if ( object instanceof Error ) {
        console.log("object is an Error instance");
} else if ( object instanceof Blob ) {
        console.log("object is a Blob instance");
} else {
        console.log("object is an unknown instance");
}
```

The output is:

```
date is a Date instance
error is an Error instance
blob is a Blob instance
object is an unknown instance
```

How It Works

The `instanceof` operator is a useful tool for detecting instances of constructors, especially when you want to determine the finer points of an objects inheritance. It is vitally important to remember that `instanceof` will not work on any literals, such as number literals or string literals. As a rule of thumb, `instanceof` only works on values that have a `typeof` of `"object"`, so you could be ultra cautious by checking the `typeof` a value, followed by checking `instanceof` the object, only if the `typeof` is `"object"`.

Determining an Object's Direct Instance with the Constructor Property

Problem

Some objects are created from the result of a constructor (such as `Date`), but they also inherit from their parent constructor objects. For example, a `Date` object will return `true` for `instanceof Date`, but will also return `true` for `instanceof Object`. This becomes a problem when trying to find the direct descendant of an object.

Solution

Every object that has a constructor and can be created by using the `new` keyword will have a `constructor` property. This is set to the constructor function, so for example `new Date()`'s constructor property is `Date`.

The Code

Listing 1-32. Determining an Object's Direct Instance with the Constructor Property

```
var date = new Date();
var error = new Error();

var blob =  new Blob();
var object = {};

if ( date.constructor === Date ) {
    console.log("date is a Date instance");
} else if ( date.constructor === Error ) {
    console.log("date is an Error instance");
} else if ( date.constructor === Blob ) {
    console.log("date is a Blob instance");
} else {
    console.log("date is an unknown instance");
}
```

```
if ( error.constructor === Date ) {
    console.log("error is a Date instance");
} else if ( error.constructor === Error ) {
    console.log("error is an Error instance");
} else if ( error.constructor === Blob ) {
    console.log("error is a Blob instance");
} else {
    console.log("error is an unknown instance");
}

if ( blob.constructor === Date ) {
    console.log("blob is a Date instance");
} else if ( blob.constructor === Error ) {
    console.log("blob is an Error instance");
} else if ( blob.constructor === Blob ) {
    console.log("blob is a Blob instance");
} else {
    console.log("blob is an unknown instance");
}

if ( object.constructor === Date ) {
    console.log("object is a Date instance");
} else if ( object.constructor === Error ) {
    console.log("object is an Error instance");
} else if ( object.constructor === Blob ) {
    console.log("object is a Blob instance");
} else {
    console.log("object is an unknown instance");
}
```

The output is:

```
date is a Date instance
error is an Error instance
blob is a Blob instance
object is an unknown instance
```

How It Works

The constructor property is very useful for determining the direct descendant of an object. It is also useful for getting the constructor itself, which can be useful for cloning an instance or making new instances of the same type. It also illustrates the main difference between instanceof and constructor.

Determining If Something Is a Plain Object

Problem

You want to be able to assert that an object is not a descendant of a resulting constructor function, and instead asserting that an object is a plain object—one that was created using new Object() or an object literal ({}). instanceof will assert that the object is an instance of the object constructor. instanceof also asserts on any descendants of the object's constructor such as the Date instances.

Solution

Just like in Listing 1-30, determining the direct descendant of an object should use the .constructor property. Determining if an object is a "plain" object (e.g., is not an instance of another constructor, such as date) requires the same process, even for object literals ({}).

The Code

Listing 1-33. Determining If Something Is a Plain Object

```
var date = new Date();
var error = new Error();
var object = new Object();
var plainObject = {};

if ( date.constructor === Object ) {
    console.log("date is a plain object");
} else {
    console.log("date is not a plain object");
}

if ( error.constructor === Object ) {
    console.log("error is a plain object");
} else {
    console.log("error is not a plain object");
}

if ( object.constructor === Object ) {
    console.log("object is a plain object");
} else {
    console.log("object is not a plain object");
}

if ( plainObject.constructor === Object ) {
    console.log("plainObject is a plain object");
} else {
    console.log("plainObject is not a plain object");
}
```

The output is:

```
date is not a plain object
error is not a plain object
object is a plain object
plainObject is a plain object
```

How It Works

This is another important example of how the constructor property can sometimes be more useful than instanceof. The instanceof property will "walk the prototype chain"; that is, it will check not only the direct descendant, but the descendant of that, and that, and that, and so on. This means objects like Date are instances of Object (in fact, nearly everything is), however "plain" objects are the only objects where the .constructor property should be Object.

Creating an Array and Assigning and Retrieving Values

Problem

You need to create a list of values and store them in an ordered manner.

Solution

Using arrays is the best way to create an ordered list of values. Each value has a unique, numerical identifier and so, unlike objects, there is an explicit order to arrays.

The Code

Listing 1-34. Creating an Array and Assigning and Retrieving Values

```
var register = ['Annie', 'Cathy', 'Jessica', 'Sally'];
console.log(register[0]);
console.log(register[1]);
console.log(register[2]);
console.log(register[3]);
var places = ['First', 'Second', 'Third'];
console.log(places.length);
console.log(places[2]);

var bytes = new Array(2);
console.log(bytes.length);
console.log(bytes[0]);
```

The output is:

```
Annie
Cathy
Jessica
Sally
3
Third
2
`undefined`
```

How It Works

Arrays are ordered lists of values. You can get to any individual value inside an array by using the staple-notation ([and]) with a numeric index of the key. The numerical index starts from 0 and counts up by 1 for each new value in the array. Arrays also include a .length property, which is set to the total number of items in the array. Arrays can be created with an initial length, by using the array constructor with the new keyword, and a length parameter. For example, new Array(3) will create an array with three undefined values in it.

Choosing Between Objects and Arrays

Problem

You are unsure when to use an object over an array, or are unsure of the merits of using either one.

Solution

Both arrays and objects store values against keys—they are "key-value stores". The benefits of an array over an object are that the keys are predictable sequential numbers for each new item in the array, and that they explicitly maintain their sort order. Objects, on the other hand, do not have an explicit sort order and have unpredictable keys, they also cannot determine their length easily. An array's key sequence is strictly sequential, so this has a side effect that if you create new values with large key numbers, the previous empty keys are backfilled to be undefined values.

The benefit of objects is that keys can be given a name decided by you, which can be very useful for object-oriented programming. Typically you would use objects for storing some kind of record, e.g., attributes about a person or place. You would likely use arrays for lists, perhaps a list of people or rankings. Refer to Table 1-3 for an object-array comparison.:

Table 1-3. *Objects versus Arrays Comparison*

	Objects	Arrays
Key Types	String	Number
Key Sequence	Up to the user	Sequential numbers
Key Predictability	Low	High
Lowest Key Value	Unknown	0
Highest Key Value	Unknown	theArray.length - 1
Value	Any	Any
Duplicate Values Allowed	Yes	Yes
Duplicate Keys Allowed	No	No

Creating a Regular Expression Literal

Problem

You need to be able to match a string against a particular pattern and need a concise way to do it.

Solution

Using regular expressions is the most powerful way to match patterns or test for patterns against a string value. It is a powerful tool that exists in many programming languages, including Ruby, C++11, Java, and Perl, and is even built into command-line tools such as Awk and Sed.

The Code

Listing 1-35. Creating a Regular Expression Literal

```
var testString = 'hello world';

if ( /hello/.test(testString) ) {
    console.log('testString contains "hello"!');
} else {
    console.log('testString does not contain "hello"');
}

if ( /world/.test(testString) ) {
    console.log('testString contains "world"!');
} else {
    console.log('testString does not contain "world"');
}
```

```
var testStringMatch = testString.match(/(\b\w+\b)+/g); // A complex pattern!
if ( testStringMatch ) {
    console.log('testString contains ' + testStringMatch.length + ' words!');
} else {
    console.log('testString does not contain any words');
}
```

The output is:

```
testString contains "hello"!
testString contains "world"!
testString contains 2 words!
```

How It Works

Regular expressions are almost a miniature language alongside JavaScript (as well as many other languages), which allow for very powerful string finding and matching. The syntax is very complex, but with it comes a lot of power. Not only can you match parts of a string, as in the first two examples, but you can also match complex patterns such as words, number patterns, word boundaries, character ranges, and a lot more. You can also extract parts of a string based on these patterns or replace parts of a string. Regular expressions are covered in extensive detail in Chapter 20.

Injecting Variables into a String with Template Literals

▪ **Caution**   Template literals are an ECMAScript 6 (ES6) feature. Older browsers still in use, such as Internet Explorer 11 and below and Safari 7 and below, do not support this feature (they work off of the ECMAScript 5, or ES5 standard). In fact, at the time of writing only the Taceur Compiler tool could support template string literals. Check out `http://kangax.github.io/es5-compat-table/es6/` for the current compatibility charts.

Problem

You want to do variable substitution inside of a string.

Solution

JavaScript ES6 features template literals, which fix a wide range of issues with existing JavaScript strings, the biggest of which is injecting variables into strings. Template literals use backticks (` and `), whereas normal strings use quotes ("" or ' ').

The Code

Listing 1-36. Injecting Variables into a String with Template Literals

```
var name = 'Bob';
console.log( 'Hello ' + name + '!' ); // The old way to do this, cumbersome and error prone
console.log( `Hello ${name}!` ); // Template Literals, shorter, more succinct, and less
error prone
var otherName = 'Mary';
var thirdName = 'Jim';
console.log( 'Hello ' + otherName + ', how is ' + thirdName + '?' ); // Can get very messy
console.log( `Hello ${otherName}, how is ${thirdName}?` ); // Much cleaner
```

The output is:

```
Hello Bob!
Hello Bob!
Hello Mary, how is Jim?
Hello Mary, how is Jim?
```

How It Works

Template string literals are specially tuned to let the JavaScript interpreter know that variable substitution needs to take place. Every time a template substitution (${}) is encountered, it will inject the known variable in its place, as you'd expect. The same scoping rules for variables apply here, as they do everywhere else. Template string literals are much more powerful than simple variable substitution—they behave very differently from strings with regard to escaping characters, and can be passed into custom functions to build complex formatting and template engines. Template string literals are covered in Chapter 14 of this book.

CHAPTER 2

Working with Expressions

Performing an Addition with the + Operator

Note   String concatenation is covered in more detail in Chapter 3.

Problem

You want to add some numbers together.

Solution

JavaScript has a set of recognizable math operators, including the addition (+) operator, which you can use to add numbers (or variables of numbers) together.

The Code

Listing 2-1. Performing an Addition with the + Operator

```
console.log(2 + 1);
var myNum = 14;
var anotherNum = 22;
console.log(anotherNum + myNum);
console.log(myNum + 0.23);
console.log(anotherNum + 16 + myNum + 14);
console.log('45' + '3'); // the two Strings are concatenated, because + is the concatenation operator
console.log('45' + '6'); // the two Strings are concatenated, because + is the concatenation operator
```

The output is:

```
3
36
14.23
66
453
456
```

© Russ Ferguson and Keith Cirkel 2017
R. Ferguson and K. Cirkel, *JavaScript Recipes*, DOI 10.1007/978-1-4302-6107-0_2

How It Works

As you can see, JavaScript's addition operator is simple reflection of the same mathematical operator. You can add number literals together, or variables of numbers, or a mixture. Additions can happen multiple times in one statement. Essentially everything you expect from the Math operator, you can do in JavaScript. It should be noted that adding number variables together does not affect the underlying variable.

If you attempt to add two strings together, you'll actually get both of those strings combined into one new string, rather than the addition of those numbers. For example, '1' + '1' actually gives you 11, not 2. This is because + is also the string concatenation operator (see Chapter 3 for more info on string concatenation).

Performing a Subtraction with the - Operator

Problem

You want to subtract some numbers from each other.

Solution

JavaScript has a set of recognizable math operators, including the subtraction (-) operator, which you can use to subtract numbers (or variables of numbers) from each other.

The Code

Listing 2-2. Performing a Subtraction with the - Operator

```
console.log(2 - 1);
var myNum = 14;
var anotherNum = 22;
console.log(anotherNum - myNum);
console.log(myNum - 0.23);
console.log(anotherNum - 16 - myNum - 14);
console.log('45' - '3'); // the two Strings are coerced into Numbers
```

The output is:

```
1
8
13.77
-22

42
```

How It Works

Just like the mathematical operators in JavaScript, the subtraction operator works pretty much identically to its mathematical equivalent. Importantly: variables you use as operands in the statement will not be modified as part of the operation.

Internally, the subtraction operator also coerces the value using the internal ToNumber function (section 7.1.3 in ES6, section 9.3 in ES5), which has the same effect as using the number constructor (discussed in Chapter 1). In other words, '1' - '1' is the same as '1 - 1'. This is a big difference between how the subtraction and addition operators behave. While subtraction will coerce the values into numbers, addition does not (well, it would do, but when using + with two strings, it actually becomes the string concatenation operator, discussed in Chapter 3).

Performing Multiplication with the * Operator

Problem

You want to multiply some numbers together.

Solution

JavaScript has a set of recognizable mathematical operators, including the multiplication (*) operator, which you can use to multiply numbers (or variables of numbers) together.

The Code

Listing 2-3. Performing Multiplication with the * Operator

```
console.log(2 * 1);
var myNum = 14;
var anotherNum = 22;
console.log(anotherNum * myNum);
console.log(myNum * 0.23);
console.log(anotherNum * 16 * myNum * 14);
console.log('45' * '3'); // the two Strings are coerced into Numbers
```

The output is:

```
2
308
3.22
68992
135
```

How It Works

Just like all other mathematical operators, the multiplication operator works pretty much identically to the mathematical equivalent. Importantly, variables you use as operands in the statement will not be modified as part of the operation.

Internally, the multiplication operator also coerces the value using the internal ToNumber function (section 7.1.3 in ES6, section 9.3 in ES5), which has the same effect as using the number constructor (discussed in Chapter 1). In other words, `'1' * '1'` is the same as `1 * 1`.

Performing Division with the / Operator

Problem

You want to divide some numbers.

Solution

JavaScript has a set of recognizable mathematical operators, including the division (/) operator, which you can use to divide numbers (or variables of numbers) together.

The Code

Listing 2-4. Performing Division with the / Operator

```
console.log(2 / 1);
var myNum = 14;
var anotherNum = 22;
console.log(anotherNum / myNum);
console.log(myNum / 0.23);
console.log(anotherNum / 16 / myNum / 14);
console.log('45' / '3'); // the two Strings are coerced into Numbers
```

The output is:

```
2
1.5714285714285714
60.869565217391305
0.00701530612244898
15
```

How It Works

Just like the other mathematical operators in JavaScript, the division operator works pretty much identically to the mathematical equivalent. Importantly: any variables you use as operands in the statement will not be modified as part of the operation.

Internally, the division operator also coerces the value using the internal ToNumber function (section 7.1.3 in ES6, section 9.3 in ES5), which has the same effect as using the number constructor (discussed in Chapter 1). In other words, `'1' / '1'` is the same as `1 / 1`.

Getting the Remainder of a Division Operation with the Modulo (%) Operator

Problem

You want to get the remainder of a division operation (modulus) of some numbers.

Solution

As in many programming languages, JavaScript has a modulo operator that will return the remainder of an Euclidean division. In other words, it will return the remainder of a division that has been divided into whole parts. For example, getting the modulo of 3 and 1 is 0, as 1 divides equally into three parts; however, the modulo for 3 % 2 returns 1, as 2 goes into 3 with 1 remaining.

The Code

Listing 2-5. Getting the Remainder of a Division Operation with the Modulo (%) Operator

```
console.log(6 % 1); // 0
console.log(6 % 2); // 0
console.log(6 % 3); // 0
console.log(6 % 4); // 2
console.log(6 % 5); // 1
console.log(6 % 6); // 0
var myNum = 14;
var anotherNum = 22;
console.log(anotherNum % myNum);
console.log(myNum % 0.23);
console.log(anotherNum % 16 % myNum % 14);
```

The output is:

```
0
0
0
2
1
0
8
0.1999999999999994
6
```

How It Works

The modulo operator uses Euclidean division to work out the amount of whole numbers of the right hand operand go into the left hand operand, and retains the remaining amount. This may seem pretty useless at first, but it's actually a very useful way to work out number properties inside loops, such as odd and even numbers (number % 2) or rows of numbers (number % n). This has such prevalent use in programming that almost all computer languages implement modulo operators as either using the % sign or using the keyword mod.

Internally, the modulo operator also coerces the value using the internal ToNumber function (section 7.1.3 in ES6, section 9.3 in ES5), which has the same effect as using the number constructor (discussed in Chapter 1). In other words, `'1' % '1'` is the same as `1 % 1`.

Determining If a Value Is Less Than Another with the < Operator

Problem

You want to determine if one number is less (smaller) than another number.

Solution

JavaScript comes with a specific operator to assert if a number is less than another number, called the less than operator, <.

The Code

Listing 2-6. Determining If a Value Is Less Than Another with the < Operator

```
if (1 < 2) {
    console.log('1 is a smaller Number than 2')
}
if (2 < 1) {
    console.log('2 is a smaller Number than 1');
}
if (2 < 2) {
    console.log('2 is a smaller Number than 2');
}
var myNum = 14;
var otherNum = -9;
if (myNum < otherNum) {
    console.log('myNum is a smaller Number than otherNum');
}
if (otherNum < myNum) {
    console.log('otherNum is a smaller Number than myNum');
}
var stringNum = '-18'; // note this is a string
if (stringNum < otherNum) {
    console.log('stringNum is a smaller Number than otherNum');
}
```

The output is:

```
1 is a smaller Number than 2
otherNum is a smaller Number than myNum
stringNum is a smaller Number than otherNum
```

How It Works

The less than operator simply asserts that the left hand operand has a smaller numerical value than the right hand operand. If it does, then the expression will return the Boolean `true`. If the left hand operand's numerical value is equal to or greater than the right hand operand, then it will return the Boolean `false`.

Just like pretty much all numerical/mathematical operations in JavaScript, the less than operator coerces both operands to be numbers using the internal `ToNumber` function (section 7.1.3 in ES6, section 9.3 in ES5), which has the same effect as using the number constructor (discussed in Chapter 1). In other words, `'1' < '1'` is the same as `1 < 1`.

Determining If a Value Is Greater than Another with the > Operator

Problem

You want to determine if one number is greater (bigger) than another number.

Solution

JavaScript comes with a specific operator to assert if a number is greater than another number, called the greater than operator, `>`.

The Code

Listing 2-7. Determining If a Value Is Greater Than Another with the > Operator

```
if (1 > 2) {
    console.log('1 is a bigger Number than 2')
}
if (2 > 1) {
    console.log('2 is a bigger Number than 1');
}
if (2 > 2) {
    console.log('2 is a bigger Number than 2');
}
var myNum = 14;
var otherNum = -9;
if (myNum > otherNum) {
    console.log('myNum is a bigger Number than otherNum');
}
if (otherNum > myNum) {
    console.log('otherNum is a bigger Number than myNum');
}
var stringNum = '-18'; // note this is a string
if (otherNum > stringNum) {
    console.log('otherNum is a bigger Number than stringNum');
}
```

The output is:

```
2 is a bigger Number than 1
myNum is a bigger Number than otherNum
otherNum is a bigger Number than stringNum
```

How It Works

The greater than operator simply asserts that the left hand operand is a greater numerical value than the right hand operand. If it is, then the expression will return the Boolean true. If the left hand operand's numerical value is equal to or smaller than the right hand operand, then it will return the Boolean false.

Just like pretty much all numerical/mathematical operations in JavaScript, the greater than operator coerces both operands to be numbers using the internal ToNumber function (section 7.1.3 in ES6, section 9.3 in ES5), which has the same effect as using the number constructor (discussed in Chapter 1). In other words, '1' > '1' is the same as 1 > 1.

Determining If a Value Is Less than or Equal to Another with the <= Operator

Problem

You want to determine if one number is less (smaller) than another number, or exactly the same size.

Solution

JavaScript comes with a specific operator to assert if a number is greater than, or equal to another number, called the less than or equal operator, <=.

The Code

Listing 2-8. Determining If a Value Is Less Than or Equal to Another with the <= Operator

```
if (1 <= 2) {
    console.log('1 is a smaller Number than 2, or equal to 2')
}
if (2 <= 1) {
    console.log('2 is a smaller Number than 1, or equal to 1');
}
if (2 <= 2) {
    console.log('2 is a smaller Number than 2, or equal to 2');
}
var myNum = 14;
var otherNum = -9;
if (myNum <= otherNum) {
    console.log('myNum is a smaller Number than otherNum, or equal to otherNum');
}
```

```
if (otherNum <= myNum) {
    console.log('otherNum is a smaller Number than myNum, or equal to myNum');
}
var stringNum = '-18'; // note this is a string
if (stringNum <= otherNum) {
    console.log('stringNum is a smaller Number than otherNum, or equal to otherNum');
}
```

The output is:

```
1 is a smaller Number than 2, or equal to 2
2 is a smaller Number than 2, or equal to 2
otherNum is a smaller Number than myNum, or equal to myNum
stringNum is a smaller Number than otherNum, or equal to otherNum
```

How It Works

The less than equal operator simply asserts that the left hand operand is a smaller or equal numerical value than the right hand operand. If it is, then the expression will return the Boolean true. If the left hand operand's numerical value is greater than the right hand operand, then it will return the Boolean false. The crucial difference between this and the less than operator is what Boolean is returned when both operands are equal. In the case of the less than or equal operator, it's true (whereas the less than operator will return false).

Just like pretty much all numerical/mathematical operations in JavaScript, the less than or equal operator coerces both operands to be numbers using the internal ToNumber function (section 7.1.3 in ES6, section 9.3 in ES5), which has the same effect as using the number constructor (discussed in Chapter 1). In other words, '1' <= '1' is the same as 1 <= 1.

Determining If a Value Is Greater than or Equal to Another with the >= Operator

Problem

You want to determine if one number is greater (bigger) than another number, or exactly the same size.

Solution

JavaScript comes with a specific operator to assert if a number is greater than or equal to another number, called the greater than or equal operator, >=.

The Code

Listing 2-9. Determining If a Value Is Greater Than or Equal to Another with the >= Operator

```
if (1 >= 2) {
    console.log('1 is a bigger Number than 2, or equal to 2')
}
if (2 >= 1) {
    console.log('2 is a bigger Number than 1, or equal to 1');
}
if (2 >= 2) {
    console.log('2 is a bigger Number than 2, or equal to 2');
}
var myNum = 14;
var otherNum = -9;
if (myNum >= otherNum) {
    console.log('myNum is a bigger Number than otherNum, or equal to otherNum');
}
if (otherNum >= myNum) {
    console.log('otherNum is a bigger Number than myNum, or equal to myNum');
}
var stringNum = '-18'; // note this is a string
if (otherNum >= stringNum) {
    console.log('otherNum is a bigger Number than stringNum, or equal to stringNum');
}
```

The output is:

```
2 is a bigger Number than 1, or equal to 1
2 is a bigger Number than 2, or equal to 2
myNum is a bigger Number than otherNum, or equal to otherNum
otherNum is a bigger Number than stringNum, or equal to stringNum
```

How It Works

The greater than or equal operator simply asserts that the left hand operand is a greater or equal numerical value than the right hand operand. If it is, then the expression will return the Boolean true. If the left hand operand's numerical value is smaller than the right hand operand, then it will return the Boolean false. The crucial difference between this and the greater than operator is what Boolean is returned when both operands are equal. In the case of the greater than or equal operator, it's true (whereas the greater than operator will return false).

Just like pretty much all numerical/mathematical operations in JavaScript, the greater than or equal operator coerces both operands to be numbers using the internal ToNumber function (section 7.1.3 in ES6, section 9.3 in ES5), which has the same effect as using the number constructor (discussed in Chapter 1). In other words, '1' <= '1' is the same as 1 <= 1.

Determining If a Value Is Equivalent to Another Using the == Operator

Problem

You want to loosely determine the equality of two values—to assert that are identical values, while not necessarily being the same type.

Solution

JavaScript's abstract equality operator, ==, compares the two operands for equality, while coercing the types of each operand to be the same.

The Code

Listing 2-10. Determining If a Value Is Equivalent to Another Using the == Operator

```
if (3 == 3) {
    console.log('3 is (abstractly) equal to 3');
}
if (3 == 2) {
    console.log('3 is (abstractly) equal to 2');
}
if ('hello' == 'hello') {
    console.log('"hello" is (abstractly) equal to "hello"');
}
if ('hello' == 'hi') {
    console.log('"hello" is (abstractly) equal to "hi"');
}
if ('3' == 3) {
    console.log('"3" is (abstractly) equal to 3');
}
if (false == false) {
    console.log('false is (abstractly) equal to false');
}
if (true == true) {
    console.log('true is (abstractly) equal to true');
}
if (false == true) {
    console.log('false is (abstractly) equal to true');
}
if (false == 0) {
    console.log('false is (abstractly) equal to 0');
}
if (true == 1) {
    console.log('true is (abstractly) equal to 1');
}
var myObject = {};
var otherObject = {};
```

```
if (myObject == myObject) {
    console.log('myObject is (abstractly) equal to myObject');
}
if (myObject == otherObject) {
    console.log('myObject is (abstractly) equal to otherObject');
}
if (myObject == {}) {
    console.log('myObject is (abstractly) equal to {}');
}
var myArray = [];
var otherArray = [];
if (myArray == myArray) {
    console.log('myArray is (abstractly) equal to myArray');
}
if (myArray == otherArray) {
    console.log('myArray is (abstractly) equal to otherArray');
}
if (myArray == []) {
    console.log('myArray is (abstractly) equal to []');
}
```

The output is:

```
3 is (abstractly) equal to 3
"hello" is (abstractly) equal to "hello"
"3" is (abstractly) equal to 3
false is (abstractly) equal to false
true is (abstractly) equal to true
false is (abstractly) equal to 0
true is (abstractly) equal to 1
myObject is (abstractly) equal to myObject
myArray is (abstractly) equal to myArray
```

How It Works

The abstract equality operator works similarly to the strict equality operator, but it does not fail after type checking, instead, it coerces types to match. If the types of both operands match, it simply performs a strict equality check, but if they don't, then it will attempt to coerce them using the rules in Figure 2-1 (the X axis being the right hand operand, the Y axis being the left hand operand, and the resulting cell being the type that both operands are coerced into).

Right Hand Operand

Left Hand Operand	Number	String	Undefined	Null	Boolean	Other
Number		Numbers (ToNumber)			Numbers (ToNumber)	Numbers (ToNumber)
String	Numbers (ToNumber)				Numbers (ToNumber)	Strings (ToString)
Undefined				Booleans (ToBoolean)		
Null			Booleans (ToBoolean)			
Boolean	Numbers (ToNumber)	Numbers (ToNumber)				Numbers (ToNumber)
Other	Numbers (ToNumber)	Strings (ToString)			Numbers (ToNumber)	

Figure 2-1. *Abstract equality type coercions*

After coercing the types to be the same (where possible), it will then behave the same as a strict equality check; if the types are not the same, it will return the Boolean false. If they are numbers of the same size, strings of the same content, Booleans of the same value, or objects/arrays that point to the same reference in memory, then the strict equality operator returns the Boolean true. If they don't match any of these criteria, then it will return the Boolean false, with the exception of NaN, which you will need to use Number.isNaN() for (as discussed in Chapter 1).

Because of the added complexity in an abstract equality operator versus a strict equality operator, it is always recommended to use the strict version, unless you absolutely have a reason to use the abstract one. Also remember you can cast values to different types yourself using the constructor methods mentioned throughout Chapter 1.

Determining If a Value Is Strictly Equal to Another Using the === Operator

Problem

You want to determine the equality of two values—to assert that they are identical values.

Solution

JavaScript's strict equality operator, ===, compares the two operands for equality.

The Code

Listing 2-11. Determining If a Value Is Strictly Equal to Another Using the === Operator

```
if (3 === 3) {
    console.log('3 is equal to 3');
}
if (3 === 2) {
    console.log('3 is equal to 2');
}
if ('hello' === 'hello') {
    console.log('"hello" is equal to "hello"');
}
if ('hello' === 'hi') {
    console.log('"hello" is equal to "hi"');
}
if ('3' === 3) {
    console.log('"3" is equal to 3');
}
if (false === false) {
    console.log('false is equal to false');
}
if (true === true) {
    console.log('true is equal to true');
}
if (false === true) {
    console.log('false is equal to true');
}
if (false === 0) {
    console.log('false is equal to 0');
}
if (true === 1) {
    console.log('true is equal to 1');
}
var myObject = {};
var otherObject = {};
if (myObject === myObject) {
    console.log('myObject is equal to myObject');
}
```

```
if (myObject === otherObject) {
    console.log('myObject is equal to otherObject');
}
if (myObject === {}) {
    console.log('myObject is equal to {}');
}
var myArray = [];
var otherArray = [];
if (myArray === myArray) {
    console.log('myArray is equal to myArray');
}
if (myArray === otherArray) {
    console.log('myArray is equal to otherArray');
}
if (myArray === []) {
    console.log('myArray is equal to []');
}
```

The output is:

```
3 is equal to 3
"hello" is equal to "hello"
false is equal to false
true is equal to true
myObject is equal to myObject
myArray is equal to myArray
```

How It Works

The strict equality operator first checks that both operands are the same type (e.g., they are both numbers). If they are not the same type, it will return the Boolean false. If they are numbers of the same size, strings of the same content, Booleans of the same value, or objects/arrays that point to the same reference in memory, then the strict equality operator returns the Boolean true. If they don't match any of these criteria, then it will return the Boolean false. This makes it the best way to determine the equality of two values. There is one exception to this rule—and that is the literal value NaN, if either (or both) of the operands is NaN then it will return the Boolean false. Quizzically, this makes the statement NaN === NaN return the Boolean false. If you want to assert that something is NaN, you'll need to use Number.isNaN(), as discussed in Chapter 1. See Figure 2-2 for an illustration of this flow.

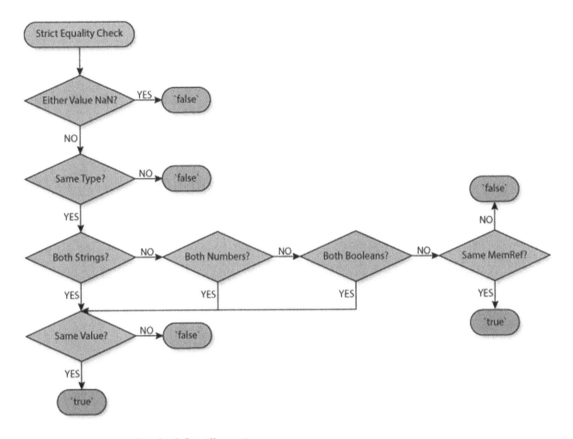

Figure 2-2. *Strict equality check flow illustration*

Determining If a Value Is Not Equivalent to Another Using the != Operator

Problem

You want to loosely determine the inequality of two values—to assert that are not identical values, even when coerced to be the same type.

Solution

JavaScript's abstract inequality operator, ! =, compares the two operands for inequality, while coercing the types of each operand to be the same.

The Code

Listing 2-12. Determining If a Value Is Not Equivalent to Another Using the != Operator

```
if (3 != 3) {
    console.log('3 is not equal to 3');
}
if (3 != 2) {
    console.log('3 is not equal to 2');
}
if ('hello' != 'hello') {
    console.log('"hello" is not equal to "hello"');
}
if ('hello' != 'hi') {
    console.log('"hello" is not equal to "hi"');
}
if ('3' != 3) {
    console.log('"3" is not equal to 3');
}
if (false != false) {
    console.log('false is not equal to false');
}
if (true != true) {
    console.log('true is not equal to true');
}
if (false != true) {
    console.log('false is not equal to true');
}
if (false != 0) {
    console.log('false is not equal to 0');
}
if (true != 1) {
    console.log('true is not equal to 1');
}
var myObject = {};
var otherObject = {};
if (myObject != myObject) {
    console.log('myObject is not equal to myObject');
}
if (myObject != otherObject) {
    console.log('myObject is not equal to otherObject');
}
if (myObject != {}) {
    console.log('myObject is not equal to {}');
}
var myArray = [];
var otherArray = [];
if (myArray != myArray) {
    console.log('myArray is not equal to myArray');
}
```

```
if (myArray != otherArray) {
    console.log('myArray is not equal to otherArray');
}
if (myArray != []) {
    console.log('myArray is not equal to []');
}
```

The output is:

```
3 is not (abstractly) equal to 2
"hello" is not (abstractly) equal to "hi"
false is not (abstractly) equal to true
myObject is not (abstractly) equal to otherObject
myObject is not (abstractly) equal to {}
myArray is not (abstractly) equal to otherArray
myArray is not (abstractly) equal to []
```

How It Works

The abstract inequality operator works almost identically to the abstract equality operator, except that it returns the opposing Boolean value. It performs the same type coercions as mentioned in Table 2-1. After coercing the types to be the same (where possible), it will then behave the same as a strict inequality check; if the types are not the same, it will return the Boolean true. If they are numbers of the same size, strings of the same content, Booleans of the same value, or objects/arrays that point to the same reference in memory, then the strict equality operator returns the Boolean false. If they don't match any of these criteria, then it will return the Boolean true, with the exception of NaN, which you will need to use Number.isNaN() for (as discussed in Chapter 1).

Because of the added complexity in an abstract inequality operator versus a strict inequality operator, it is always recommended to use the strict version, unless you absolutely have a reason to use the abstract one. Also remember that you can cast values to different types yourself, using the constructor methods mentioned throughout Chapter 1.

Determining If a Value Is Strictly Not Equal to Another Using the !== Operator

Problem

You want to determine the inequality of two values - to assert that are *not* identical values.

Solution

JavaScript's Strict Inequality Operator, !==, compares the two operands it is given for inequality.

The Code

Listing 2-13. Determining If a Value Is Strictly Not Equal to Another Using the !== Operator

```javascript
if (3 !== 3) {
    console.log('3 is not equal to 3');
}
if (3 !== 2) {
    console.log('3 is not equal to 2');
}
if ('hello' !== 'hello') {
    console.log('"hello" is not equal to "hello"');
}
if ('hello' !== 'hi') {
    console.log('"hello" is not equal to "hi"');
}
if ('3' !== 3) {
    console.log('"3" is not equal to 3');
}
if (false !== false) {
    console.log('false is not equal to false');
}
if (true !== true) {
    console.log('true is not equal to true');
}
if (false !== true) {
    console.log('false is not equal to true');
}
if (false !== 0) {
    console.log('false is not equal to 0');
}
if (true !== 1) {
    console.log('true is not equal to 1');
}
var myObject = {};
var otherObject = {};
if (myObject !== myObject) {
    console.log('myObject is not equal to myObject');
}
if (myObject !== otherObject) {
    console.log('myObject is not equal to otherObject');
}
if (myObject !== {}) {
    console.log('myObject is not equal to {}');
}
var myArray = [];
var otherArray = [];
if (myArray !== myArray) {
    console.log('myArray is not equal to myArray');
}
```

```
if (myArray !== otherArray) {
    console.log('myArray is not equal to otherArray');
}
if (myArray !== []) {
    console.log('myArray is not equal to []');
}
```

The output is:

```
3 is not equal to 2
"hello" is not equal to "hi"
"3" is not equal to 3
false is not equal to true
false is not equal to 0
true is not equal to 1
myObject is not equal to otherObject
myObject is not equal to {}
myArray is not equal to otherArray
myArray is not equal to []
```

How It Works

The Strict Inequality Operator works almost identically to the Strict Equality operator, except that the Boolean values are reversed. It checks that both operands are the same type (e.g. they are both numbers), if they are not the same type, it will return the Boolean true. If they are numbers of the same size, Strings of the same content, Booleans of the same value, or Objects/Arrays that point to the same reference in memory, then the Strict Equality Operator returns the Boolean false. If they don't match any of these criteria, then it will return the Boolean true. This makes it the best way to determine the inequality of two values. Similarly to the Strict Equality Operator, if either (or both) of the operands is NaN then it will return the Boolean true, meaning NaN !== NaN return the Boolean true. If you want to assert that something is *not* NaN, you'll need to use Number.isNaN() as discussed in Chapter 1. Refer to Figure 2-3 for an illustration of this flow.

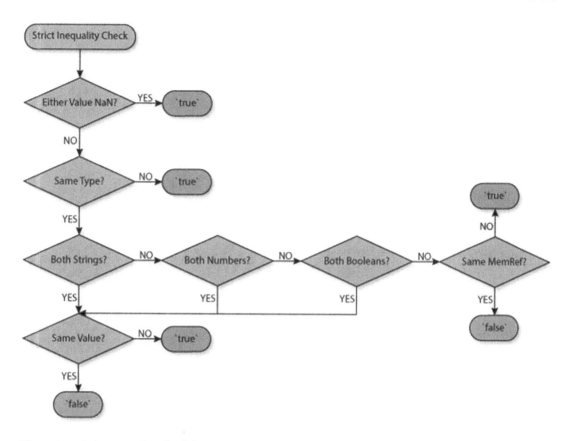

Figure 2-3. *Strict inequality check flow illustration*

Using the Increment (++) Operator to Increase the Value of a Number Variable

Problem

You want a simple way to increment a number by 1, for example, while iterating over an array in a for loop.

Solution

Because it is such a common task to perform in programming, JavaScript comes with the increment operator (++). You can use the increment operator with a variable to set the value to value + 1. It comes in two flavors—prefix (putting the ++ before the value) and postfix (putting the ++ after the value), and they have some subtle differences.

The Code

Listing 2-14. Using the Increment (++) Operator to Increase the Value of a Number Variable

```
var myVar = 1;
++myVar; // increments myVar to 2
console.log(myVar); // logs 2
console.log(++myVar); // Increments myVar to 3, logs 3
console.log(myVar); // logs 3

myVar = 1;
myVar++; // increments myVar to 2
console.log(myVar); // logs 2
console.log(myVar++); // logs 2, increments myVar to 3
console.log(myVar); // logs 3
```

The output is:

```
2
3
3
2
2
3
```

How It Works

The increment operators take the variable from the statement, adds one to it, and then sets the variable to the new value. The difference between postfix and prefix operators comes from how the interpreter treats them. The postfix operation is treated as a "left hand side expression," which puts its code equivalent to value += 1. The prefix operation is treated as a "unary expression," which is an expression with one operand, a standalone operation. It puts its code equivalent to something like value = value + 1.

The practical difference between these is that the postfix operation (coincidentally to its name) will return the original value, and then increment it after the statement has been parsed, while the prefix operation increments the value, and then returns it. Unless you have a specific reason to use the postfix operator, it is always recommended to use the prefix operator. If you ever try to assign a value upon increment using the postfix operator, it will assign the previous value, not the incremented version.

Using the Decrement (--) Operator to Decrease the Value of a Number Variable

Problem

You want a simple way to decrement a number by 1, for example, while iterating over an array in a for loop.

Solution

Just like the commonly used increment operator, JavaScript also comes with the complementary decrement operator. It uses two dashes (--) either as a prefix operator (before variable or literal) or postfix operator (after variable or literal) to decrement the given number by 1.

The Code

Listing 2-15. Using the Decrement (--) Operator to Decrease the Value of a Number Variable

```
var myVar = 3;
--myVar; // decrements myVar to 2
console.log(myVar); // logs 2
console.log(--myVar); // decrements myVar to 1, logs 1
console.log(myVar); // logs 1

myVar = 3;
myVar--; // decrements myVar to 2
console.log(myVar); // logs 2
console.log(myVar--); // logs 2, decrements myVar to 1
console.log(myVar); // logs 1
```

The output is:

```
2
1
1
2
2
1
```

How It Works

Decrement operators work in the same way as the increment operators, except they subtract 1 rather than add 1. The same rules around postfix and prefix operators apply here too, so once again be very careful and if in doubt, use the prefix operator (--value). Using the postfix operator will not assign the incremented value to a variable, but instead assign the old value, and then increment the number.

Using the Unary Addition (+) Operator to Coerce an Object to a Number

Problem

You need an easy and concise way to convert a numeric string into an actual number, for later number-based operations.

Solution

The addition (+) operator is actually used in a few different ways. While its main use may be adding two numbers together, it can also be used as a unary operator (that is, it only has one operand) to coerce a value into a number.

The Code

Listing 2-16. Using the Unary Addition (+) Operator to Coerce an Object to a Number

```
console.log( + "42" ); // Coerces String to the Number 42
console.log( + '3.142' ); // Coerces String to the Number 3.142
console.log( + "-1e3" ); // Coerces String to the Number -1000
var myNum = '1.231'; // The String '1.231'
console.log( + myNum ); // Coerces String to the Number 1.231
console.log( + {} ); // NaN (Not a Number)
console.log( + 'foo' ); // NaN (Not a Number)
console.log( + + + + '1' ); // Operator can be repeated (value is the Number 1)
```

The output is:

```
42
3.142
-1000
1.231
NaN
NaN
1
```

How It Works

The JavaScript interpreter specifically picks up the + sign with no preceding value as a "unary + operator" (section 12.4.9 of the ES6 spec, or section 11.4.6 of the ES5 spec). When found, it takes the value following it and tries to convert it to a numeric value. If it is unable to, it will convert it into the NaN (Not a Number) object.

Internally, it coerces the value using the internal ToNumber function (section 7.1.3 in ES6, section 9.3 in ES5), which has the same effect as using the number constructor (discussed in Chapter 1). In other words, +4 is the same as Number(4). Because of this similarity, it is probably better to just use the number constructor syntax (Chapter 1), as it reads much easier.

Using the Unary Subtraction (-) Operator to Flip the Sign of a Number

Problem

You have a number that is positive or negative, and you want to change it to the opposing sign.

Solution

The subtraction (-) operator also doubles up as a unary operator (that is, it only has one operand) to flip the sign of a number. It also will coerce any given values to numbers before flipping their sign.

The Code

Listing 2-17. Using the Unary Negation (-) Operator to Flip the Sign of a Number

```
console.log( - 1 ); // The Number -1
console.log( - -1 ); // The Number 1 (+1)
console.log( - 1e3 ); // The Number -1000
console.log( - '123' ); // The Number -123
console.log( - '-123' ); // The Number 123
console.log( - {} ); // NaN (Not a Number)
console.log( - 'foo' ); // NaN (Not a Number)
console.log( - - - - 1 ); // Operator can be repeated (value is the Number -1)
```

The output is:

```
-1
1
-1000
-123
123
NaN
NaN
1
```

How It Works

The JavaScript interpreter specifically picks up the - sign with no preceding value as a "unary - operator" (section 12.4.10 of the ES6 spec, or section 11.4.7 of the ES5 spec). When found, it takes the value and simply flips the sign from a + to a -, or a - to a +.(-)

Internally, it coerces the value using the internal ToNumber function (section 7.1.3 in ES6, section 9.3 in ES5), which has the same effect as using the number constructor (discussed in Chapter 1). It does this before it swaps the sign, so can be useful to swap signs on implicit numbers (e.g., numerical strings).

Using the Logical NOT (!) Operator to Toggle a Boolean Value

Problem

You want a simple way to toggle the value of a Boolean, from either true to false, or from false to true.

Solution

The logical NOT operator is a unary expression (that is, it only has one operand), which allows you to toggle Boolean values between true and false. It has the added ability of coercing implicit Boolean values to Booleans before flipping them (for example, a number of 0 or 1).

The Code

Listing 2-18. Using the Logical Negation (!) Operator to Toggle a Boolean Value

```
console.log( ! true ); // False
console.log( ! false ); // True
console.log( ! 0 ); // True
console.log( ! 1 ); // False
console.log( ! ! 1 ); // Can be used multiple times to flip values again, this value is True
```

The output is:

```
false
true
true
false
true
```

How It Works

The first thing the logical NOT operator does is convert the value into a Boolean using the ToBoolean internal function (discussed in Chapter 1 in much more detail, and section 7.1.2 of the ES6 spec or section 9.2 of the ES5 spec). After it has done this, it very simply converts a value of true to false and false to true.

The logical NOT operator can be seen in the wild mostly inside if statements, as it is a easy way to assert something is the Boolean opposite of its value, which makes it ideal for control flow. Of all of the unary operators that exist, it is safe to say that the logical NOT operator is the most widely used.

Deleting an Object, Property, or Array Element with the Delete Operator

Problem

You need to delete a property on an object or array and remove the property name from the list of keys in the object or array.

Solution

The delete unary operator (that is, it only has one operand) is the way to remove properties from objects or arrays.

The Code

Listing 2-19. Deleting an Object, Property, or Array Element with the Delete Operator

```
var house = { floors: 3, bedrooms: 4, garden: true };
console.log( 'House has', house.floors , 'floors' );
console.log( delete house.floors ); // delete returns true
console.log( delete house.floors ); // delete returns true
console.log( 'House has', house.floors , 'floors' );
console.log( delete house );

var primes = [ 2, 3, 5, 7, 11 ];
console.log( delete primes[11] ); // delete returns false
console.log( delete primes[2] ); // delete returns true
console.log( primes );
console.log( delete primes );
```

The output is:

```
House has 3 floors
true
true
House has undefined floors
false
true
true
2, 3, undefined, 7, 11 // this may be logged as [2, 3, 3: 7, 4: 11] in some consoles, but it
represents the same values
false // You may see true here if using eval() or using a console that uses it (for
example Firefox's)
```

How It Works

delete works by removing a property from an object or array. It is important to note that delete *does not* work on variables or declared functions—that is, it cannot delete things that are not properties of objects or arrays.

A common misconception around delete is that it is useful for freeing up memory. Delete does not free up any memory as a direct result of its operation. For example, if you have an object that is referenced elsewhere in your code, as well as in an object you are deleting from, then the object still has a hard reference, and therefore will not be freed. The only way delete will ever appear to be freeing memory is if the deleted property was the only hard reference to an object, function, or array. Consider the code in Listing 2-20.

Listing 2-20. Deleting an Object, Property, or Array Element with the Delete Operator

```
var license1234 = { id: 1234, expiry: '2022-01-01' };
var person = { name: 'Bob', license: license1234 }; // person's 'license' property is linked
to 'license1234'
console.log( delete person.license ); // Removes the 'license' property from  the 'person' object
console.log( license1234.id ); // License 1234 still exists, as it is referenced by the
variable 'license1234', and so no memory has been freed by deleting it from the 'person' object.
```

The output is:

```
true
1234
```

As you can see, no memory is freed by using the delete operator, as the license1234 variable still exists and is referencing the same object. Any memory freed by the delete operator is merely a side-effect. In fact, there is no way in JavaScript to manually free memory. You can set variable values to undefined to "dereference" their existing values, but this is not a guaranteed way of freeing memory. JavaScript's GC (Garbage Collector) is the only way memory is freed, and it automatically runs when the particular implementation detects there is "garbage" or no-longer-referenced objects to be removed from memory. This is done using the mark-and-sweep algorithm. Using this algorithm, each object will be marked as "in use" and therefore referenced by other objects. When no references can be made the object is not considered to be in use, and at that time memory is then released.

Evaluating an Expression Without a Return Value with the Void Operator

Problem

You want to evaluate an expression, but explicitly ignore its return value, instead returning undefined.

Solution

The void operator is another unary operator (that is, it only has one operand), which allows you to evaluate an expression and explicitly return undefined from the expression. Simply prefix any expression with void and the expression will return undefined.

The Code

Listing 2-21. Evaluating an Expression Without a Return Value with the Void Operator

```
console.log( void( 0 ) ); // returns Undefined
var object = { one: 1, two: 2 };
delete object.one; // returns true
console.log( void( delete object.one ) ); // returns Undefined
console.log( object.two ); // returns the Number 2
console.log( void( object.two ) ); // returns Undefined
function addNumbers(a, b) {
    return a + b
}
console.log( addNumbers(1, 2) ); // returns 3
console.log( void( addNumbers(1, 2) ) ); // returns Undefined
```

The output is:

```
undefined
undefined
2
undefined
3
undefined
```

How It Works

The JavaScript interpreter reads the void keyword and executes the expression after it. It explicitly always returns undefined, unless of course the remaining expression throws an Error.

While this has pretty limited utility, it can be useful in some cases. One case, for example, is when using arrow function syntax (described in Chapter 13), which uses the last expressions value as the implicit return value. You can use void to always ensure you're returning undefined.

Another example of real-world usage you may frequently see are developers using void 0 in place of undefined. This is due to a bug in the ES3 spec (and therefore older browsers) allowing the undefined literal value to be overridden. Because undefined was not guaranteed to be the undefined literal value, some developers chose to program defensively, and use void 0 as a syntactical replacement, which is guaranteed to be undefined. Generally this should be avoided, as today almost all browsers follow the ES6 or ES5 spec, which explicitly tell implementers that the undefined value is not writable (ES6 section 18.1.3, ES5 section 15.1.1.3).

Determining the Type of a Variable with the typeof Operator

■ **Caution**   Symbols are an ES6 feature. Older browsers still in use, such as Internet Explorer 11 and below, or Safari 7 and below, do not support this feature.

Problem

You want to be able to determine the type of a literal value.

Solution

The typeof unary operator (that is, it only has one operand) is the easiest way to determine the type of some literal values. Unfortunately, it does not work with all values, but literals do work.

The Code

Listing 2-22. Determining the Type of a Variable with the typeof Operator

```
console.log( typeof 0 ); // "number"
console.log( typeof Infinity ); // "number"
console.log( typeof NaN ); // "number"
console.log( typeof 'Hi' ); // "string"
console.log( typeof "Hi" ); // "string"
console.log( typeof true ); // "boolean"
console.log( typeof false ); // "boolean"
console.log( typeof undefined ); // "undefined"
console.log( typeof new Symbol() ); // "symbol" - (careful, only in ES6)
console.log( typeof {} ); // "object"
console.log( typeof [] ); // "object"
console.log( typeof new Date() ); // "object"
console.log( typeof /^$/ ); // "object"
console.log( typeof null ); // "object"
console.log( typeof new String() ); // "object"
console.log( typeof new Number() ); // "object"
console.log( typeof typeof {} ); // "string"
```

The output is:

```
number
number
number
string
string
boolean
boolean
undefined
symbol
object
object
object
object
object
object
object
string
```

How It Works

The typeof operator checks predefined internal values using the specification (ES6 section 12.4.6, ES5 section 11.4.3). If the operand given is a literal value with a defined typeof value, then the operator returns that value. If not, the operator returns "object". The return value of typeof is *always* a string, hence typeof typeof will *always* evaluate to a string. See Table 2-1 for a summary of return types.

Table 2-1. *Return Values for the typeof Operator*

Operand Type	Return Value
String literal ("" or '')	`"string"`
Number literal	`"number"`
Boolean literal (true or false)	`"Boolean"`
Undefined literal	`"undefined"`
Null literal	`"null"`
Symbol	`"symbol"`
Function	`"function"`
Anything else	`"object"`

Using instanceof to Determine If a Variable Is an Instance of an Object

▦ **Note** Instances and the prototype chain are covered in more detail in Chapter 18.

▦ **Caution** Symbols are an ES6 feature. Older browsers still in use, such as Internet Explorer 11 and below, or Safari 7 and below, do not support this feature.

Problem

You want to be able to check if a non-literal value inherits from an object, such as the date constructor.

Solution

The `typeof` operator only asserts against literal values, which makes it useless for asserting against more complex objects, such as the Date object. Instead, the `instanceof` can be used to determine if a variable or object is an instance of a particular constructor.

The Code

Listing 2-23. Using instanceof to Determine If a Variable Is an Instance of an Object

```
var myDate = new Date();
if (myDate instanceof Date) {
    console.log('myDate is a Date instance');
}
if (myDate instanceof Array) {
    console.log('myDate is an Array instance');
}
```

```
if (myDate instanceof Symbol) {
    console.log('myDate is a Symbol instance');
}
if (myDate instanceof Object) {
    console.log('myDate is an Object instance');
}

var mySymbol = new Symbol();
if (mySymbol instanceof Date) {
    console.log('mySymbol is a Date instance');
}
if (mySymbol instanceof Array) {
    console.log('mySymbol is an Array instance');
}
if (mySymbol instanceof Symbol) {
    console.log('mySymbol is a Symbol instance');
}
if (mySymbol instanceof Object) {
    console.log('mySymbol is an Object instance');
}

var myArray = new Array();
if (myArray instanceof Date) {
    console.log('myArray is a Date instance');
}
if (myArray instanceof Array) {
    console.log('myArray is an Array instance');
}
if (myArray instanceof Symbol) {
    console.log('myArray is a Symbol instance');
}
if (myArray instanceof Object) {
    console.log('myArray is an Object instance');
}

var myObject = new Object();
if (myObject instanceof Date) {
    console.log('myObject is a Date instance');
}
if (myObject instanceof Array) {
    console.log('myObject is an Array instance');
}
if (myObject instanceof Symbol) {
    console.log('myObject is a Symbol instance');
}
if (myObject instanceof Object) {
    console.log('myObject is an Object instance');
}
```

The output is:

```
myDate is a Date instance
myDate is an Object instance
mySymbol is a Symbol instance
mySymbol is an Object instance
myArray is an Array instance
myArray is an Object instance
myObject is an Object instance
```

How It Works

The `instanceof` unary operator checks to see if the left hand operator is an instance of the right hand operator. It knows if a particular object has been instantiated by a constructor because of a piece of JavaScript internals known as the *prototype*.

JavaScript's prototype allows objects to inherit properties and methods from constructors. Constructors define a `.prototype` property that is an object of properties and functions to assign to new objects. When a constructor gets called with the new keyword (e.g., new `Date()`), it creates a new object, whose __proto__ property is set to a reference of the constructor's `.prototype` property. `instanceof` essentially asserts that the left hand operand's __proto__ property is equal to the right hand's `.prototype` property. But it goes further than that, because `instanceof` will also check the constructor's __proto__ property, and that constructor's __proto__ property, and so on. This is called the "prototype chain," and it means that you can assert against an object's ancestry. As a side note, all non-literal values have an ancestry starting with object, which is why all constructors and instances will assert that they are instances of object. This may seem like a complex topic, and that's because it is—but it's covered in much more detail later in the book.

Finding Properties in an Object with the in Operator

■ **Note** Enumerability and defining object meta properties are discussed more in Chapter 9.

Instances and the prototype chain are covered in more detail in Chapter 18.

Problem

You want to determine if an object contains (in itself or as part of its prototype) a particular property or function.

Solution

JavaScript's in operator is a great way to check for the existence of property names inside an object or its ancestor objects (the prototype chain).

The Code

Listing 2-24. Finding Properties in an Object with the in Operator

```javascript
var house = { bedrooms: 4, floors: 3 };
if ('bedrooms' in house) {
    console.log('house has a "bedrooms" property');
}
if ('floors' in house) {
    console.log('house has a "floors" property');
}
if ('style' in house) {
    console.log('house has a "style" property');
} else {
    console.log('house does not have a "style" property');
}
var bedroomPropertyName = 'bedrooms';
if (bedroomPropertyName in house) {
    console.log('house has a ' + bedroomPropertyName + ' property');
}

var qualifiers = ['First', 'Second', 'Third', 'DNF'];
if (0 in qualifiers) {
    console.log('qualifiers has a "0" item');
}
if (3 in qualifiers) {
    console.log('qualifiers has a "3" item');
}
if (8 in qualifiers) {
    console.log('qualifiers has an "8" item');
} else {
    console.log('qualifiers does not have an "8" item');
}

var myDate = new Date();
if ('setDay' in myDate) {
    console.log('myDate has a "setDay" method');
}
```

The output is:

```
house has a "bedrooms" property
house has a "floors" property
house does not have a "style" property
house has a bedrooms property
qualifiers has a "0" item
qualifiers has a "3" item
qualifiers does not have an "8" item
```

How It Works

The in operator checks for the existence of a property inside of an object, even if that property is not enumerable (enumerability refers to if a property appears in loops, it is discussed much more in Chapter 8) or even if is set to the undefined literal.

It will also check for properties or methods that it has inherited from constructors it has been created from (the same kind of ancestry pattern we see in instanceof). These might not be directly attached to the object, but will be part of the Object's prototype. For more on how JavaScript's prototype works, read ahead to Chapter 18.

Using Logical AND (&&) for Combining Boolean Expressions in an if Statement, with Short-Circuit Evaluation

Problem

You want to combine a set of expressions in an if statement, ending the evaluation of all statements upon the first false one.

Solution

The logical AND operator (&&) is an incredibly useful tool for short-circuit evaluation of a series of expressions. It will executes each expression, continuing if the expression is true, until the first expression that returns false, and will exit early at that point. This is useful for combining Boolean expressions in a useful and performant way.

The Code

Listing 2-25. Using Logical AND (&&) Short-Circuit Evaluation in an if Statement

```
var myBoolean = true, otherBoolean = true;
if (myBoolean && otherBoolean) {
    console.log('Both operands were true');
} else {
    console.log('One or both operands were false');
}

myBoolean = false;
if (myBoolean && otherBoolean) {
    console.log('Both operands were true');
} else {
    console.log('One or both operands were false');
}

myBoolean = true;
otherBoolean = false;
if (myBoolean && otherBoolean) {
    console.log('Both operands were true');
} else {
```

```
    console.log('One or both operands were false');
}

var house = { bedrooms: 4, floors: 3 };
if (house.bedrooms && house.bedrooms > 3) {
    console.log('House has more than 3 bedrooms');
}
if (house.floors && house.bedrooms && house.bedrooms > house.floors) {
    console.log('House has more bedrooms than floors');
}
```

The output is:

```
Both operands were true
One or both operands were false
One or both operands were false
House has more than 3 bedrooms
House has more bedrooms than floors
```

How It Works

The JavaScript interpreter will separate each expression on either side of the logical AND operator and run them serially (in sequence, one after the other). If an expression returns false, it will exit the entire statement early and return false. If it gets to the end of all expressions—each one returning true—then the entire statement will return true.

Short-circuit evaluation is the crux of control flow in almost any programming language. It keeps things performant by ending at the first false expression, which means developers seeking for performant control flow can easily order their expressions from most performant to least. JavaScript performance is not something this book will dive into, as it's a vast topic in and of itself, but there are many great books you can read on the topic of performance.

Using Logical OR (||) Short-Circuit Evaluation in an if Statement

Problem

You want to combine a set of expressions in an if statement, ending the evaluation of all statements upon the first true one.

Solution

The logical OR OPERATOR (||) is pretty much the antithesis of the logical AND operator. It will execute each expression continuing if the expression is false, until the first expression that returns true, and will exit early at that point. This is useful for combining Boolean expressions in a useful and performant way.

The Code

Listing 2-26. Using Logical OR (||) Short-Circuit Evaluation in an if Statement

```
var myBoolean = true, otherBoolean = true;
if (myBoolean || otherBoolean) {
    console.log('Both operands were true');
} else {
    console.log('One or both operands were false');
}

myBoolean = false;
if (myBoolean || otherBoolean) {
    console.log('Both operands were true');
} else {
    console.log('One or both operands were false');
}

myBoolean = true;
otherBoolean = false;
if (myBoolean || otherBoolean) {
    console.log('Both operands were true');
} else {
    console.log('One or both operands were false');
}

var house = { bedrooms: 4, floors: 3, driveway: 1 };
if (house.floors === 4 || house.bedrooms === 4) {
    console.log('House has either 4 floors OR 4 bedrooms');
}
if (house.streetParking || house.garage || house.driveway) {
    console.log('House has some parking space');
}
```

The output is:

```
Both operands were true
Both operands were true
Both operands were true
House has either 4 floors OR 4 bedrooms
House has some parking space
```

How It Works

The JavaScript interpreter will separate each expression on either side of the logical OR operator and run them serially (in sequence, one after the other). If an expression returns true, it will exit the entire statement early and return true. If it gets to the end of all expressions—each one returning false—then the entire statement will return false. This is effectively the opposite behavior of the logical AND operator.

Short-circuit evaluation is the crux of control flow in almost any programming language. It keeps things performant by ending at the first true expression, which means developers seeking for performant control flow can easily order their expressions from most performant to least. JavaScript performance is not something this book will dive into, as it's a vast topic in and of itself, but there are many great books you can read on the topic of performance.

Simplifying Variable Assignments Using the Conditional (?) Operator

Problem

You want a more concise way of assigning a variable to a value based on a condition and using an if/else is too complex for simple variable assignment. A terser way accomplish the same goals is preferable.

Solution

The conditional ternary (that is, it takes three expressions) operator (?) is a quick-fire way to assign a variable based on a condition. Simply begin a variable assignment as you would normally, followed by a condition, followed by two potential values. This is better than than the overly verbose if(condition) { value } else { otherValue }.

The Code

Listing 2-27. Simplifying Variable Assignments Using the Conditional (?) Operator

```
var retake = false;
var passMark = retake ? 180 : 150;
console.log('The pass mark is ' + passMark);

var retake = true;
var passMark = retake ? 180 : 150;
console.log('The pass mark is ' + passMark);

var score = 180, retake = true;
var passFail = retake ? (score >= 180 ? 'pass' : 'fail') : (score >= 150 ? 'pass': 'fail');
console.log('You scored ' + score + ' which is a ' + passFail);

var score = 150, retake = false;
var passFail = retake ? (score >= 180 ? 'pass' : 'fail') : (score >= 150 ? 'pass': 'fail');
console.log('You scored ' + score + ' which is a ' + passFail);

var score = 150, retake = true;
```

```
var passFail = retake ? (score >= 180 ? 'pass' : 'fail') : (score >= 150 ? 'pass': 'fail');
console.log('You scored ' + score + ' which is a ' + passFail);

var score = 120;
var grade =  score >= 180 ? 'A' :
             score >= 150 ? 'B' :
             score >= 120 ? 'C' :
             score >= 100 ? 'D' :
             score >= 80 ? 'E' :
             'F';
var anOrA = (grade === 'B' || grade === 'C' || grade === 'D') ? 'a' : 'an';
console.log('You scored ' + score + ' which is ' +  anOrA + ' ' + grade);

var score = 40;
var grade =  score >= 180 ? 'A' :
             score >= 150 ? 'B' :
             score >= 120 ? 'C' :
             score >= 100 ? 'D' :
             score >= 80 ? 'E' :
             'F';
var anOrA = (grade === 'B' || grade === 'C' || grade === 'D') ? 'a' : 'an';
console.log('You scored ' + score + ' which is ' +  anOrA + ' ' + grade);
```

The output is:

```
The pass mark is 150
The pass mark is 180
You scored 180 which is a pass
You scored 150 which is a pass
You scored 150 which is a fail
You scored 120 which is a C
You scored 40 which is an F
```

How It Works

The conditional ternary operator uses a ? to denote that the left hand expression should be treated as a conditional expression, then the remaining two expressions—separated by :—will be used based on the resulting conditional value. If the conditional expression returns true, the value left of the : is used. If the conditional expression returns false, the value right of the : is used. It behaves exactly like an if/else statement that assigns one value, in that the conditional is coerced using the same ToBoolean internal function, and the resulting expressions will become the variable's value.

Because each operand can be a full expression you can also create complex expressions, such as combining short-circuit evaluation or multiple conditional ternary operators—as demonstrated in the examples—this can become messy very quickly. As a good rule of thumb, use this only for setting single values based on a single condition; if you find yourself nesting conditional ternary operators, it is most likely going to be clearer as an if statement.

Specifying Multiple Expressions Using the Comma Operator

Problem

You want to be able to specify multiple expressions in one statement, for example inside a for loop, a variable declaration, or a conditional ternary operator.

Solution

The comma operator has some caveats but is a great way to express multiple expressions in a single statement, which has various uses.

The Code

Listing 2-28. Specifying Multiple Expressions Using the Comma Operator

```
var names = ['bob', 'jim', 'sue'],
    greetings = { warm: 'hello' },
    count = names.length;
// Here the comma operator is used in the last statement
// of a for loop to mutate two numbers at once
for (var i = 0, n = names.length; i < count; ++i, --n) {
    console.log(greetings.warm + ' ' + names[i] + ' (' + n + ' people left)');
}
// vs:
for (var i = 0, n = names.length; i < count; ++i) {
    --n;
    console.log(greetings.warm + ' ' + names[i] + ' (' + n + ' people left)');
}

// Here, the comma operator can be used in a while loop
// which clarifies what the while loop is searching for
// in a cleaner way:
function findFirstParentTag(position, tag) {
    while (position = position.parent(), position.tagName !== tag);
    return position;
}
// vs:
function findFirstParentTag(position, tag) {
    position = position.parent();
    while (position.tagName !== tag) {
        position = position.parent();
    }
    return position;
}

// Confusing use of the operator to assign variables:
var a = (1, 2, 3, 4); // 'a' is set to 4, as that is the last evaluated statement
```

The output is

```
hello bob (3 people left)
hello jim (2 people left)
hello sue (1 people left)
hello bob (2 people left)
hello jim (1 people left)
hello sue (0 people left)
```

How It Works

The JavaScript interpreter treats the comma operator as a separation of expressions. It works similarly to the semicolon (which explicitly closes a statement). It has limited use, and in fact it can be quite confusing to use. It works best inside for and while loops (as demonstrated).

Another popular use of the comma operator is attempting to use them in place of semicolons. Many large libraries, such as Zepto.JS, feature little to no semicolons in their source code, and rely on the comma operator instead, as they believe this reads better. This is completely not recommended, as it is trivially easy to get stung by doing this, especially because JavaScript has a feature called ASI (automatic semicolon insertion), which will cause the parser to automatically insert semicolons in your code to close of statements, sometimes in undesirable places. This book doesn't cover ASI rules simply because if you stick to the best practice of using semicolons, your code will work.

CHAPTER 3

Working with Strings

Understanding Unicode Strings

> **Caution** Unicode code point escape codes are an ES6 feature. Some browsers still in use, such as Internet Explorer 11 and below, or Safari 7 and below, do not support this feature. Check out `http://kangax.github.io/es5-compat-table/es6/` for the current compatibility charts.

Problem

You want to have a better understanding of Unicode strings.

Solution

JavaScript uses the Unicode standard of encoding characters. In JavaScript Unicode, character points can be manually expressed using the \uXXXX (Unicode code unit format) or \u{XXXXX} (Unicode code point format). Unicode code point format only works in ES6 compatible browsers.

The Code

Listing 3-1. Understanding Unicode Strings

```
console.log('\u0068\u0065\u006c\u006c\u006f');
console.log('\u{68}\u{65}\u{6c}\u{6c}\u{6f}');
console.log('\u0061\u0041\u0062\u0042\u0063\u0043');
console.log('you can mix \u0075nicode escape codes');
```

The output is:

```
hello
hello
aAbBcC
you can mix unicode escape codes
```

© Russ Ferguson and Keith Cirkel 2017
R. Ferguson and K. Cirkel, *JavaScript Recipes*, DOI 10.1007/978-1-4302-6107-0_3

How It Works

JavaScript strings are actually a collection of 16-bit integers; the underlying language does not have a concept of characters like A, B or C like we do. It uses these 16-bit integers in combination with the Unicode UTF-16 encoding format, which tells JavaScript interpreters how to represent these 16-bit integers. Every unique integer has a unique character to go with it; for example, the integer 65 (0x41 in Hexadecimal) represents the character 'A' (Latin Capital Letter A), 66 (0x42) represents the letter 'B' (Latin Capital Letter B), and so on (for the curious, you can see the huge selection of Unicode character references at http://unicode-table.com/).

Unicode calls these 16-bit integers *code units*. Each code unit is usually represented in Hexadecimal, as four Hexadecimal digits. When you type a UTF-16 character in a string (for example, 'A') it is converted to the 16-bit integer, the exception being escape codes (which are covered a bit more later in this chapter). You can manually enter in UTF *code units* by using the \u character escape code, followed by four hexadecimal characters, and JavaScript will convert this into a Unicode UTF-16 *code unit*, just like the rest of the string. Consider the string "hello"; this is actually the string "\u0068\u0065\u006C\u006C\u006F". Each character is comprised of a UTF-16 hexadecimal (as an aside, you can actually express the string as "\u0068\u0065\u006C\u006C\u006F" and JavaScript interpreters will represent it as "hello"; the two strings are identical in JavaScript).

The character set in UTF that spans from \u0000 to \uFFFF is called the Basic Multilingual Plane or BMP, and it covers the Latin Alphabet (for example, \u0061 is the Latin Small Case A "A"), and many, many others, including Japanese Katakana Character characters (for example \u30C1 is the Japanese Katakana Letter Ti "チ"). In fact the BMP covers most languages' alphabets and syllabaries, and includes special ranges, such as the Unicode Private Use Area (\uE00 to \uF8FF), which is specifically unspecified and designed for users of Unicode to define for themselves. There is another specific range worth mentioning inside the BMP, and that is the Surrogates range (\uD800 to \uDFFF).

To extend the Unicode range past the initial 65,535 characters that can be expressed in a four-digit Hexadecimal, there are other planes (17 in total, including the BMP) that extend the character set from 16 bits to 24 bits, such as the SMP (Supplementary Multilingual Plane), which contains more esoteric blocks such as Byzantine Musical Symbols, Domino Tiles. and Alchemical Symbols, as well as the popular Emoticons range of characters. To access the extra characters on these planes in JavaScript, you have to use the Surrogate Pairs special range in the BMP.

Surrogates Pairs are special Unicode characters that on their own do not represent a single character. When a *High Surrogate* (\uD800 to \uDBFF) is combined with a *Low Surrogate* (\uDC00 to \uDFFF), the resulting 32-bit character may represent a single character; this is known as a *Surrogate Pair*. Some parts of the *High Surrogate* range are used as shortcuts to denote character blocks on different planes, such as the SMP. When a Unicode aware program such as a JavaScript interpreter sees the *High Surrogate code unit*, it knows to expect a *Low Surrogate code unit* afterward.

Take, for example, the Emoticon character "Open Book" (\uD83D\uDCD6): the High Surrogate - \uD83D - covers the SMP 0x1F400 to 0x1F7FF range, which includes Emoticons (which range from 0x1F600 to 0x1F64F). The Low Surrogate - \uDCD6 - specifies Open Book Emoticon inside that range (for further examples, \uD83D\uDCD7 is *Green Book Emoticon* and \uD83D\uDCD8 is *Black Book Emoticon*). In ES6 compatible browsers, surrogate pairs can be defined using the Unicode Code Point Escape Code (\u{XXXXX}), as single hex codes; for example \uD83D\uDCD8 becomes \u{1F4D6}.

Because Unicode has so many character sets, often overlapping in terms of appearance, it has a problem with what are known as "confusables." Take for example the Greek Lowercase Letter Alpha (α, \u03B1). In certain typefaces, especially when capitalized (A, \u0391), this letter can look identical to the Latin Capital Letter A (\u0041 for capital A, \u0061 for lowercase a). There is a potential for phishing or spoofing attacks by generating lookalike names unless properly validated by your program. As an example, if your name was "Alan" ('\u0041\u006C\u0061\u6E' all Latin characters), a would-be attacker could write this as "Alan" ('\u0391\u006C\u0430\u006E'), that is, a Greek Capital Letter Alpha, a Latin Lowercase Letter L, a Cyrillic Lowercase Letter A and a Latin Lowercase Letter N. This string uses over 50% different characters, but to the human eye, it's almost indiscernible.

Using Special Characters (Escape Codes) in Strings

Problem

You want to be able to express certain characters in a string, such as a newline, tab indentation, backslashes, or quotes.

Solution

JavaScript strings have a set of escape characters, denoted by the backslash. The character directly after the backslash is used to determine the specific escape code. Earlier, you learned about the unicode escape sequence, \u. There are eight others: \' (single quote), \" (double quote), \\ (backslash), \n (newline), \r (carriage return), \t (tab), \b (backspace), and \f (form feed).

The Code

Listing 3-2. Using Special Characters in Strings

```
console.log('this\nis\na\nmultiline\nstring');
console.log('\tthis\tstring\thas\ttabs\tinstead\tof\tspaces');
console.log('this string uses \'single quotes\', and includes escaped \'single quotes\' inside it');
```

The output is:

```
This
is
a
multiline
string
        this string has tabs instead of spaces
this string uses 'single quotes', and includes escaped 'single quotes' inside it
```

How It Works

JavaScript strings are evaluated against any escape characters (the \ character). If a string contains a \ character, then the interpreter will expect the character directly after it to be an escape code sequence. Primarily, they are useful for entering characters you couldn't otherwise normally enter.

Comparing Two Strings for Equality

Problem

You want to determine if two strings have the same or different content.

Solution

As described in Chapter 2, the easiest way to compare two string values is with the equality operators.

The Code

Listing 3-3. Comparing Two Strings for Equality

```
if ('hello' === 'goodbye') {
    console.log('"hello" is equal to "goodbye"');
} else {
    console.log('"hello" is NOT equal to "goodbye"');
}

if ('A' === 'a') {
    console.log('"A" is equal to "a"');
} else {
    console.log('"A" is NOT equal to "a"');
}

if ('hello' === '\u0068\u0065\u006c\u006c\u006f') {
    console.log('"hello" is equal to "\u0068\u0065\u006c\u006c\u006f"');
} else {
    console.log('"hello" is NOT equal to "\u0068\u0065\u006c\u006c\u006f"');
}

if ('Alan' === '\u0391\u006C\u0430\u006E') {
    console.log('"Alan" is equal to "\u0391\u006C\u0430\u006E" ("Alan")');
} else {
    console.log('"Alan" is NOT equal to "\u0391\u006C\u0430\u006E" ("Alan")');
}
```

The output is:

```
"hello" is NOT equal to "goodbye"
"A" is NOT equal to "a"
"hello" is equal to "hello"
"Alan" is NOT equal to "Alan" ("Alan")
```

How It Works

The equality operators are a built-in part of JavaScript and are low-level building blocks that can be used for all datatypes, including strings. More detail on each of the equality operators can be found in Chapter 2.

Strings that are literal values are compared for their content; the interpreter goes through each Unicode code unit in each string and compares the numeric values. If any Unicode code unit in the left hand operand differs with the code unit in the right hand operand, then the string is not equal and the operation returns `false`. If all Unicode code units are the same value across the whole string, the operation returns `true`. The reason this concept is important to grasp is because, as suggested in the first section of this chapter, a user could make two subtly different strings that would be unequal.

Determining a String's Length

Problem

You want to determine how long a string is, in characters.

Solution

When every string is created in JavaScript, it is assigned the `.length` property, which can be used to ascertain how many characters make up the string

The Code

Listing 3-4. Determining a String's Length

```
console.log( '"hello" is ' + ( 'hello'.length ) + ' characters long' );
console.log( '"1234" is ' + ( '1234'.length ) + ' characters long' );
console.log( '"0061" is ' + ( '0061'.length ) + ' characters long' );
console.log( '"\u0061" is ' + ( '\u0061'.length ) + ' characters long' );
console.log( '"length" is ' + ( 'length'.length ) + ' characters long' );
console.log( '"Mixed\u0055nicode" is ' + ( 'Mixed\u0055nicode'.length ) + ' characters long' );
console.log( '"\uD83D\uDCD6" is ' + ( '\uD83D\uDCD6'.length ) + ' characters long' );
```

The output is:

```
"hello" is 5 characters long
"1234" is 4 characters long
"0061" is 4 characters long
"a" is 1 characters long
"length" is 6 characters long
"MixedUnicode" is 12 characters long
"••" is 2 characters long
```

How It Works

The `.length` property is an "automatic" property (it is referred to as a *getter*, which is a type of function that is called when the property is accessed; read more about getters in Chapter 15). It cannot be assigned a value, but when accessed it will return the value of the total number of characters in a string.

There is a small caveat with a string's length—it actually represents the number of Unicode code units, and not individual characters (or code points) inside of a string. As established earlier, the Emoticon character Open Book Emoticon is actually comprised of two Unicode code units, \uD83D and \uDCD6. The problem herein lies that JavaScript's `.length` property only reads code points and as such the character Open Book Emoticon has a length of 2 (`'\uD83D\uDCD6'.length === 2`). Note that this behavior is the same in many other programming languages, such as Java, Perl, or C#, and .NET. On the other hand, Python 3 and Ruby tend to count code points and not code units and so display the "correct" length.

If you concatenate large strings or perform this often, you may run into performance issues. Because strings are immutable, performance over time suffers from creating new strings based on the previous strings.

Concatenating Strings with the + Operator

Problem

You want to be able to combine two strings together, to form one string.

Solution

As briefly mentioned, you may use the + operator to concatenate two string literals. This works differently than the addition operator, which adds numbers together. If the first operand is a string then the addition operator will concatenate the right hand operand as a string to the first, resulting in a new string.

The Code

Listing 3-5. Concatenating Strings with the + Operator

```
console.log( 'hello ' + 'world' );
console.log( 'hello' + ' ' + 'world' );
console.log( 'strings' + ' ' + 'can' + ' ' + 'be' + ' ' + 'concatenated' + ' ' + 'multiple'
+ ' ' + 'times');
console.log('A' + '\uD83D');
console.log('A' + '\uD83D' + '\uDCD6');
```

The output is:

```
hello world
hello world
strings can be concatenated multiple times
A
A••
```

How It Works

The addition operator (+) with a string left hand operand will concatenate the right hand operand as a string, not the add the values together as numbers (described in Chapter 2). It is important to note that this operation is idempotent—any strings used in the operation remain unaffected.

Like most of JavaScript's string operations, surrogate characters can play an interesting role with string concatenation. If you concatenate a string ending in a *Hi*gh Surrogate code unit and a Low Surrogate code unit, the combined string will feature that Surrogate code point, as you may expect. For example, 'A\uD83D' + '\uDCD6' will result in 'A\uD83D\uDCD6' (the Latin Capital Letter A followed by a Open Book Emoticon).

Getting a Single Character from a String

Problem

You want to retrieve a single character from a string, at a given index (position).

Solution

Strings can be treated similarly to arrays (discussed in Chapter 7), in that you can extract any index using *bracket notation* ([ ]). It returns either a single character string, or undefined if the index you supply is out of range (longer than the length of the string). The alternative is to use the method `String.prototype.charAt()`, which exists on all string objects and primitives. It takes one argument, which is a number index value that corresponds to the character you want to retrieve. It always returns either a single character string or an empty string if the index you supply is out of range or is not a number.

The Code

Listing 3-6. Getting a Single Character from a String

```
console.log( 'abc'[0] );
console.log( 'abc'[1] );
console.log( 'abc'[2] );
console.log( 'abc'[4] );
console.log( 'abc'.charAt(0) );
console.log( 'abc'.charAt(1) );
console.log( 'abc'.charAt(2) );
console.log( 'abc'.charAt(4) );
```

The output is:

```
A
b
c
undefined
a
b
c
(an empty string, '')
```

How It Works

Bracket notation is a specific piece of syntax in JavaScript that works on strings, arrays, and objects. Every string has a set of properties from 0 to the length of the string, which can be accessed using this. For example, the string 'hello' has the properties 0 ('h'), 1 ('e'), 2 ('l'), 3 ('l') and 4 ('o'). You access each property by passing the appropriate numerical key in between the square brackets, for example 'hello'[4] returns 'o'. Each property represents a UTF code unit at the given position.

`String.prototype.charAt()` retrieves the UTF code unit at the given index. The index is coerced into a number (using the `ToInteger` function—section 7.1.4 in ES6, section 9.4 in ES5), meaning numerical strings will be coerced to a number value. If the resulting value is NaN then the function will return an empty string (`' '`). The index number starts from 0, being the first character, 1 being the second, and so on until the string's total length.

Like most string functions, both the bracket notation and `String.prototype.charAt()` only deal with code units, not individual characters (or code points) inside of a string. This is fine for most strings, but you can run into problems. As established earlier, the Emoticon character Open Book Emoticon is actually comprised of two Unicode code units, `\uD83D` and `\uDCD6`. Meaning the expression `'\uD83D\uDCD6'[0]` or `'\uD83D\uDCD6'.charAt(0)` returns `'\uD83D'` which is not a valid UTF code point on its own (it's a High Surrogate Value). This can be avoided in ES6 platforms by using `String.prototype.codePointAt()`.

It should be pointed out that bracket notation for strings was first introduced in ES5 and so really old browsers that are ES3 compatible, such as Internet Explorer 7, can't actually use this syntax. But virtually no one uses non-ES5 compatible browsers today, so you should have no problems.

Creating a String of UTF Character Code Units with fromCharCode()

Problem

You want to be able to create a string using number-based character codes as input. String literals with Unicode escaping (e.g., \u0061) will not suffice.

Solution

Unicode escape characters, as mentioned, will only work when you hard-code strings. `String.fromCharCode()`, however, can be used to make strings programmatically using character codes. `String.fromCharCode()` takes numbers as arguments and turns them into UTF string characters. It takes unlimited arguments and returns a combined string of each character code.

The Code

Listing 3-7. Creating a String of UTF Character Code Units with fromCharCode()

```
console.log( String.fromCharCode(0x61) );
console.log( String.fromCharCode(0x61) + String.fromCharCode(0x61) );
console.log( String.fromCharCode(0x68, 0x65, 0x6C, 0x6C, 0x6F) );
console.log( String.fromCharCode(119, 111, 114, 108, 100) );
console.log( String.fromCharCode('0x61') ); // note this is a String of a hexadecimal
console.log( String.fromCharCode(0xD83D, 0xDCD6) ); // Open Book Emoticon
console.log( String.fromCharCode(0x10102) ); // Number > 16 bits
```

The output is:

```
A
aa
hello
world
a
•• (UTF character "Open Book")
Ă
```

How It Works

`String.fromCharCode()` can take any numerical value, even strings that contain numeric values, as the function coerces each argument to a number before using it. Actually, more specifically the number is converted to a 16-bit integer, and any value greater than 16 bits is truncated to the first 16 bits, as shown in the code example, where 0x10102 (Aegean Check Mark "••") is truncated to 0x0102 (Latin Capital Letter A with Breve "Ă").

As you'd expect, you can also use UTF-16 Surrogate Pairs within `String.fromCharCode()`, meaning the archetypal Open Book Emoticon is able to be successfully rendered in the example. Also noted in the example, string concatenation works with the resulting return values, since those resulting return values are string literals.

Creating a String of UTF Code Points with fromCodePoint()

■ **Caution**   `String.fromCodePoint()` is an ES6 feature. Some browsers still in use, such as Internet Explorer 11 and below, or Safari 7 and below, do not support this feature. Check out `http://kangax.github.io/es5-compat-table/es6/` for the current compatibility charts.

Problem

You want to be able to create a string from a whole UTF code point (sometimes comprised of multiple code units).

Solution

`String.fromCodePoint()` works almost the same as `String.fromCharCode()`, with the exception that it can handle numbers (or Hexadecimal numbers) larger than 8 bits. This makes it ideal for creating strings using the upper planes of Unicode, such as Emoticons. `String.fromCodePoint()` takes numbers as arguments and turns them into UTF string characters. It takes unlimited arguments and returns a combined string of each character code.

The Code

Listing 3-8. Creating a String of UTF Code Points with fromCodePoint()

```
console.log( String.fromCodePoint(0x61) );
console.log( String.fromCodePoint(0x61) + String.fromCodePoint(0x61) );
console.log( String.fromCodePoint(0x68, 0x65, 0x6C, 0x6C, 0x6F) );
console.log( String.fromCodePoint(119, 111, 114, 108, 100) );
console.log( String.fromCodePoint('0x61') ); // note this is a String of a hexadecimal
console.log( String.fromCodePoint(0xD83D, 0xDCD6) ); // Open Book Emoticon
console.log( String.fromCodePoint(0x1F4D6) ); // Open Book Emoticon
console.log( String.fromCodePoint(0x10102) ); // Number > 16 bits
```

The output is:

```
A
aa
hello
world
a
••
••
••
```

How It Works

String.fromCodePoint() can take any numerical value, even strings that contain numeric values, as the function coerces each argument to a number before using it. As opposed to String.fromCharCode(), which truncates numbers to 16-bit integers (you can see in the previous example, 0x0102 outputs String.fromCodePoint()) will actually throw a RangeError. While this is an inconsistency between the two methods, throwing an error is preferred, and String.fromCharCode() does not, for legacy compatibility reasons.

You can also use UTF-16 Surrogate Pairs within String.fromCodePoint(), although there is little point over using the actual code points. But it is important to note when passing multiple arguments, as it may trip you up. Also noted in the example, string concatenation works with the resulting return values, as the resulting return values are string literals.

Getting a Single Character's UTF Code Unit from a String with charCodeAt()

Problem

You want to retrieve the code unit at a given point in a string.

Solution

`String.prototype.charCodeAt()` works similarly to `String.prototype.charAt()` discussed previously and it's a method that exists on all string objects and primitives. It takes one argument, which is a number index value that corresponds to the character code unit you want to retrieve. It always returns a number, relating to the Unicode code unit, or NaN if the index you supply is out of range (longer than the length of the string).

The Code

Listing 3-9. Getting a Single Character's UTF Code Unit from a String with charCodeAt()

```
console.log( 'a'.charCodeAt(0) ); // 97
console.log( 'aa'.charCodeAt(1) ); // 97
console.log( 'hello'.charCodeAt(4) ); // 111
console.log( 'abc'.charCodeAt(4) ); // NaN
console.log( '\uD83D\uDCD6'.charCodeAt(0) ); // 55357
console.log( '\uD83D\uDCD6'.charCodeAt(1) ); // 56534
console.log( '\u{1F4D6}'.charCodeAt(1) ); // 56534
```

The output is:

```
97
97
111
NaN
55357
56534
56534
```

How It Works

`String.prototype.charAt()` retrieves the UTF code unit at the given index. The index is coerced into a number (using `ToNumber` function—section 7.1.3 in ES6, section 9.3 in ES5), meaning the numerical strings will be coerced to a number value. If the resulting value is NaN then the function will return NaN. If the number provided is greater than the string's `.length` property, then the resulting return value will be NaN.

Like most string functions, it only deals with code units, not individual characters (or code points) inside of a string. This is fine for most strings, but you can run into problems. As established earlier, the Emoticon character Open Book Emoticon is actually comprised of two Unicode code units, `\uD83D` and `\uDCD6`. This means the expression `'\uD83D\uDCD6'.charAt(0)` returns `'\uD83D'` (well, it returns 55357, which is the decimal representation of 0xD38D), which is not a valid UTF character. This can be avoided in ES6 platforms by using `String.prototype.codePointAt()`.

Getting a Single Character's UTF Code Point from a string with codePointAt()

░ **Caution** `String.prototype.codePointAt()` is an ES6 feature. Browsers such as Internet Explorer 11 do have support for this feature. However, Safari does not.

Problem

You want to retrieve the code unit at a given point in a string.

Solution

`String.prototype.codePointAt()` works similarly to `String.prototype.charCodeAt()` discussed previously, and it's a method that exists on all string objects and primitives. It takes one argument, which is a number index value that corresponds to the character code point (which may consist of multiple code units) you want to retrieve. It always returns either a number representing the hexadecimal value of the code point, or undefined if the index you supply is out of range (longer than the length of the string).

The Code

Listing 3-10. Getting a Single Character's UTF Code Point from a String with codePointAt()

```
console.log( 'a'.codePointAt(0) ); // 97
console.log( 'aa'.codePointAt(1) ); // 97
console.log( 'hello'.codePointAt(4) ); // 111
console.log( 'abc'.codePointAt(4) ); // undefined
console.log( '\uD83D\uDCD6'.codePointAt(0) ); // 128214
console.log( '\uD83D\uDCD6'.codePointAt(1) ); // 56534

console.log( '\u{1F4D6}'.codePointAt(1) ); // 56534
```

The output is:

```
97
97
111
undefined
128214
56534
56534
```

How It Works

`String.prototype.codePointAt()` retrieves the UTF code point at the given index. The index is coerced into a number (using ToNumber function (section 7.1.3 in ES6, section 9.3 in ES5), meaning numerical strings will be coerced to a number value. If the resulting value is NaN then the function will return undefined.

   `String.prototype.codePointAt()` specifically deals with code points, as opposed to the norm, code units. This means characters such as the Emoticon character Open Book Emoticon will be returned as the full code point. In this case the number 128214 (0x1F4D6 in hex); however, characters in the BMP (Basic Multilingual Plane), which are comprised of single code units, will be the same values as using `String.prototype.charCodeAt()`, for example, `'a'.codePointAt()` returns 97 (0x61 in hex), just as `'a'.charCodeAt()` does.

Iterating Over a String's code Units Using for...in

Problem

You want to iterate over all code units in a string.

Solution

With a `for...in` loop you can iterate over all of the keys in a string. Each key in a string represents a code point, and so you can iterate over a string's code unit values by combining a `for...in` with bracket notation, as discussed earlier in this chapter.

The Code

Listing 3-11. Iterating Over a String's Code Units Using for...in

```
var myString = 'abc';
for(var i in myString) {
    console.log('Character at position ' + i + ' is ' + myString[i]);
}
```

   The output is:

```
Character at position 0 is a
Character at position 1 is b
Character at position 2 is c
```

How It Works

`for...in` loops will check the "enumerable keys" of an object or primitive value. In the case of a string, its enumerable properties are index keys for each code unit in the string, from 0 to the value of `String.prototype.length`. This means that the left hand operand of the `for...in` statement (the variable) gets assigned to each index of the string, and the block is executed over and over, each time reassigning the variable until it is equal to `String.prototype.length`. This makes `for(var i in string)` the equivalent of `for(var i = 0; i < string.length; ++i)`. Because you only get the key values, you still need to extract the individual characters with *bracket notation*, for example `myString[i]`.

Just like most string methods and behaviors, this does not deal well with code points. Using the `for...in` loop combined with `String.prototype.codePointAt()` will also give very undesirable results, because you're iterating over code units and extracting code points. For this, use a `for...of` loop instead (discussed later in this chapter).

Iterating Over a String's Code Points Using for...of

■ **Caution**   `for...of` symbols and iterators are ES6 features. Older browsers still in use, such as Internet Explorer 11 and below, or Safari 7 and below, do not support this feature. Check out `http://kangax.github.io/es5-compat-table/es6/` for the current compatibility charts.

Problem

You want to iterate over all code points in a string. A `for...in` loop will not work because it iterates over code units, giving you undesirable effects.

Solution

With a `for...of` loop you can iterate over all of the code units in a string. It uses the string's (hidden) underlying `String.prototype[Symbol.iterator]` function, which will iterate over each code point in a string, returning a string for each iteration, which is a code point for that position.

The Code

Listing 3-12. Iterating Over a String's Code Units Using for...in

```
var myString = 'abc\uD83D\uDCD6';
for(var v of myString) {
    console.log(v);
}
```

The output is:

```
"a"
"b"
"c"
▯
```

How It Works

for...of works surprisingly different than for...in (described previously). for...in simply iterates over enumerable keys of the right hand operand (in this case a string), but for...of uses the right hand operand's [Symbol.iterator] method and calls it for each iteration until it has no more iterations left. The [Symbol.iterator] property is a built-in symbol used by the language. You can read more about the built-in symbols, like [Symbol.iterator] in Chapter 17. String.prototype[Symbol.iterator] is an iterator (discussed in Chapter 15), which when called will return each code point in sequence, one by one, until there are none left. It specifically returns each code point as a string value. If you wanted to retrieve the numerical code point, a simple call to v.codePointAt(0) on each iteration would suffice.

Because String.prototype[Symbol.iterator] returns a string value of each code point, and not an index referencing each point. The use case for both for...of and for...in still exist, so do not discount either looping mechanism over.

Repeating a String with repeat()

▓ **Caution**   String.prototype.repeat() is an ES6 feature. Browsers such as Internet Explorer and Opera do not support this feature.

Problem

You want to be able to repeat a string.

Solution

In ES6 compatible JavaScript engines, String.prototype.repeat() is available. It takes one argument, which is a number representing the number of repetitions you want. If you pass a number less than 0 or pass infinity, it will throw a RangeError. It always returns a string, which is the result of repeating the given string.

The Code

Listing 3-13. Repeating a String with repeat()

```
console.log( 'a '.repeat(6) );
console.log( 'ab '.repeat(6) );
console.log( 'echo '.repeat(4) );
console.log( '\uD83D\uDCD6 '.repeat(2) );
console.log( 'return value will be empty'.repeat(0) );
```

The output is:

```
Aiea
ababababababab
echo echo echo echo
□ □)
    (an empty string, '')
```

How It Works

`String.prototype.repeat()` repeats the attached string a given number of times. The argument passed to it is coerced into a number (using the `ToInteger` function (section 7.1.4 in ES6, section 9.4 in ES5), meaning numerical strings will be coerced to a number value and then floored (the decimal place is removed). If the resulting value is NaN or 0 then the return value is an empty string.

`String.prototype.repeat()`, like all string methods, is *idempotent*—that is, it does not mutate the original string value. Also, like other string methods, it works on code units and so you need to be aware of UTF-8 surrogate characters (described earlier in this chapter).

Determining If a String Contains a Smaller String Using contains()

▨ **Caution** `String.prototype.contains()` is an ES6 feature. Older browsers still in use, such as Internet Explorer 11 and below, or Safari 7 and below, do not support this feature. Check out `http://kangax.github. io/es5-compat-table/es6/` for the current compatibility charts.

Problem

You want to find out if a string contains another string (substring) anywhere within the parent string.

Solution

`String.prototype.contains()` is a method that exists on all string objects and primitives, used to search for a substring inside of a string value. It takes two arguments: the first is a string to search for (the substring or "needle" to the parent string's "haystack"), the second is an optional argument that determines the start position to search from which defaults to 0. It returns a Boolean that indicates if the string was found (`true`) or not (`false`).

The Code

Listing 3-14. Determining If a String Contains a Smaller String Using contains()

```
if ('abc'.contains('a')) {
    console.log('The string "abc" contains the letter a');
} else {
    console.log('The string "abc" does not contain the letter a');
}
if ('abc'.contains('d')) {
    console.log('The string "abc" contains the letter d');
} else {
    console.log('The string "abc" does not contain the letter d');
}
if ('abc'.contains('a', 1)) {
    console.log('The string "abc" contains the letter a past the first character');
} else {
    console.log('The string "abc" does not contain the letter a past the first character');
}
```

```
if ('Surprise!'.contains('!')) {
    console.log('The string "Surprise!" contains the letter !');
} else {
    console.log('The string "Surprise!" does not contain the letter !');
}

var greeting = 'Hello Jim, how are you';
if (greeting.contains('Jim')) {
    console.log('The string ' + greeting + ' contains the word Jim');
} else {
    console.log('The string ' + greeting + ' does not contain the word Jim');
}
if (greeting.contains('jim')) {
    console.log('The string ' + greeting + ' contains the word jim');
} else {
    console.log('The string ' + greeting + ' does not contain the word jim');
}

if (greeting.contains('Jim', greeting.length / 2)) {
    console.log('The string ' + greeting + ' contains the word Jim in the second half of the
    String');
} else if(greeting.contains('Jim')) {
    console.log('The string ' + greeting + ' contains the word Jim in the first half of the
    String');
} else {
    console.log('The string ' + greeting + ' does not contain the word Jim');
}
```

The output is:

```
The string "abc" contains the letter a
The string "abc" does not contain the letter d
The string "abc" does not contain the letter a past the first character
The string "Surprise!" contains the letter !
The string Hello Jim, how are you contains the word Jim
The string Hello Jim, how are you does not contain the word jim
The string Hello Jim, how are you contains the word Jim in the first half of the String
```

How It Works

String.prototype.contains() will search for the string given inside the parent string. The first argument passed to it is coerced into a string (using the ToString function; ES6 section 7.1.12, ES5 section 9.8). The second argument, the starting position, is coerced to an integer number (using the ToInteger function—section 7.1.4 in ES6, section 9.4 in ES5), meaning numerical strings will be coerced to a number value and then floored (the decimal place is removed) and any NaN values will be converted to 0, and the search will begin at 0.

`String.prototype.contains()` has some very predictable results, for example, if the starting search position is greater than the parent string's length, then it will always return `false`. Similarly, if the substring to search for (the proverbial "needle") is longer than the parent string ("haystack") then the return value will also always be `false`. It is worth bearing this in mind, and perhaps executing these checks beforehand to optimize for performance. It also, like many string methods, uses code units not code points.

If you are using an older browser that's not ES6 compliant, you can still achieve the same functionality as `String.prototype.contains()` by using `String.prototype.indexof()`, for example `'abcabc'.indexOf('b', 3) !== -1` is the same as `'abcabc'.contains('b', 3)`.

Determining If a String Starts with a Smaller String using startsWith()

▓ **Caution**   `String.prototype.startsWith()` is an ES6 feature. Older browsers still in use, such as Internet Explorer 11 and below, or Safari 7 and below, do not support this feature. Check out `http://kangax.github.io/es5-compat-table/es6/` for the current compatibility charts.

Problem

You want to find out if a string contains another string (substring), and you want to know that the parent string specifically starts with the substring.

Solution

`String.prototype.startsWith()` is a method that exists on all string objects and primitives, used to search for substrings that begin at a specific position inside a string. It takes two arguments: the first is a string to search for (the substring or the "needle" to the parent string's "haystack"), the second is an optional argument that determines the start position to search from which defaults to 0. It returns a Boolean that indicates if the string was found (`true`) or not (`false`).

The Code

Listing 3-15. Determining If a String Starts with Substring Using startsWith()

```
if ('abc'.startsWith('a')) {
    console.log('The string "abc" starts with the letter a');
} else {
    console.log('The string "abc" does not start with the letter a');
}

if ('abc'.startsWith('b')) {
    console.log('The string "abc" starts with the letter b');
} else {
    console.log('The string "abc" does not start with the letter b');
}
```

```
if ('abc'.startsWith('a', 1)) {
    console.log('The string "abc" starts with the letter a from the first character');
} else {
    console.log('The string "abc" does not start with the letter a from the first
    character');
}

if ('Surprise!'.startsWith('!')) {
    console.log('The string "Surprise!" starts with the letter !');
} else {
    console.log('The string "Surprise!" does not start with the letter !');
}

var greeting = 'Hello Jim, how are you';
if (greeting.startsWith('Jim')) {
    console.log('The string ' + greeting + ' starts with the word Jim');
} else {
    console.log('The string ' + greeting + ' does not start with the word Jim');
}

if (greeting.startsWith('Jim', 6)) {
    console.log('The string ' + greeting + ' starts with the word Jim from the letter 6');
} else {
    console.log('The string ' + greeting + ' does not start with the word Jim from the letter 6');
}
```

The output is:

```
The string "abc" starts with the letter a
The string "abc" does not start with the letter b
The string "abc" does not start with the letter a from the first character
The string "Surprise!" does not start with the letter !
The string Hello Jim, how are you does not start with the word Jim
The string Hello Jim, how are you starts with the word Jim from the letter 6
```

How It Works

`String.prototype.startsWith()` will search for the string given inside the parent string, expecting to see the string at the exact starting position you specify (or, if not specified, the end of the string). The first argument passed to it is coerced into a string (using the `ToString` function; ES6 section 7.1.12, ES5 section 9.8). The second argument, the starting position, is coerced to an integer number (using the `ToInteger` function—section 7.1.4 in ES6, section 9.4 in ES5), meaning numerical strings will be coerced to a number value and then floored (the decimal place is removed) and any NaN values will be converted to 0, and the search will begin at 0.

   `String.prototype.startsWith()` has some very predictable results, for example, if the starting search position is greater than the parent string's length, then it will always return `false`. Similarly if the substring to search for (the proverbial "needle") is longer than the parent string ("haystack"), then the return value will also always be `false`. It is worth bearing this in mind, and perhaps executing these checks beforehand to optimize for performance. It also, like many string methods, uses code units not code points.

Determining If a String Ends with a Smaller String Using endsWith()

■ **Caution** `String.prototype.endsWith()` is an ES6 feature. Older browsers still in use, such as Internet Explorer 11 and below, or Safari 7 and below, do not support this feature. Check out `http://kangax.github.io/es5-compat-table/es6/` for the current compatibility charts.

Problem

You want to find out if a string contains another string (substring), and also want to determine if the parent string specifically ends with the substring.

Solution

`String.prototype.endsWith()` is a method that exists on all string objects and primitives; it's used to search for substrings that end at a specific position inside a string. It takes two arguments: the first is a string to search for (the substring or the "needle" to the parent string's "haystack"), the second is an optional argument that determines the ending position to search from which defaults to the string's length. It returns a Boolean that indicates if the string was found (`true`) or not (`false`).

The Code

Listing 3-16. Determining If a String Ends with Substring Using endsWith()

```
if ('abc'.endsWith('a')) {
    console.log('The string "abc" ends with the letter a');
} else {
    console.log('The string "abc" does not end with the letter a');
}
if ('abc'.endsWith('c')) {
    console.log('The string "abc" ends with the letter c');
} else {
    console.log('The string "abc" does not end with the letter c');
}

if ('abc'.endsWith('a', 2)) {
    console.log('The string "abc" ends with the letter a from the second character');
} else {
    console.log('The string "abc" does not end with the letter a from the second
    character');
}
```

```
if ('Surprise!'.endsWith('!')) {
    console.log('The string "Surprise!" ends with the letter !');
} else {
    console.log('The string "Surprise!" does not end with the letter !');
}

var greeting = 'Hello Jim, how are you';
if (greeting.endsWith('Jim')) {
    console.log('The string ' + greeting + ' ends with the word Jim');
} else {
    console.log('The string ' + greeting + ' does not end with the word Jim');
}

if (greeting.endsWith('Jim', 13)) {
    console.log('The string ' + greeting + ' ends with the word Jim');
} else {
    console.log('The string ' + greeting + ' does not end with the word Jim');
}
```

The output is:

```
The string "abc" does not end with the letter a
The string "abc" ends with the letter c
The string "abc" does not end with the letter a from the second character
The string "Surprise!" ends with the letter !
The string Hello Jim, how are you does not end with the word Jim
The string Hello Jim, how are you does not end with the word Jim
```

How It Works

`String.prototype.endsWith()` will search for the string given inside the parent string, expecting to see the string at the exact ending position you specify (or, if not specified, the end of the string). The first argument passed to it is coerced into a string (using the ToString function; ES6 section 7.1.12, ES5 section 9.8). The second argument, the starting position, is coerced to an integer number (using the ToInteger function—section 7.1.4 in ES6, section 9.4 in ES5), meaning numerical strings will be coerced to a number value and then floored (the decimal place is removed) and any NaN values will be converted to 0, and the search will begin at 0. It is important to emphasize that the ending position (second argument) is a reverse index—it effectively truncates the string before the assertion. If you look closely at the examples, you'll see how this works.

`String.prototype.endsWith()` has some very predictable results. For example, if the starting search position is greater than the parent string's length, then it will always return `false`. Similarly if the substring to search for (the proverbial "needle") is longer than the parent string ("haystack"), then the return value will also always be `false`. It is worth bearing this in mind, and perhaps executing these checks beforehand to optimize for performance. It also, like many string methods, uses code units not code points.

111

Finding the Index of an Occurring Substring with indexOf()

Problem

You want to find the index of the first occurring substring that is contained within the parent string.

Solution

`String.prototype.indexOf()` is a method that exists on all string objects and primitives, and will return the index of a substring that occurs in the parent string. It takes two arguments: the first is a string to search for (the substring or the "needle" to the parent string's "haystack"), the second is an optional argument that determines the starting position to search from, which defaults to 0. It returns a whole number that indicates at which position in the string the substring exists; if the substring is not found, it returns -1.

The Code

Listing 3-17. Finding the Index of an Occurring Substring with indexOf()

```
console.log('letter a in "abc" is in position ' + 'abc'.indexOf('a') );
console.log('letter b in "abc" is in position ' + 'abc'.indexOf('b') );

var directory = '/var/www/javascriptrecipes.com/'
if (directory.indexOf('/') === 0) {
    console.log('directory is absolute');
} else if (directory.indexOf('../') === 0) {
    console.log('directory is relative');
}

var directory = '../var/www/javascriptrecipes.com/'
if (directory.indexOf('/') === 0) {
    console.log('directory is absolute');
} else if (directory.indexOf('../') === 0) {
    console.log('directory is relative');
}

var userAgent = 'Mozilla/4.0 (compatible; MSIE 7.0; Windows NT 6.1; Trident/6.0)';
if (userAgent.indexOf('Trident') === -1) {
    console.log('user agent is not Internet Explorer');
} else {
    console.log('user agent is Internet Explorer');
}

var userAgent = 'Mozilla/5.0 (Macintosh; Intel Mac OS X 10.9; rv:27.0) Gecko/20100101
Firefox/27.0';
if (userAgent.indexOf('Trident') === -1) {
    console.log('user agent is not Internet Explorer');
} else {
    console.log('user agent is Internet Explorer');
}
```

The output is:

```
letter a in "abc" is in position 0
letter b in "abc" is in position 1
directory is absolute
directory is relative
user agent is Internet Explorer
user agent is not Internet Explorer
```

How It Works

`String.prototype.indexOf()` will search for the string given inside the parent string. The first argument passed to it is coerced into a string (using the `ToString` function; ES6 section 7.1.12, ES5 section 9.8). The second argument, the starting position, is coerced to an integer number (using the `ToInteger` function—section 7.1.4 in ES6, section 9.4 in ES5), meaning numerical strings will be coerced to a number value and then floored (the decimal place is removed) and any NaN values will be converted to 0. The search will begin at 0.

　　`String.prototype.indexOf()` will return `-1` if the substring is not found at all in the parent string, and predictably, if the substring is longer than the parent string or the search position is greater than the parent string's length. It is important to note that it may sometimes return 0 if the substring is at the start of a string. Be careful with this and with Boolean coercions that will convert 0 to `false`. Like many string methods, it also will search using code units not code points, meaning you can use it to find halves of Unicode Surrogate Pairs.

Finding the Index of the Last Occurrence of a Substring with lastIndexOf()

Problem

You want to find the index of the last occurring substring that is contained within the parent string.

Solution

`String.prototype.lastIndexOf()` is a method that exists on all string objects and primitives and will return the index of a substring that occurs in the parent string. It takes two arguments: the first is a string to search for (the substring or the "needle" to the parent string's "haystack"), the second is an optional argument that determines the starting position to search from which defaults to the length of the string. It returns a whole number that indicates at which position in the string the substring exists; if the substring is not found, it returns `-1`.

The Code

Listing 3-18. Finding the Index of an Occurring Substring with indexOf()

```
console.log('letter a in "abc" is in position ' + 'abc'.lastIndexOf('a') );
console.log('letter b in "abc" is in position ' + 'abc'.lastIndexOf('b') );
```

```
var directory = '../var/www/javascriptrecipes.com/'
if (directory.lastIndexOf('/') === directory.length - 1) {
    console.log('directory has a trailing slash');
} else {
    console.log('directory does not have a trailing slash');
}

var mySentence = 'Lorem ipsum dolor sit amet';
if (mySentence.lastIndexOf('.') === directory.length - 1) {
    console.log('sentences must end in a . mySentence ends in a .');
} else {
    console.log('sentences must end in a ., but mySentence does not');
}
```

The output is:

```
letter a in "abc" is in position 0
letter b in "abc" is in position 1
directory has a trailing slash
sentences must end in a ., but mySentence does not
```

How It Works

`String.prototype.lastIndexOf()` is similar to `String.prototype.indexOf()`, except it searches the string backwards, for the last occurring substring's index. The first argument passed to it is coerced into a string (using the `ToString` function; ES6 section 7.1.12, ES5 section 9.8). The second argument, the starting position, is coerced to an integer number (using the `ToInteger` function—section 7.1.4 in ES6, section 9.4 in ES5), meaning numerical strings will be coerced to a number value and then floored (the decimal place is removed) and any `NaN` values will be converted to 0. The search will begin at 0.

   `String.prototype.lastIndexOf()` will return `-1` if the substring is not found at all in the parent string, and also (predictably), if the substring is longer than the parent string or the search position is less than the substring's length. It is also important to note that it may sometimes return 0 if the substring is at the start of a string. Be careful with this and with Boolean coercions that will convert 0 to `false`. Like many string methods, it also will search using code units not code points, meaning you can use it to find halves of Unicode Surrogate Pairs.

Finding Many Matches of a Substring with match()

Problem

You want to be able to determine how many times a particular substring occurs in a string, or you'd like to use a regular expression and determine how many occurrences of a regular expression are in a string.

Solution

`String.prototype.match()` is a method that exists on all string objects and primitives and will return an array of matches pertaining to the regular expression or string given to it as the first argument. If it finds no matches, it will return `null`.

The Code

Listing 3-19. Finding Many Matches of a Substring with match() Using Firefox

```
console.log('/var/www/javascriptrecipes/'.match('/'));
console.log('/var/www/javascriptrecipes/'.match('/var/www/'));
console.log('/var/www/javascriptrecipes/'.match(/\//g));
console.log('/var/www/javascriptrecipes/'.match(/[^\/]+/g));
console.log('There are ' + 'javascript'.match('a').length + ' letter "a"s in the word javascript');
```

The output is:

```
["/"]
["/var/www/"]
["/", "/", "/", "/"]
["var", "www", "javascriptrecipes"]
There are 1 letter "a"s in the word javascript
```

How It Works

`String.prototype.match()` actually uses regular expressions (discussed at length in Chapter 20) to search for matches inside of the parent String. If the first argument passed to it is not a regular expression, it will convert it to one (using the RegExp constructor function). This means simply using a string is mostly fine, as long as you don't cross swords with regular expression syntax.

`String.prototype.match()` will return an array of all of the matched values as strings. The array will always contain strings and no other value. If no results are found, `null` is returned.

It is worth mentioning that just using a string as the first argument will not match all occurrences (because of the way regular expressions work). To match all occurrences of a substring in a string, you need to convert it to a greedy regular expression. For example, `'abc'` becomes `/abc/g` (note the /g part means "greedy"). Once again, regular expressions are discussed in depth in Chapter 20.

Replacing Parts of a String with replace()

Problem

You want to be able to replace part of a string with another string.

Solution

`String.prototype.replace()` is a method that exists on all string objects and primitives and will replace parts of the parent string ("haystack") with another string, using a string or regular expression to find the replacement part. The first argument is the "needle" string or regular expression, the second the string (or function) used to replace the matched parts. The resulting return value is always a string.

The Code

Listing 3-20. Replacing Parts of a String with replace()

```
console.log('javascript'.replace('java', 'ecma'));
console.log('/var/www/javascriptrecipes/'.replace('/', '--'));
console.log('/var/www/javascriptrecipes/'.replace(/\//g, '--'));
console.log('/var/www/javascriptrecipes/'.replace('/var/www/', '/home/sites/'));
console.log('/var/www/javascriptrecipes/'.replace(/[^\/]+/g, function (str) {
    return str.toUpperCase();
}));
```

   ·   The output is:

```
Ecmascript
--var/www/javascriptrecipes/
--var--www--javascriptrecipes--
/home/sites/javascriptrecipes/
/VAR/WWW/JAVASCRIPTRECIPES/
```

How It Works

`String.prototype.replace()` actually uses regular expressions (discussed at length in Chapter 20) to search for matches inside of the parent string. If the first argument passed to it is not a regular expression, it will convert it to one (using the RegExp constructor function). This means simply using a string is mostly fine, as long as you don't cross swords with regular expression syntax.

The second argument can be a string or a function—both are treated specially. If it is a string, it uses a $ as a string escape pattern, as is common in many languages. This is useful for shortcuts based on complex regular expression pattern matching. $$ returns a $, $& will return the matched substring, $` returns the portion of the string preceding the matched substring, and $' returns the portion of the string following the matched substring. You can also use $n or $nn to replace parts of the string with other matched substrings. This can get very complicated, especially using the scope of regular expressions, and so once again, it's covered in more detail in Chapter 20.

`String.prototype.replace()` will always return a string based on the original string, with the necessary replacements made. If the search substring ("needle") is not found within the parent string, the return result will be a copy of the parent string, as noted in the example code.

It is worth mentioning that just using a string as the first argument will not match all occurrences (because of the way regular expressions work). To match all occurrences of a substring in a string, you need to convert it to a greedy regular expression. For example, `'abc'` becomes `/abc/g` (note the `/g` part means "greedy"). Once again, regular expressions are discussed in depth in Chapter 20.

Searching a String Using a Regular Expression with search()

Problem

You want to be able to determine if a string contains more abstract strings using regular expressions (Chapter 20).

Solution

`String.prototype.search()` is a method that exists on all string objects and primitives. It is very similar to `String.prototype.contains()`, with the exception that it takes a regular expression rather than a string, to determine a substring match. That means that it allows for much more complex string matching. It does not have a second argument (a dissimilarity with `String.prototype.contains()`). It will always return a Boolean value based on if it found a match (`true`) or not (`false`).

The Code

Listing 3-21. Searching a String Using a Regular Expression with search()

```
console.log('the word javascript has the letter a in position ' + 'javascript'.search('a'));
console.log('the last word in "lorem ipsum dolor" is in position ' + 'lorem ipsum dolor'.
search(/\w+$/));

var myName = 'Keith'
if (myName.search(/[^a-z]/i) !== -1) {
    console.log('variable myName contains non-alphabetical characters!');
} else {
    console.log('variable myName contains only alphabetical characters');
}

var myName = 'not a name'
if (myName.search(/[^a-z]/i) !== -1) {
    console.log('variable myName contains non-alphabetical characters!');
} else {
    console.log('variable myName contains only alphabetical characters');
}
```

The output is:

```
the word javascript has the letter a in position 1
the last word in "lorem ipsum dolor" is in position 12
variable myName contains only alphabetical characters
variable myName contains non-alphabetical characters!
```

How It Works

`String.prototype.search()` uses regular expressions (discussed at length in Chapter 20) to search for matches inside of the parent string. If the first argument passed to it is not a regular expression, it will convert it to one (using the `RegExp` constructor function). This means simply using a string is mostly fine, as long as you don't cross swords with regular expression syntax.

Getting a Substring Form a String with slice()

Problem

You want to be able to extract part of a string using its index.

Solution

`String.prototype.slice()` is a method that exists on all string objects and primitives and it's used to extract a substring from a string, given a start and end index. The first argument is the starting index number, and the second is the ending index number, which is optional and defaults to the strings length. It will always return a string based on the parent string.

The Code

Listing 3-22. Getting a Substring from a String with slice()

```
console.log('abc'.slice(1));
console.log('Hello World'.slice(6));
console.log('It was the best of times'.slice(-5));
console.log('It was the best of times'.slice(7, -6));
```

The output is:

```
Bc
World
times
the best of
```

How It Works

`String.prototype.slice()` coerces both its arguments into integer numbers (using the `ToInteger` function—section 7.1.4 in ES6, section 9.4 in ES5), meaning numerical strings will be coerced to a number value and then floored (the decimal place is removed) and any `NaN` values will be converted to 0.

`String.prototype.slice()` will return an empty string if both arguments are the same number, or if the first argument is longer than the parent string's length. It also works on code units, and so using our archetypal Open Book character (\uD83D\uDCD8), '\uD83D\uDCD8'.slice(0, 1) would equal '\uD83D'. The ending index number can also be a negative number. If that is the case, the browser is treated as first `stringLength`, last index.

Splitting Strings with .split()

Problem

You want to be able to split a string into an array of strings, given a specific substring (or regular expression) to split them by.

Solution

`String.prototype.split()` is a method that exists on all string objects and primitives and it's used to dice up a string into an array of strings at a given split market. The first argument is the string or regular expression to split the parent string by, and the second argument is the limit—the number of times the string should be split. The second argument is optional and defaults to 9,007,199,254,740,991 (that's nine quadrillion or so— an Unsigned 53-bit integer's maximum value). The return result is always an array.

The Code

Listing 3-23. Splitting Strings with .split()

```
console.log('abc'.split('a'));
console.log('/var/www/site/javascriptrecipes'.split('/'));
console.log('/var/www/site/javascriptrecipes'.split(/\//g));
console.log('/var/www/site/javascriptrecipes'.split('/', 2));
```

The output is:

```
["", "bc"]
["", "var", "www", "site", "javascriptrecipes"]
["", "var", "www", "site", "javascriptrecipes"]
["", "var"]
```

How It Works

`String.prototype.split()` uses regular expressions (discussed at length in Chapter 20) to search for matches inside of the parent string. If the first argument passed to it is not a regular expression, it will convert it to one (using the `RegExp` constructor function). This means simply using a string is mostly fine, as long as you don't cross swords with regular expression syntax. The second argument can be used to limit the amount of splits that happen. It defaults to 2^{53}-1 (9,007,199,254,740,991) and if you attempt to enter a larger value (e.g., 9,007,199,254,740,992), 2^{53}-1 will be used. It's a hard cap on the amount of splits that can occur in a string. Realistically this is a limit that you're very unlikely to hit.

Using the limit integer will not affect the split marks in a string, that is to say that the split will still happen on the whole string, but the returned array will just be limited to the first *n* strings from the resulting split operation.

`String.prototype.split()` will then search for the first occurrence that matches the string or regular expression, and will split at the index, until the length of the substring, meaning the actual contents of the substring are removed. For example, `'a-b-c'.split('-')` results in `['a', 'b', 'c']`. The dashes have been removed. You can sometimes mitigate this depending on the string used with regular expression capture groups (discussed more in Chapter 20). For example, `'a-b-c'.split(/-/)` results in `['a', '-', 'b', '-', 'c']`. If you absolutely must keep the extra characters you're splitting by then you are likely better off using `String.prototype.match()`.

Changing String Case with toUpperCase() and toLowerCase()

Problem

You want to be able to convert the case of a string to uppercase or lowercase.

Solution

The methods `String.prototype.toUpperCase()` and `String.prototype.toLowerCase()` are available to all string objects and primitives and will take an entire string and convert all letters to the respective case. The resulting string will have *only* one case of lettering (uppercase or lowercase, depending on the method).

The Code

Listing 3-24. Changing String Case with toUpperCase and toLowerCase()

```
console.log('lowercase'.toUpperCase());
console.log('uppercase'.toLowerCase());
console.log('Hello'.toLowerCase());
console.log('#@!?'.toLowerCase());
console.log('The ligature \uFB02 has a length of ' + '\uFB02'.length);
console.log('The ligature \uFB02 capitalized has a length of ' + '\uFB02'.toUpperCase().
length);
```

The output is:

```
LOWERCASE
uppercase
hello
#@!?
The ligature fl has a length of 1
The ligature fl capitalized has a length of 2
```

How It Works

JavaScript interpreters have a set of hard-coded tables for converting Unicode characters between upper- and lowercase values (the reference Unicode table can be found at `http://unicode.org/Public/UCD/latest/ucd/UnicodeData.txt`). The methods take each Unicode code point and use a lookup table to see if there is an available conversion. If there is, then it will convert the case to the opposing case; if not, then it will leave the existing code point in place.

The intricacies of the case map are complex. Some scripts, such as Japanese Kanji, Hiragana, or Katakana do not have upper- and lowercase variants, and so cannot convert case with these methods. In fact it is mostly "modern" languages that have case, such as Latin, Greek, Armenian, and Cyrillic.

Some specific characters also can make things confusing—for example both Greek Small Letter Final Sigma (`'\u03C2'` "σ") and Greek Small Letter Sigma (`'\u03C3'` "σ")capitalize as Greek Capital Sigma (`'\u03A3'` "σ"). The lowercase of Greek Capital Sigma (`'\u03A3'` "σ") is Greek Small Letter Sigma (`'\u03C3'` "σ"), meaning the conversion back and forth actually changes the character (`'\u03C2'.toUpperCase().toLowerCase()` returns `'\u03C3'`).

Also, sometimes "decomposition" can occur. For example, with the *Ligature* (a combined set of characters for visual appeal). Latin Small Ligature FL (`'\uFB02'` `"fl"`) does not have an uppercase variant of its own, but instead is converted to its individual letters: Latin Capital Letter F (`'\u0046'`) and Latin Capital Letter L (`'\u004C'`), meaning that `'\uFB02'.length` is 1, while `'\uFB02'.toUpperCase().length` is 2.

Some of these caveats can really trip developers up, so remember to be mindful of them when working with the case-swapping methods. For the most part you will be fine, but it is worth *boundary testing* for these edge cases, as they can present attack vectors for your application!

Stripping Blank Spaces with trim()

Problem

You want to be able to remove trailing and leading whitespace from a string.

Solution

It's a common need in programming to remove any whitespace from the beginning or end of a string, and `String.prototype.trim()` does exactly that. Available on all string objects and primitives, it takes no arguments, and the return value is always a string.

The Code

Listing 3-25. Stripping Blank Spaces with trim()

```
console.log(' hello '.trim());
console.log('\r\n\r\nFile start...\r\n...\r\nFile end...\r\n');
console.log('\r\n\r\nFile start...\r\n...\r\nFile end...\r\n'.trim());
```

The output is:

```
hello
File start...
...
File end...
File start...
...
File end...
```

How It Works

`String.prototype.trim()` simply looks at the start and end of a string, truncating the string until the first non-whitespace character. "Whitespace" is considered to be one of the following characters: \u0009 Tab, \u000B Vertical Tab, \u000C Form Feed, \u0020 Space, \u00A0 No-Break Space, and \uFEFF Byte Order Mark, as well as "Line Terminators" \u000A Line Feed, \u000D Carriage Return, \u2028 Line Separator, and \u2029 Paragraph Separator.

Determining If a String "Comes Before" Another with localeCompare()

■ **Caution**   Although `String.prototype.localeCompare()` is part of the ES5 specification, browsers such as Internet Explorer 10 and below, and Safari 7 and below still do not support this feature. The additional second and third arguments in this method also come from the supplementary ES Internationalisation API Specification, and so may not be supported in all browsers.

Problem

You want to check if a particular string should precede another, in terms of ordering within a particular locale. For example in English a "comes before" b, as a precedes b in the English alphabet.

Solution

Comparing two strings for their supposed ordering is quite complex and relies on various levels of information. `String.prototype.localeCompare()` is the method available to all string objects and primitives to try and execute a comparison between a given string and the parent string. The first argument is the string to compare the parent string against, the second is a string (or array of strings) representing a BCP-47 language tag. For example, `"en-US"` for the United States or `"en-GB"` for Great Britain. This argument is optional and will default to the user's locale. The final option is an object of options properties. The return value will always be a number that is negative if the parent string comes before the string argument, positive if the parent string comes after the string argument, or 0 if they are in the same order.

The Code

Listing 3-26.   Determining If a String "Comes Before" Another with localeCompare()

```
if ('Mike'.localeCompare('John') === -1) {
    console.log('Mike comes before John');
} else if ('Mike'.localeCompare('John') === 1) {
    console.log('John comes before Mike');
} else {
    console.log('John and Mike are both in the same position');
}

if ('Jan'.localeCompare('John') === -1) {
    console.log('Jan comes before John');
} else if ('Jan'.localeCompare('John') === 1) {
    console.log('John comes before Jan');
} else {
    console.log('John and Jan are both in the same position');
}
```

```
if ('a'.localeCompare('á') === -1) {
    console.log('a comes before á');
} else if ('a'.localeCompare('á') === 1) {
    console.log('á comes before a');
} else {
    console.log('a and á are the same kind of letter');
}

if ('Michelle'.localeCompare('Michéllé') === -1) {
    console.log('Michelle comes before Michéllé');
} else if ('Michelle'.localeCompare('Michéllé') === 1) {
    console.log('Michéllé comes before Michelle');
} else {
    console.log('Michéllé and Michelle are both in the same position');
}
```

The output is:

```
John comes before Mike
Jan comes before John
a comes before á
Michelle comes before Michéllé
```

How It Works

Using `String.prototype.localeCompare()` can get very complex, because of the complexities of language. The options object of `String.prototype.localeCompare()` can add a lot of complexity—it has various options that change the behavior of the function. The `localeMatcher` property will decide which algorithm to use and must be a string of either "lookup" or "best fit" (the default). The sensitivity property changes how similar characters are compared, for example the "Base" value will compare "a", "á", and "A" as 0 (the same character), while "Accents" will compare "a" and "A" as 0 (the same), but "á" as different, the "Case" value compares "a" and "á" as 0 (the same) but "A" as different. Finally, "variant"—the default—compares "a", "á", and "A" as all different. The exact sensitivity you pick will be entirely up to your exact application. Other properties, such as `ignorePunctuation`, `numeric`, and `caseFirst` are reasonably self-explanatory, and will be left as an exercise for you to explore should you need to, especially as these options are part of a separate ECMAScript Spec (the *ECMAScript Internationalisation API Specification 1st Edition*, which could warrant its own book).

Counting the Occurrences of a Substring

Problem

You want to be able to count the occurrences of a substring in a given parent string, but no methods exist for this natively in JavaScript.

Solution

There are many ways to solve this particular problem, some using regular expressions, others using `String.prototype.split()`, but the simplest and most effective (also the fastest) is to iterate over the string while using `String.prototype.indexOf()`.

123

The Code

Listing 3-27. Counting the Occurrences of a Substring

```
function findOccurrences(string, substring) {
  var occurrenceCount = 0, position = 0;
  while ((position = string.indexOf(substring, position)) !== -1)  {
      occurrenceCount++;
      position += substring.length;
  }
  return occurrenceCount;
}


console.log('javascript contains ' + findOccurrences('javascript', 'a') + ' letter "a"s');
console.log('antidisestablishmentarianism contains ' + findOccurrences('antidisestablishment
arianism', 's') + ' letter "s"s');
console.log('"echo echo echo" contains the word "echo" ' + findOccurrences('echo echo echo',
'echo') + ' times');
var sentence = 'once you, like, find that, like, you hear people saying like a lot, it gets
really like, irritating';
console.log('That sentence had the word "like" ' + findOccurrences(sentence, 'like') + ' times');


var name = 'Robert';
if (findOccurrences(name.toLowerCase(), 'e') === 1) {
    console.log('Your name contains the letter E once, good for you!');
} else if(findOccurrences(name.toLowerCase(), 'e') > 2) {
    console.log('Wow, your name has a lot of Es in it!');
} else {
    console.log('Strange, the letter E is the most common vowel, but your name has none');
}


var name = 'Ebraheem';
if (findOccurrences(name.toLowerCase(), 'e') === 1) {
    console.log('Your name contains the letter E once, good for you!');
} else if(findOccurrences(name.toLowerCase(), 'e') > 1) {
    console.log('Wow, your name has a lot of Es in it!');
} else {
    console.log('Strange, the letter E is the most common vowel, but your name has none');
}
```

The output is:

```
javascript contains 2 letter "a"s
antidisestablishmentarianism contains 4 letter "s"s
"echo echo echo" contains the word "echo" 3 times
That sentence had the word "like" 4 times
Your name contains the letter E once, good for you!
Wow, your name has a lot of Es in it!
```

How It Works

A high-level overview of this function is that it uses a loop to recurse through the string, each time finding the first occurrence since the last. When it cannot find an occurrence, it breaks the loop and returns the total tally. Let's investigate this line by line to get a better understanding.

Padding a String with a Custom Function

■ **Caution**   `String.prototype.repeat()`, *default function parameters, and the use of* `let` *to declare local variables* are ES6 features. Older browsers still in use, such as Internet Explorer 11 and below, or Safari 7 and below, only support some of these features. Check out `http://kangax.github.io/es5-compat-table/es6/` for the current compatibility charts.

Problem

You want to be able to "pad" a string to ensure it is of a given length. If it is too short, you want to fill the remainder with characters of your own choosing.

Solution

The solution here is to mix a blend of various string methods. The biggest part will be `String.prototype.repeat()` and using the string's `.length` property to determine how much additional padding needs to be added. We'll make a function that takes a string to pad as the first argument, the second argument will be the desired length after padding, the third will be the string to pad with, and the fourth and final argument will be the desired direction to pad. Negative numbers will pad left, positive numbers will pad right, and 0 will pad in both directions, but favor the right if there is an uneven number. The function will also cater to multi-character pad strings.

The Code

Listing 3-28. Padding a String with a Custom Function

```
function pad(string, desiredLength = 0, padString = ' ', direction = -1) {
    var repetition = (desiredLength - string.length) / padString.length;
    if (repetition && direction > 0) {
        return string + padString.repeat(repetition);
    } else if (repetition && direction < 0) {
        return padString.repeat(repetition) + string;
    } else if (repetition && direction === 0) {
        var left = Math.floor(repetition/2),
            right = repetition - left;
        return padString.repeat(left) + string + padString.repeat(right);
    }
    return string;
}
```

```
console.log(pad('indent', 10));
console.log(pad('indent', 14));
console.log(pad('01', 12, '0'));
console.log('0x' + pad('61', 4, '0'));
console.log(pad('echo', 8, 'o', 1));
console.log(pad('trails off', 22, '.', 1));
console.log(pad('equal indent', 20, ' ', 0));
console.log(pad('double padded', 20, '-', 0));
```

The output is:

```
    Indent
        indent
000000000001
0x0061
echooooo
trails off...........
    equal indent (extra whitespace on the right hand side)
---double padded----
```

How It Works

As a high-level overview of this function, it calculates to see if it needs to repeat any characters. It then repeats them using `String.prototype.repeat()` based on the desired direction. If the direction is "both" it will calculate the left side as an integer and calculate the right using the leftover length, as this way will provide the most reliable desired length at the cost of having uneven padding (which favors the right). Let's examine further to get an understanding of how it works:

```
function pad(string, desiredLength = 0, padString = ' ', direction = 1) {
```

pad has been declared as a function with four arguments (three of them are optional). Chapter 14 goes in a lot more detail about argument defaults and how to use them. This specific syntax requires an ES6 compatible interpreter—read Chapter 14 for the alternative ES5 compatible version.

```
    var repetition = (desiredLength - string.length) / padString.length;
```

This line does a simple bit of math—it calculates the amount the given string is short by ((`desiredLength` - `string.length`)) and divides it by `padString`'s length. This way repetition becomes the amount of times `padString` needs to repeat, rather than the amount of characters that the given string is lacking.

```
    if (repetition && direction > 0) {
        return string + padString.repeat(repetition);
```

Here is the first block of the `if` statement (while not strictly one line, both lines are simple enough to explain as one). The `if` statement checks repetition is a significant value (i.e., not 0) and if the direction is a positive number (our semantics indicate that means pad to the right). Repetition is checked because there is no point entering the `if` block to only return the given string, as `String.prototype.repeat()` will return an empty string if repetition is 0, so we may as well save the method call and not enter this block. If repetition is

0, it will fall down the if statement until it hits the final line of the function: `return string;`. This is where it will simply return back the given string, in other words a "no op".

```
} else if (repetition && direction < 0) {
    return padString.repeat(repetition) + string;
```

This block has the same fundamentals as the previous block, the only difference being that this block adds padding to the left of the string.

```
} else if (repetition && direction === 0) {
    let left = Math.floor(repetition/2),
        right = repetition - left;
    return padString.repeat(left) + string + padString.repeat(right);
}
```

This block is more complex than the others. This is path when the direction is "both," in other words you should expect equal amount of padding on the left and on the right. Obviously, the method should get as close to the desired length as possible, and each side should be even—but that might not be possible because of the structure of the strings, but the string certainly shouldn't be longer than the desired length. Because of this desired behavior, the first step is to create two variables, left and right, and have them set to roughly half of the amount of repetitions needed. More specifically though, the left side is set to half (rounded down to the nearest whole number) and the right side takes the remaining amount of padding (repetition - left). The return line should be self-explanatory by now. If you wanted your implementation to favor the right side, as opposed to the left, you could simply swap the left and right variable statements around.

```
    return string;
}
```

The last block is a fallback just in case any of these if statements do not work and the method falls through all if statements; the method should always return a string so that it is a reliable method for developers to use. We simply return the original string here because there is nothing else we can really do—the interpreter will only end up here if the repetitions count is 0, or if the direction is set to a non-numeric value. We could check the type of the direction early on to ensure it is a number (using typeof) and if not throw a TypeError, to ensure the API is followed accurately, but that is generally an uncommon practice in JavaScript, although feel free to add this for your own implementations.

Truncating a String with a Custom Function

■ **Caution**   Default function parameters are an ES6 feature. Older browsers still in use, such as Internet Explorer 11 and below, or Safari 7 and below, do not support this feature. Check out `http://kangax.github.io/es5-compat-table/es6/` for the current compatibility charts.

Problem

You want to be able to truncate a string to a particular length, while also ensuring word integrity.

Solution

The solution for this may seem quite simple—you simply slice the given string by the given amount—however for it to be a robust solution we need to be more intelligent, especially when considering the preservation of whole words.

The Code

Listing 3-29. Truncating a String with a Custom Function

```
function truncate(string, desiredLength, addendum = '\u2026') {
    if (string.length <= desiredLength) {
        return string;
    }
    return string.slice(0, string.lastIndexOf(' ', desiredLength - addendum.length)) + addendum;
}
console.log( truncate('The truncate function will shorten strings to the nearest word', 20) );
console.log( truncate('The addendum can be customized to be any desired substring', 35, '
(read more...)') );
```

The output is:

```
The truncate...
The addendum can be (read more...)
```

How It Works

A high-level overview of this function is as follows: it takes the string, and, using `String.prototype.slice()`, it chops the end off of the string. The ending index is decided upon the first space at the end of the string before the truncation index—the `desiredLength`. The returned string is then given an addendum, which defaults to the Horizontal Ellipsis character \u2026. Looking at this code piece by piece provides more insight:

```
function truncate(string, desiredLength, addendum = '\u2026') {
```

truncate has been declared as a function with three arguments (one of them is optional). Chapter 14 goes in a lot more detail about argument defaults and how to use them. This specific syntax requires an ES6-compatible interpreter—read Chapter 14 for the alternative ES5 compatible version.

```
if (string.length <= desiredLength) {
    return string;
}
```

This if statement provides an early exit to the function if the given string's length is under or the same as the `desiredLength` threshold; for example if `string.length` is 20 and the `desiredLength` is 20, there is no point truncating this string. It simply returns string here, making this particular path a "no op".

```
return string.slice(0, string.lastIndexOf(' ', desiredLength - addendum.length)) + addendum;
```

Here is where all of the logic lies. The solution in this particular implementation is simple, perhaps a little naive. Much more complex solutions exist for the same problem. This also generally only works with LTR (Left to Right) languages such as English or French. `String.prototype.slice()` is given two arguments, the first is 0 (the beginning of the string) the next is more complex.

Here the function calls `String.prototype.lastIndexOf()`. It calls it with a `' '` (space) character, the idea being it should look for the last space character in the string, which would indicate the index between the last and second to last word. Except it's actually passed a second argument, `desiredLength - addendum. length`, which tells `String.prototype.lastIndexOf()` to look further down the string. This means that `String.prototype.lastIndexOf()` actually finds the nearest space, left-most of the `desiredLength` cutoff point. This makes the function a little greedy, oftentimes coming in under the `desiredLength`, but the use case of this means it's better to be under than over.

The line as a whole, one can see, simply returns the newly sliced string with the addendum string concatenated onto the end. If you wanted to use this implementation but did not want additional strings concatenated on, you could simply pass an empty string (`''`) as the third argument, which would have the same effect.

Making a ROT13 Cypher with a Custom Function

Problem

You want a function that will convert text using the famous ROT13 cypher (a crude form of encryption on the Latin alphabet that moves every letter right by 13 characters, e.g., a becomes n, b becomes m, and so on).

Solution

Using a combination of `String.prototype.replace()`, `String.prototype.toLowerCase()`, `String. prototype.charCodeAt()`, and `String.fromCharCode()`, we can create a custom function that will turn the first and only argument (the given string) into a string that has been "encoded" with ROT13. It always expects a string and always returns a string.

The Code

Listing 3-30. Padding a String with a Custom Function

```
function rot13(string) {
    return string.replace(/[a-z]/ig, function (character) {
        var moveNumber = character.toLowerCase() < 'n' ? 13 : -13;
        character = character.charCodeAt(0) + moveNumber;
        return String.fromCharCode(character);
    });
}

console.log(rot13('hello'));
console.log(rot13('HELLO'));
console.log(rot13('uryyb'));
console.log(rot13('URYYB'));
console.log(rot13('This is a secret message'));
console.log(rot13('Guvf vf n frperg zrffntr'));
```

The output is:

```
Uryyb
URYYB
hello
HELLO
Guvf vf n frperg zrffntr
This is a secret message
```

How It Works

The core of this function utilizes `String.prototype.replace()` and the function facility to process each Latin alphabet character, by shifting the character code up 13 characters. A line-by-line look at this will give more insight.

```
function rot13(string) {
```

Here the function `rot13` is declared and takes one argument, a string. For more on functions, read Chapter 14.

```
    return string.replace(/[a-z]/ig, function (character) {
```

This is the call to `String.prototype.replace()`, which, as discussed earlier in this chapter, can take a regular expression as the first argument and a function as the second. The first argument given is a reasonably simple regular expression: `/[a-z]/ig`. Splitting this regular expression into its component parts, the first bit—`[a-z]`—says match any character between lowercase a and z, including a and z. The regular expression then has two flags: i and g. The i flag means "insensitive" as in case insensitive, and means that the regular expression will now capture both upper- and lowercase characters. The g flag means "greedy," that is, it will capture all occurrences of the match rather than just the first. So in total this regular expression says "greedily match all characters from A to Z, regardless of case," it'll capture each character, one by one, and evaluate it against the second argument. For more on regular expressions, read Chapter 20.

The second argument is a function that itself has one argument, a named character. `String.prototype.replace()` will execute this function, passing it a set of arguments. The first of which is the matched string from the given regular expression. It will replace the matched point with whatever the function returns.

```
        var moveNumber = character.toLowerCase() < 'n' ? 13 : -13;
```

ROT13 typically moves Latin alphabet characters 13 places forward, taking into account that the letter after z loops back to a again, so the letter z moved 13 places forward becomes m. That would be too complex to try and implement literally in code, so we cheat. If the character given is an n or lower, then we add 13, but if it is higher than an n, we take away 13. This gives exactly the same effect as moving forward on an infinitely looping alphabet.

This works by taking the existing string and comparing it to the less than operator (discussed in Chapter 2) against the character n. As mentioned, all strings are effectively a series of 16-bit integers, and so comparing a one-character string (for example 'a' - 0x61 or 97 in decimal) to another one-character string (in this case 'n' - 0x6e or 110 in decimal) will compare the integer values. Because we are effectively comparing integers, 'a' < 'n' works and evaluates to `true`, the same as 97 < 110 does. However, capital letters have a completely different set of character codes—while 'a' is 0x61, 'A' is 0x41 (65 in decimal). Having capital letters a value of 32 less than their lowercase counterparts would break our cheat to evaluate which direction to move, so we have to use `String.prototype.toLowerCase()` to normalize any uppercase characters to fit within our pattern. This does not affect the final result because we only use it here to compare the integer value, not to return a lowercase string. The remainder of this line is simply a conditional operator to determine if moveNumber is +13 or -13. Read more on conditional operators in Chapter 2.

```
character = character.charCodeAt(0) + moveNumber;
```

Here, `String.prototype.charCodeAt(0)` extracts the given character into a character code. You could alternatively use `String.prototype.codePointAt(0)` for the same effect. We know because of our regular expression we are only dealing with single characters from the Latin alphabet. The resulting character code is then added or subtracted to, based on the value of moveNumber (-13 or +13). This is the line of code that actually does the ROT13 conversion—we now have a character code that is 13 places away from the original one.

```
return String.fromCharCode(character);
```

Of course, this line actually converts the character variable into a number. It does not give back a string character but a character code. So the last line cannot simply return a character; it needs to do the conversion back from character code to actual string character, enter `String.fromCharCode()`.

Calculating the Levenshtein Distance Between Two Strings with a Custom Function

---

■ **Caution**   Let variables are an ES6 feature. Older browsers still in use, such as Internet Explorer 11 and below, or Safari 7 and below, do not support this feature. Check out `http://kangax.github.io/es5-compat-table/es6/` for the current compatibility charts. If you would like to use this function in ES5 compatible browsers, simply replace all `lets` for `vars`.

Problem

You want to use the Levenshtein Distance algorithm to denote the numerical similarity between two words. Levenshtein distance is the algorithm used to predict spelling corrections or auto-correct, and counts the number of single character edits between two words, to get from one word to the other. For example, the Levenshtein distance between "cat" and "hat" is 1 (change the c to h), while "cat" and "care" is 2 (change the t to r, add the e). A naive implementation might just count the different letters, but we want the most efficient way to change this.

Solution

This code relies fairly little on the string's prototype manipulation functions, and more on the mathematics behind strings. It utilizes `for` loops to iterate over what we call a "two-dimensional matrix"—an array of arrays. This is done to simulate the Levenshtein Distance algorithm. You could use this function, for example, in a Spell Checking engine. You have a spelling dictionary (literally a list of all available English words) and if a given word is not available in that list then you could find the closest word to it by calculating the Levenshtein Distance of each word in the dictionary, and taking the top-N (say, five) of those words to offer as suggestions for spelling corrections.

The Code

Listing 3-31. Calculating the Levenshtein Distance Between Two Strings with a Custom Function

```
function lev(string1, string2) {
    var string1Length = string1.length,
        string2Length = string2.length,
        matrix = new Array(string1Length + 1);
    for (var i = 0; i <= string1Length; i++) {
        matrix[i] = new Array(string2Length + 1);
        matrix[i][0] = i;
    }
    for (let i = 0; i <= string2Length; i++) {
        matrix[0][i] = i;
    }

    for (let i = 1; i <= string1Length; i++) {
        for (let n = 1; n <= string2Length; n++) {
            var add = matrix[i - 1][n] + 1,
                remove = matrix[i][n - 1] + 1,
                change = matrix[i - 1][n - 1] + Number(string1.charAt(i - 1) !== string2.
                charAt(n - 1));
            matrix[i][n] = Math.min(add, remove, change);
        }
    }
    return matrix[string1Length][string2Length];
}

console.log('Distance between pea and part is ' + lev('pea', 'part'));
console.log('Distance between foo and four is ' + lev('foo', 'four'));
console.log('Distance between matrix and mattress is ' + lev('matrix', 'mattress'));
console.log('Distance between honey and money is ' + lev('honey', 'money'));
console.log('Distance between tape and hate is ' + lev('tape', 'hate'));
```

The output is:

```
Distance between pea and part is 3
Distance between foo and four is 2
Distance between matrix and mattress is 4
Distance between honey and money is 1
Distance between tape and hate is 2
```

How It Works

The Levenshtein algorithm defines a way to calculate the cheapest combination of operations that will change the first string into the second, or vice versa. The crux of the Levenshtein algorithm is the matrix, or grid. Table 3-1 shows an example of how the initial grid should look.

Table 3-1. *A Basic Levenshtein Grid Set Up to Convert "PEA" to "PART"*

		P	A	R	T
	0	1	2	3	4
P	1				
E	2				
A	3				

In Table 3-1, the initial row of numbers has been set up so that they count sequentially for each letter. In this case for PEA and PART the numbers (starting at 0) count to 3 for PEA and 4 for PART. These numbers represent the cost of converting an empty string to the respective word, for example to convert an empty string to 'P' it costs 1, to convert an empty string to 'PE' it costs 2, 'PEA' would cost 3. The same applies to the 'PART' word going across. The empty cells will be full of similar numbers, which we have the task of calculating.

For each empty cell, we need to fill in the cell with one of three values, whichever is the least. It is important that each cell represents the string up until that point, so cell C3 (the cross-section between P and P) represents the change from 'P' to 'P', which of course is no change, meaning we can put a 0 here. Cell C5 (the cross-section between the P in PART and the A in PEA) will represent the change from 'PE' to 'P', which is one deletion so we can put 1 here. For each string you can do three operations: remove letters, change letters, and add letters. Each operation costs 1 point, but each one has different rules about how that number is taken:

- If you want to add a letter, you need to take the number left of the cell and add 1.

- If you want to remove a letter, you need to take the number above the cell and add 1.

- If you want to change a letter, you need to take the number above-left of the cell and add 0.

- If you want to do nothing, simply take the number above-left of the cell.

Now we have the rules to what numbers to put down, we can calculate each of the cells and fill out the whole table. For the example in Table 3-1, a filled out version will look like Table 3-2. To help work out how each change has been made, all new digits are suffixed with **E** (equal), **A** (add), **R** (remove), or **C** (change).

Table 3-2. *A Completed Basic Levenshtein Grid Converting "PEA" to "PART"*

		P	A	R	T
	0	1	2	3	4
P	1	0E	1A	2A	3A
E	2	1R	1S	2S	3S
A	3	2R	1E	2S	3S

From here, we can simply take the bottom-right number, which is 3. This is the least amount of operations to convert "PEA" to "PART". The operations to complete this would be to **add** the letter A to 'pea' to make 'paea', **change** the letter E to the letter R, changing 'paea' to 'para'. And finally to **change** the letter A to the letter T, meaning 'para' becomes 'part'. This is categorically the shortest way to change the word 'PEA' to the word 'PART'.

Once you have understood how this grid works, you can decipher what happens in the function. Essentially exactly the same thing, but in code, a "2D matrix" (array of arrays) is set up and each cell is calculated, then finally the bottom-right cell is taken as the Levenshtein Distance. Let's look closer—piece by piece—to understand this function:

```
var string1Length = string1.length,
    string2Length = string2.length,
    matrix = new Array(string1Length + 1);
```

Here we store the string lengths, for easier later reference, and also create the initial array with a length of the first string's length + 1. This array will form our virtual Levenshtein grid, just like the tables demonstrated.

```
for (var i = 0; i <= string1Length; i++) {
    matrix[i] = new Array(string2Length + 1);
    matrix[i][0] = i;
}
```

This `for` loop will count from 0 until the length of the first string, for each iteration it adds a new array into the right position in matrix. It sets the first position of this new array to `i`, which is an incremental counting up, so we have an array of arrays that looks something like [[0], [1], [2], [3], [4]] (given our "PART", "PEA" example). This has created the X axis of our string.

```
for (let i = 0; i <= string2Length; i++) {
    matrix[0][i] = i;
}
```

This `for` loop does the same thing for the Y axis—simply looping through the length of `String2` and adding incremental numbers throughout the array. Given our "PART"/"PEA" example, the array now looks something like [[0, 1, 2, 3], [1], [2], [3], [4]]. This effectively looks like an unfinished Levenshtein grid.

```
for (let i = 1; i <= string1Length; i++) {
    for (let n = 1; n <= string2Length; n++) {
        let add = matrix[i - 1][n] + 1,
            remove = matrix[i][n - 1] + 1,
            change = matrix[i - 1][n - 1] + Number(string1.charAt(i - 1) !== string2.
                charAt(n - 1));
        matrix[i][n] = Math.min(add, remove, change);
    }
}
```

This is the main meat of the function—it's a nested `for` loop, as we need to enter each of the nested arrays, and then look at each item in each of the sub-arrays. This simulates a human behavior of filling out the grid, simply filling out each cell, one by one. When inside the inner-most loop, we create the three allowed rules, so we can naively determine which one is the quickest for this individual cell: adding a character (matrix[i - 1][n] + 1, that is, getting the number from the row above and adding 1), removing a character (matrix[i][n - 1] + 1, that is, getting the number from the row to the left and adding 1), and changing the character, if possible (matrix[i - 1][n - 1] + Number(string1.charAt(i - 1) !== string2.charAt(n - 1)), that is, taking the above-left number, and adding 1 if the character needs changing, or 0 if it doesn't. Here we use the number constructor converting a Boolean; if the strings are not equal the Boolean operation will return `true`, which is coerced to 1, meaning we want a change operation; otherwise it'll return `false`, which is coerced to 0, meaning we don't want a change operation because the strings are equal.

The last line of this loop assigns this cell to the lowest value of the three rules—add, remove, or change. It uses Math.min (discussed in Chapter 4), which will choose the smallest number out of a given set of numbers. This means that each cell is filled with the smallest number out of the given operations.

```
return matrix[string1Length][string2Length];
```

The last line of the function once again copies how you could manually calculate the Levenshtein distance. It takes the bottom-right value out of its grid (matrix, the two-dimensional array).

As you can see, most of the complexity with the Levenshtein Distance algorithm actually lies within its concept, but once it's understood, it is reasonably trivial to implement into any language, including JavaScript. While the algorithm itself mostly relies on the use of arrays (Chapter 7) and numbers and mathematics (Chapter 4), it certainly deserves its place in this chapter, having huge utility in comparing the closeness of strings.

CHAPTER 4

Working with Numbers and Math

Converting Strings to Numbers

Problem

Receive a value as a string and convert it to a number.

■ **Caution**   Methods attached to the Number object are part of ECMAScript 6 (ES6, the new standard of JavaScript). Older browsers that still in use, such as Internet Explorer 11 and below and Safari 7 and below, do not support these features (they work to the older ECMAScript 5 or ES5 standard). Check out http://kangax. github.io/es5-compat-table/es6/ for the current compatibility charts.

Solution

There are several ways to make this conversion. Global methods parseInt and parseFloat will convert strings into numbers as long as the strings are not using letters. Variables with numbers as strings can also be converted to numbers. The last example is implicit conversion where an equation is performed on a string.

Math is a global object that does not use a constructor. This means that all properties and methods using the Math object are static. You will see this in some of the following examples.

The Code

Listing 4-1. Converting a String Into a Number

```
var x = '1 ';
Number(x);      // returns 1
Number.parseInt(x, 10) ; // returns 1 and uses a radix to make the browser use the decimal
system
Number.parseFloat(x) // returns 1
parseFloat('+1x2345x'); //returns 1
Number.parseFloat('+1234x567'); //returns 1234
typeof(parseInt(x)); // returns number
typeof(parseFloat(x)); //returns number
+x //returns 1.
```

How It Works

Because JavaScript is a loosely typed language, the interpreter will make type conversions automatically. Where most of the examples are explicit type conversion, the last instance is implicit using the unary plus operator.

The parseInt method has a second parameter called radix. The radix is the base number of unique digits. For example, using a value of 10 will ensure the parseInt method will use numbers 0 though 9. Using 10 as the radix is recommended. You can avoid unpredictable results by making parseInt use the decimal system.

The parseFloat method returns a floating-point number. If the first character cannot be converted into a number, the method will return NaN (not a number). It will parse characters up to a point where characters cannot be converted. For example, sign (+,-) numbers, with or without decimals and exponents, will be converted.

Both of these methods are included in the Number object and behave the same way. Once they are converted all the Arithmetic operators can be used.

Number.parsInt and Number.parseFloat do not work in IE 11 and below or in Safari.

Creating a Number Object

Problem

You want to create an object whose datatype is a number in order to work with numerical values.

Solution

In addition to converting strings to numbers, you can explicitly create a number object. The result is an object with the number datatype. If the value cannot be converted to number, the result will be NaN (Not a Number). Not using the new operator will result in type conversion. You can also use the global typeOf operator to check the datatype of a variable.

The Code

Listing 4-2. Creating an Object Wrapper to Work with Numbers

```
var myNumberObject = new Number(2);
console.log(myNumberObject);
if(myNumberObject.valueOf() === 2){
   console.log('we are the same');
}
console.log(typeof parseInt('2')); // returns number
console.log(typeof parseFloat('2')); //returns number
console.log(typeof parseFloat(myNumberObject)); //returns number
```

How It Works

JavaScript will take the value passed to the constructor and create a number object. If the value passed is a string, it will convert the string into a number; otherwise, it will return NaN. Because Number is a primitive value in JavaScript, to test both value and datatype the valueOf method is used to return the number.

Checking If a Value Is Not a Number

Problem

You receive data and you need to check if the value is a number.

Solution

Both the global method `isNaN` and the `Number.isNaN` method can be used. You can also check the datatype by using the `typeof` operator.

The Code

Listing 4-3. Using the isNaN Method on the Number Object to Check Value

```
var numberObject = new Number('things');
function checkIsNaN(value){
  if(typeof value !== 'number'){
    return 'is not a number';
  }else{
    return 'is a number';
  }
}
checkIsNaN('1234'); //returns is not a number
isNaN('things'); // returns true
Number.isNaN(numberObject.valueOf()); //returns true
Number.isNaN(4); //returns false
Number.isNaN(NaN); //returns true
```

How It Works

Using the global `isNaN` method, parameters are converted to numbers, then evaluated. If you were to pass a string or number to the method on the number object, it will return `false`. This makes it possible to only pass parameters that can safely be converted to NaN but are not the same value. In addition, you can use the `typeof` operator and strict equality or inequality operators. One way to think of this would be, "is this not a number?".

Formatting a Number to a Fixed Amount of Digits

Problem

You need to format numbers with a fixed amount of digits.

Solution

JavaScript contains methods that will fix the amount of digits. Depending on the method, the results may be different. The reason for this is how each method rounds numbers.

The Code

Listing 4-4. Fixing the Amount of Numbers after a Decimal Point

```
var numObj = 1.23456789;
numObj.toPrecision(); //returns 1.23456789
numObj.toPrecision(2); //returns 1.2
numObj.toPrecision(5); //returns 1.2346 Five numbers total. Notice how it is rounded up

numObj.toFixed(5); //returns 1.23457 Notice how it rounds up
numObj.toFixed(2); //returns 1.2
```

How It Works

toPrecision() and toFixed() will both return a string with the formatted numbers. Using toPrecision will set the amount of digits used. When using toFixed, the amount of digits after the decimal point will be set.

The trunc() method will remove all numbers after the decimal, but has no support in Internet Explorer.

Checking to See If a Number Is Finite

Problem

You want to make sure the number being used is a finite number.

Solution

isFinite has a global function and one that is associated with the Number object as of ES6.

The Code

Listing 4-5. Check to See If a Number Is Finite

```
var myNumberObject = new Number(2);
isFinite(myNumberObject); //returns true
isFinite(2); //returns true
isFinite('myNumberObject'); //returns false
Number.isFinite(myNumberObject.valueOf()); //returns true
Number.isFinite(myNumberObject); //returns false
Number.isFinite('myNumberObject'); //returns false
Number.isFinite(NaN); //returns false
isFinite(NaN); //returns false
isFinite(null); //returns true
Number.isFinite(null); //returns false
```

How It Works

The global isFinite function will do type conversion while the version associated with the number object does not. If you're passing a number object to the global version, it will be treated like a number due to type conversion. Passing a string that cannot be converted into a number will return false. Values like null will be converted into a number and return true, while NaN will return false.

If you're using the method associated with the number object, no type conversion happens. Strings will always return false. If a number object is being passed, you will need to use the valueOf method so the isFinite method can evaluate the number and not the object.

Checking If a Value Is an Integer

Problem

You want to determine if the number are working with is a whole number.

Solution

JavaScript does not have an integer datatype; all numbers are really floating-point numbers. For these purposes, you want a number converted to a whole number without decimals. The methods round, ceil, and floor used with the math object will return integers and will convert strings into numbers. If the string cannot be converted, it will return NaN.

The Code

Listing 4-6. Checking for Integers

```
var myNumber = 1

Number.isInteger(myNumber);//returns true does not work in IE
Number.isInteger('2'); //returns false does not work in IE

Math.floor(1.6); //returns 1
Math.floor(1.4); //returns 1
Math.floor(NaN); //returns NaN

Math.ceil(1.6); //returns 2
Math.ceil(1.4); //returns 2

Math.round(1.6); //returns 2
Math.round(1.4); //returns 1

Math.round(-1.5); //returns -1
Math.round(-1.6); //returns -2

Math.round('3.5'); //returns -4
Math.round('jenny'); //returns NaN
Math.round(null); //returns 0
```

How It Works

JavaScript does not have an integer datatype; all numbers are really floating-point numbers. The engine that is interpreting the code can store small numbers as integers unless the number grows too large or a decimal is added. ES6 adds the isInteger method. This method returns true or false it does not do type conversion.

Formatting Numbers for Date Time and Currency

Problem

You want to take numbers and format them into percentages and currency.

Solution

The number object does not have built-in formatting functions. Because of this, there are a lot of third-party libraries and APIs to give you what you need. The ECMAScript Internationalization API has methods for date time and currency. The visualization library D3 also has formatting methods. The internationalization API works with IE 11, but not in Safari and the D3 library works with IE 9 and above.

The Code

Listing 4-7. Using the D3 Library and ECMAScript Internationalization API

```
d3.format('%')(1); // returns 100%
d3.format(',')(1000000); //returns 1,000,000
d3.format("$,")(1250); //returns $1,250
d3.format("$,.2f")(1250);  //returns $1,250.00
d3.time.format('%Y-%m-%d').parse('1975-08-19');
//returns Tue Aug 19 1975 00:00:00 GMT-0400 (EDT)
new Intl.NumberFormat().format(45000);    // returns 45,000
new Intl.NumberFormat('ja-JP', { style: 'currency', currency: 'JPY' }).format(45000);
// returns ¥45,000
new Intl.DateTimeFormat('ja-JP', { weekday: 'long', year: 'numeric', month: 'long', day:
'numeric' }).format(new Date(1975, 07, 19)); //returns 1975年8月19日 火曜日
new Intl.DateTimeFormat('en-US', { weekday: 'long', year: 'numeric', month: 'long', day:
'numeric' }).format(new Date(1975, 07, 19)); // returns Tuesday, August 19, 1975
```

How It Works

If you want to use D3, you can download it from D3js.org. Once you add it to your page, you can use the formatting functions. D3 uses a lot of method chaining. The first method describes the format that you want the numbers to be converted into. The second is the number to be converted. Converting time is similar; you add the format then the parse method will take the date you want to parse. There are clear examples of how to use these methods and more here: http://koaning.s3-website-us-west-2.amazonaws.com/html/d3format.html.

The internationalization API works in a similar way where you define how the formatting will work. Then you pass over what needs to be formatted. A full breakdown can be found on Mozilla's site: https://developer.mozilla.org/en-US/docs/Web/JavaScript/Reference/Global_Objects/NumberFormat.

Creating a Random Number Generator

Problem

You want generate a random number between two values.

Solution

Use the random method in the Math object and round the results.

The Code

Listing 4-8. Creating a Random Number Generator Based on the Range of Two Numbers

```
function getRandomBetweenMinAndMax(min, max) {
  return Math.floor(Math.random() * (max - min) + min);
}
function getRandomArbitrary(min, max) {
  return Math.floor(Math.random() * (max - min + 1) + min);
}
getRandomBetweenMinAndMax(0,5);
getRandomArbitrary(0,5);
```

How It Works

On its own, the random method in the Math object returns a floating point pseudo-random number in the range of 0 or 1. The result would be a fraction of a number that would then need to be rounded using the floor method. You can set a minimum and maximum range by creating a function that will set these values.

In your function, you pass over the maximum and minimum values. In order for JavaScript to understand these values, it needs to do a little math. Inside the parentheses, you subtract the maximum number from the minimum number. By itself that should give you the value of the minimum number. This is what's called the inclusive number. Outside the parentheses, you add the minimum number back and that will give JavaScript the maximum number. This is the exclusive number. This number will not be part of the results.

This will work fine but you end up not having the high number as part of the result since it's the excluded number. In order to shift this over one, you add one to the equation in the parentheses. This will raise the maximum value so the number you want to use is included in the results.

Finding the Absolute Value of a Number

Problem

You want the real number or non-negative value without worrying about the sign.

Solution

The abs method of the Math object will give you the non-negative number.

The Code

Listing 4-9. Determine the Absolute or Non-Negative Value of a Number

```
Math.abs()   //returns NaN
Math.abs(-1)  //returns 1
Math.abs('-1')  // returns 1
Math.abs(null)  //returns 0
Math.abs('miho')   //returns NaN
Math.abs('')  //returns 0
```

How It Works

The sbs() is a static method in the Math object. Since math does not have a constructor, Math.abs(value) is the correct way to use it. This method will do type conversion before creating the real number value. Empty strings will be converted to 0, while other strings will be converted to NaN. Not passing a value to this method will also result in NaN.

Using Math.max to Determine the Highest Number

Problem

Without performing a loop or any type of comparison function, you need to determine the highest number in a list or in an array.

Solution

Math.max can take a series of numbers and return the highest number in the list or an array.

The Code

Listing 4-10. Determine the Math.max Method to Return the Highest Number

```
Math.max(1,10) //returns 10
Math.max(-100,10) //returns 10

Using apply as part of the method call can define scope of the array.
var myNumArray = [1,2,3,4,5,6,7,8,9];
Math.max.apply(null,myArray); //returns 9
This would give you the same result:
Math.max.apply(this,myArray); //returns 9

Math.max.apply(myArray) //returns –Infinity
Math.max(myArray) //Returns NaN
```

How It Works

`Math.max` is a static method so it is used as is. If no arguments are given to it, the answer is `-Infinity`. If any of the arguments cannot be converted into a number, then the answer will result in NaN.

If you are using an array and not putting values directly into the method, use the `apply` method to direct the browser to where it should find the array.

Returning the Square Root of a Number

Problem

You need to find the square root of a number.

Solution

The `Math` object has a static method called `sqrt()`. Passing any positive number to this method will result in the square root. Negative or strings will result in NaN.

The Code

Listing 4-11. Finding the Square Root of a Number

```
Math.sqrt('Roger') //result NaN
Math.sqrt(1000); //result 31.622776601683793
```

How It Works

The static `Math.sqrt()` method will return the square root of a given number.

Using Coercion and Performing Equations

Problem

Depending on the order of your variables, JavaScript will treat them as strings or convert them into numbers.

Solution

Because JavaScript does type coercion, strings can be converted into numbers and used in equations dynamically. Depending on the order of the strings, numbers, and operators (+, -), the results can be different.

The Code

Listing 4-12. Difference Between String Concatenation and Number Conversion

```
var myNumber = '15';
//adding numbers
console.log(myNumber + 5) // returns 155
console.log(5 + myNumber) //returns 515
//subtracting numbers
console.log(5 - myNumber) // returns -10
console.log(myNumber - 5) //returns 10
var testNum = '7';
    testNum += 7 // returns 77
    testumber - '1' // returns 6

var machineType = 'Tardis Type ';
    machineType += 40 // returns Tardis Type 40

var num1 = 5;
var num2= 5;
console.log ('the total is ' + (num1 + num2)); // returns the total is 10
```

How It Works

Because JavaScript is not a strongly typed language, it can change the datatype of your variables depending on context. If you start with a string on the left side and use the plus (+) operator, JavaScript will assume that you are concatenating values. This is why, in the previous examples, '15' + 5 turns into 115.

The opposite is true when using the minus operator (-). In this case, it will convert the string into a number and perform subtraction. This is why 7 – '-1' will return 6.

In the last example, JavaScript will just convert the number into a string and add it to the existing string.

If both variables are numbers, you can do the equation in parentheses and then covert them to a string later.

What's the Difference Between Math.floor() and Math.ceil()?

Problem

When working with numbers, sometimes you need to round to the lowest or highest integer.

Solution

Use Math.floor() to round to the closest lowest integer and Math.ceil() when rounding to the closest highest integer.

The Code

Listing 4-13. The Difference Between Math.floor() and Math.ceil()

```
//depending on the numbers provided the method will either round up or down to the closest
integer.
Math.floor(5.6) //returns 5
Math.ceil(5.6) //returns 6
```

How It Works

Here each method rounds to either the highest or lowest integer.

Returning a Number in Reverse

Problem

You are given a number and are asked to give that number back in reverse. For example, if you are given 123 the result should be 321.

Solution

With JavaScript, there are many ways of doing this. The fastest way is to convert everything into a string and use the reverse method then turn everything back into a number. This is also a quick way to see if a something is a palindrome if you're asked on an interview, since the results should have the value.

In the second example, you can use a while loop and remove the last number of the first variable and add it to the second, each time checking if the value of the first number is not yet 0.

The Code

Listing 4-14. Reversing a Number by Splitting It into a String then Reversing It (a Version Without String Conversion)

```
var numSequence = 1234;
 var reversedNumbers = Number(numSequence.toString().split(")").reverse().join("));
console.log(reversedNumbers) // returns 4321
//with out converting to a string
var = 123456789, b=0;
while(a > 0){
  b = b * 10;
  b = b + parseInt(a%10);
 a = parseInt(a/10);
}
console.log("Reversed number: " + b);
```

How It Works

The first example is very simple. Since you can do type conversion very quickly with JavaScript, you can chain a few methods together. All of this needs to take place inside either the Number() or parseInt() method, so the results can be converted back to the number datatype; otherwise, you end up with a string. Inside your chosen method, convert the whole number to a string using the toString() method. Chain the split('') method to that. Make sure that you have empty quotes inside the parentheses, because the split is based on the space between the characters. The result of this is now an array of strings. Add the reverse() method to reverse the order of the array. Then finally join the elements back into one string using the join('') method. To make sure you get a number datatype back, you can put the results in the browser console using the console.log() method and use typeof to return the datatype.

The second way does not use type conversion. This way, both variables are initialized. The second variable (in our case b) has a value of 0. All of the work is done inside a while loop. Each time you go through the loop, you check to see if the value of a is greater than 0. If it is, first take b and multiply it by 10. The next line will take the last number from a and add it to b, using a combination of the parseInt method and the modulo operator. This operator will take the a number divided by 10 and give you the remainder. In this case, this is the last number.

You may notice all the math is based on 10 in this example. We are using 10 in a similar way it is used in the parseInt() method as the radix. Every time we multiply b by 10, we ensure when the numbers are added together we get 987654321 and not 45.

Determining the Length of a Number

Problem

You are given a number and need to know the length, similar to knowing the length of an array.

Solution

The Number object does not have a length property. Similar to the last example, you can do this either with type conversion or without. One thing to point out—the second solution only works with positive numbers.

The Code

Listing 4-15. Determine First with String Conversion then Without

```
var myNum = 123456789;
console.log(myNum.toString().split('').length);

//without converting to a string
var length = Math.log(555555555) * Math.LOG10E + 1 | 0;
console.log(length);
```

How It Works

The first example is similar to the previous one. Convert the number to a string. Then turn the string into an array by using the split() method, then check the length.

The second example will take more time to explain. We first use the log() method of the Math object. Since it is a static method, you use it directly from the Math object. This gives you what is described as the natural logarithm of the number you provided. If it's given a negative number, it will return NaN.

Once you have that times the number by base 10, you use the LOG10E property of the Math object. This actually makes the number smaller and gets you closer to the right amount of numbers. Finally, add a bitwise OR operator. The number is then treated as a bit (1 or 0). If the value is 1, then add 1 and truncate the remaining numbers. Now you have the length of numbers.

Swapping Two Numbers Without a Temporary Variable

Problem

You need reverse the order of two numbers.

Solution

This goes under the category of questions you may get on an interview. To get this to work just involves some math that will reassign the value of each variable. The second variable is reassigned twice.

The Code

Listing 4-16. Determine First with String Conversion then Without

```
function swapNumbers(numb1, numb2){
    console.log('starting order = ' + numb1 + ',' + numb2);
    numb2 = numb2 - numb1; //is now -150
    numb1 = numb1 + numb2; //is now 50
    numb2 = numb1 - numb2; //is now 200
    console.log('ending order = ' + numb1 + ',' + numb2);
}
swapNumbers(200,50);
```

How It Works

Since we can dynamically reassign the value of our variables, we just do a little math. We immediately start to reassign the values of the variables as soon as the function starts. To help, we will use round numbers.

- num2 is reassigned to the value of 50 - 200 so now it is -150.

- num1 is reassigned to the value of 200 + (-150) so now it is 50.

- num2 is again reassigned to the value of 50 - (-150) so now it is 200.

The last line is the one to watch out for. Since it is minus a negative number, the result is the same as addition.

CHAPTER 5

Working with Bitwise Operations Against 32-Bit Integers

What Are 32-Bit Integers?

Problem

You want to be able to determine the difference between a 32-bit integer and another numeric value (such as the default number—64-bit floating point).

Solution

A 32-bit integer is vastly different from a variable bit floating-point number, which is the standard type of number in JavaScript. 32-bit integers can only be created using bitwise operators, which will be covered all throughout this chapter.

The Code

Listing 5-1. Examples of 32-Bit Integers

```
3.141; // Standard variable bit Number literal
0b; // 4, the same as ⌊2 * 2⌋
2 << 4; // 32, the same as ⌊2 * 24⌋ or ⌊2 * 16⌋
16 << 4; // 256, the same as ⌊16 * 24⌋ or ⌊16 * 16⌋
var myNum = 1234, pow = 16;
myNum << pow; // 80.871.424, the same as ⌊1234 * 216⌋ or ⌊1234 * 65536⌋
```

How It Works

The JavaScript interpreter, when encountering any bitwise operator, will coerce the given floating-point number into a 32-bit integer. It removes any decimal places from the number, because 32-bit *integers* can only be integer (whole) values. 32-bit integers are also limited in their range of values, either a *signed* range or an *unsigned* range, depending on the bitwise operator that's used.

Unsigned integers can only have positive values, and so they use the full 32-bits to designate the value of the positive integer. They have a minimum value of 0 and a maximum value of +4,294,967,295. How does this work? Well each binary bit has two values, 1 or 0, and combining 32 of them gives you 2^{32} possible values—precisely 4,294,967,296 different values—but of course the value 0 needs to be stored somehow, so that leaves 4,294,967,295 remaining values.

Signed integers have a minimum value of -2,147,483,647 and a maximum value of +2,147,483,647, this is because the first of the 32 bits is reserved to designate the "sign" (i.e., whether the integer is positive or negative). That leaves 31 bits remaining to designate the value of the integer: 2^{31} is, of course 2,147,483,648, which is enough to store 2,147,483,647 Integers, plus a 0 value. The 32nd bit is often called the "sign bit" or sometimes the MSB (Most Significant Bit). If the number is negative, the MSB is 1; if the number is positive, it's 0.

Signed integers have a further complexity: they use a system called "Two's Complement". In Two's Complement, the integer's negative values have their bits reversed and begin counting down from -1. To give an example of this, the number +9 in binary notation is 0b00000000000000000000000000001001 and the MSB or "sign bit" (left most bit, after "0b") is 0, indicating this number is a positive number. You may expect the Integer -9 to be 0b10000000000000000000000000001001, where all that has changed is the MSB is set to 1 rather than 0; however, negative integers count up from -2,147,483,647, meaning that 0b10000000000000000000000000001001 is equal to 2,147,483,657. The actual 32-bit signed integer for -9 then is 0b11111111111111111111111111110111.

Multiplying by Powers of 2 with the Left Shift (<<) Operator

Problem

You want to take a signed 32-bit integer (that is, a whole number with a maximum value of 2,147,483,647 and a minimum value of -2,147,483,647) and multiply it by a power of two.

Solution

Bitwise shift operators are useful for doing low-level binary computation, especially on numbers (although they convert them to 32-bit signed integers). The left shift bitwise operator can be used to shift binary bits to the left, which allows you to multiply a 32-bit integer by a power of 2.

The Code

Listing 5-2. Multiplying by Powers of 2 with the Left Shift (<<) Operator

```
2 << 0; // 2, the same as ⌊2 * 2⁰⌋ or ⌊2⌋. This returns a coerced 32-bit Signed Integer
2 << 1; // 4, the same as ⌊2 * 2⌋
2 << 4; // 32, the same as ⌊2 * 2⁴⌋ or ⌊2 * 16⌋
16 << 4; // 256, the same as ⌊16 * 2⁴⌋ or ⌊16 * 16⌋
var myNum = 1234, pow = 16;
myNum << pow; // 80.871.424, the same as ⌊1234 * 2¹⁶⌋ or ⌊1234 * 65536⌋
```

How It Works

The JavaScript interpreter, when the left shift bitwise operator is used, converts the number into a signed 32-bit binary integer (read more about signed 32-bit integers in the first section of this chapter).

The bitwise left shift operator simply takes the binary value of the left hand operand and moves all bits left by the specified right hand operand. Any spare bits are filled with 0 values. Take a look at Figure 5-1 to see how the number +9 can be shifted right by 1 bit, to become +18. You can see how all of the bits have moved one position to the left, and any extra spaces on the right have been filled with 0 values.

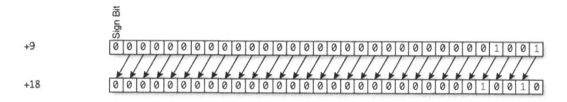

Figure 5-1. *Illustration of a bitwise left shift of 1 against +9*

There are some fairly major caveats with using bitwise shift operators that can lead to undesirable results. First, as hinted at by their mathematical equivalents, all numbers are floored (meaning the decimal values are removed). Secondly, continuing to use the left shift operator to shift bits left will eventually turn positive numbers into negative ones, as bits with a value of 1 can be shifted up. As explained, because negative numbers have reversed bits, the shifting left until you flip the sign will also produce a completely different number; for example, the operation +1073741825 << 1 returns -2,147,483,646, but +1073741825 * 2^1 is actually equal to 2,147,483,650 when not faced with the limitations of signed 32-bit integers. Figure 5-2 illustrates this concept.

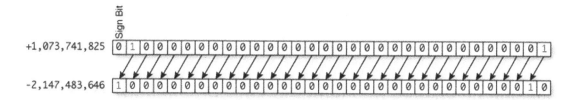

Figure 5-2. *Illustration of a bitwise left shift of 1 against +1,073,741,825*

Also, 32-bit integers have a maximum value of 2,147,483,647, so attempting to left shift numbers of a greater value leads to integer-overflows. For example, 2147483647 << 1 will return -2. See Figure 5-3 for this illustration.

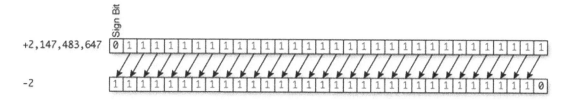

Figure 5-3. *Illustration of a bitwise left shift of 1 against +2,147,483,647*

The whole notion of bit shifting can become quite complex because of all of the caveats, and while you are generally safe with small numbers, large numbers can easily trip you up as the sign bit changes around, changing the behavior of the number. If in doubt, it is probably best to leave bitwise shift operations alone and instead use something like Math.pow(), discussed later in this book. As an illustration of how you can trip up using bitwise shift operators, Table 5-1 shows how the number +9, having its bits shifted left, can cause undesirable effects. You may see the left shift bitwise operator in real-world code, where people attempt to coerce numbers into signed 32-bit integers, using a << 0. This doesn't actually shifting any bits, but instead is simply coercing a number to 32-bit. Other real-world uses of this deal with binary data, such as image or audio data, or Node.JS binary buffers.

Table 5-1. *Bitwise Left Shift Example Scale*

Expression	Math Equivalent	Binary	Value
9 << 0	⌊9 * 2⁰⌋	0b00000000000000000000000000001001	9
9 << 1	⌊9 * 2¹⌋	0b00000000000000000000000000010010	18
9 << 2	⌊9 * 2²⌋	0b00000000000000000000000000100100	36
9 << 3	⌊9 * 2³⌋	0b00000000000000000000000001001000	72
9 << 4	⌊9 * 2⁴⌋	0b00000000000000000000000010010000	144
9 << 5	⌊9 * 2⁵⌋	0b00000000000000000000000100100000	288
9 << 6	⌊9 * 2⁶⌋	0b00000000000000000000001001000000	576
•••	•••	•••	•••
9 << 27	⌊9 * 2²⁷⌋	0b01001000000000000000000000000000	1,207,959,552
9 << 28	⌊9 * 2²⁸⌋	0b10010000000000000000000000000000	-1,879,048,192
9 << 29	⌊9 * 2²⁹⌋	0b00100000000000000000000000000000	536,870,912
9 << 30	⌊9 * 2³⁰⌋	0b01000000000000000000000000000000	1,073,741,824
9 << 31	⌊9 * 2³¹⌋	0b10000000000000000000000000000000	-2,147,483,648
9 << 32	⌊9 * 2³²⌋	0b00000000000000000000000000001001	9

Dividing by Powers of 2 with the Sign-Propagating Right Shift (>>) Operator

Problem

You want to take a signed 32bit integer (that is, a whole number with a maximum value of 2,147,483,647 and a minimum value of -2,147,483,647) and divide it by a power of two.

Solution

Bitwise shift operators are useful for doing low-level binary computation, especially on numbers (although they convert them to 32-bit signed integers). The right shift bitwise operator can be used to shift binary bits to the right, while still propagating the sign bit (in other words, it remains positive or negative), which allows you to divide a 32-bit integer by a power of 2.

The Code

Listing 5-3. Dividing by Powers of 2 with the Sign-PROPAGATING Right Shift (>>) Operator

```
2 >> 0; // 2, the same as ⌊2 ÷ 2⁰⌋or ⌊2⌋. This returns a coerced 32-bit Signed Integer
2 >> 1; // 1, the same as ⌊2 ÷ 2¹⌋ or ⌊2 ÷ 2⌋
2 >> 4; // 0, the same as ⌊2 ÷ 2⁴⌋ or ⌊2 ÷ 16⌋
16 >> 4; // 1, the same as ⌊16 ÷ 2⁴⌋ or ⌊16 ÷ 16⌋
var myNum = 1234, pow = 16;
myNum >> pow; // 0, the same as ⌊1234 ÷ 2¹⁶⌋ or ⌊1234 ÷ 65536⌋
```

How It Works

The sign-propagating right shift bitwise operator works almost the same as the left shift bitwise operator. When a sign-propagating right shift bitwise operator is used, the JavaScript interpreter converts the number into a signed 32-bit binary integer (read more about signed 32-bit integers in the first section of this chapter).

The bitwise sign-propagating right shift operator simply takes the binary value of the left hand operand and moves all bits—except for the MSB (Most Significant Bit)—right by the specified right hand operand. Any spare bits are filled with the same value as the MSB. Take a look at Figure 5-4 to see how the number +9 can be shifted right by 1 bit, to become +4. You can see how all of the bits have moved one position to the left, and any extra spaces on the right have been filled with 0 values, which is the value of the sign bit (MSB). Also notice that the number -9 shifted by 1 bit takes on the value of -5, while all new inserted bits are set to 1 (the value of the sign bit, or MSB).

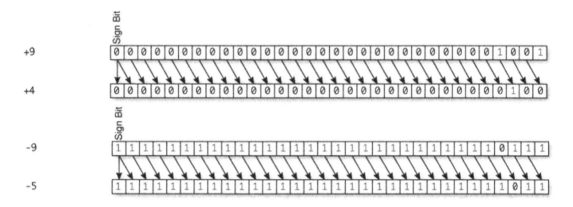

Figure 5-4. *Illustration of a bitwise sign-propagating right shift of 1 against +9 and -9*

There are some fairly major caveats with using bitwise shift operators that can lead to undesirable results.

First, as hinted at by their mathematical equivalents, all numbers are floored (meaning the decimal values are removed). Also, signed 32-bit integers have a maximum value of 2,147,483,647, so attempting to right shift numbers of a greater value leads to integer-overflows. For example 2147483648 >> 1 will return -1,073,741,824. See Figure 5-5 for this illustration.

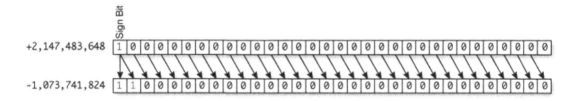

Figure 5-5. *Illustration of a sign-propagating bitwise right shift of 1 against +2,147,483,648*

The whole notion of bit shifting can become quite complex because of all of the caveats, and while you are generally safe with small numbers, large numbers can easily trip you up as the sign bit changes around, changing the behavior of the number. If in doubt, it is probably best to leave bitwise shift operations alone and instead use something like Math.pow(), discussed later in this book. As an illustration of how you can trip up using bitwise shift operators, Table 5-2 shows how the number +258, having its bits shifted right, can cause undesirable effects. You may see the sign-propagating right shift bitwise operator in real-world code, where people attempt to coerce numbers into signed 32-bit Integers using a >> 0. This doesn't actually shift any bits, but instead simply coerces a number to 32-bit. Other real-world uses of this deal with binary data, such as image or audio data, or Node.JS binary buffers.

Table 5-2. *Bitwise Sign-Propagating Right Shift Example Scale*

Expression	Math Equivalent	Binary	Value
258 >> 0	$\lfloor 258 * 2^0 \rfloor$	0b00000000000000000000000100000010	258
258 >> 1	$\lfloor 258 * 2^1 \rfloor$	0b00000000000000000000000010000001	129
258 >> 2	$\lfloor 258 * 2^2 \rfloor$	0b00000000000000000000000001000000	64
258 >> 3	$\lfloor 258 * 2^3 \rfloor$	0b00000000000000000000000000100000	32
258 >> 4	$\lfloor 258 * 2^4 \rfloor$	0b00000000000000000000000000010000	16
258 >> 5	$\lfloor 258 * 2^5 \rfloor$	0b00000000000000000000000000001000	8
258 >> 6	$\lfloor 258 * 2^6 \rfloor$	0b00000000000000000000000000000100	4
258 >> 7	$\lfloor 258 * 2^6 \rfloor$	0b00000000000000000000000000000010	2
258 >> 8	$\lfloor 258 * 2^7 \rfloor$	0b00000000000000000000000000000001	1
258 >> 9	$\lfloor 258 * 2^8 \rfloor$	0b00000000000000000000000000000000	0

Using the Zero-Fill Right Shift (>>>) Operator to Ensure a Variable Is a 32-Bit Unsigned Integer

Problem

You want to take a 32-bit unsigned integer (that is, a whole number with a maximum value of 4,294,967,295 and a minimum value of 0) and divide it by a power of two, or you want to take an existing number and coerce it into a 32-bit unsigned integer.

Solution

The zero-fill right shift operator is similar to the sign-propagating right shift operator in that it coerces a number into a 32-bit integer, and it will shift bits right based on the value of the right hand operand. There is a subtle but huge difference though—while the sign-propagating right shift operator coerces its return value into a 32-bit *signed* integer, the zero-fill right shift operator coerces its return value into an *unsigned* integer.

The Code

Listing 5-4. Use the Zero-Fill Right Shift (>>>) Operator to Ensure a Variable Is a 32-Bit Unsigned Integer

```
2 >>> 0; // 2, the same as ⌊2 ÷ 2⁰⌋or ⌊2⌋. This returns a coerced 32-bit Unsigned Integer
2 >>> 1; // 1, the same as ⌊2 ÷ 2¹⌋ or ⌊2 ÷ 2⌋
2 >>> 4; // 0, the same as ⌊2 ÷ 2⁴⌋ or ⌊2 ÷ 16⌋
16 >>> 4; // 1, the same as ⌊16 ÷ 2⁴⌋ or ⌊16 ÷ 16⌋
```

```
var myNum = 1234, pow = 16;
myNum >>> pow; // 0, the same as ⌊1234 ÷ 216⌋ or ⌊1234 ÷ 65536⌋
```

How It Works

The zero-fill right shift bitwise operator works almost the same as the sign-propagating right shift bitwise operator, but because it uses *UNSIGNED* integers the resulting conversions can be drastically different. The zero-fill right shift operator will not copy bits from the MSB to any new bits (i.e., it doesn't propagate the sign), instead filling them with zeros. The right hand operand will be converted into an *unsigned* 32-bit binary integer, which is to say a number ranging from 0 to 4,294,967,295 (read more about signed 32-bit integers in the first section of this chapter).

There are no reserved bits on an unsigned integer; every bit is used up to calculate the number, unlike a signed integer which reserves the MSB for the sign.

The bitwise zero-fill right shift operator simply takes the binary value of the left hand operand and moves all bits right by the specified right hand operand; any spare bits are filled with zeros. Take a look at Figure 5-6 to see how the number +9 can be shifted right by 1 bit to become +4.

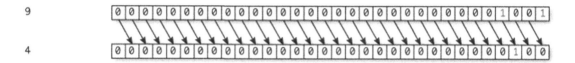

Figure 5-6. *Illustration of a bitwise zero-fill right shift of 1 against +9*

There are some fairly major caveats with using bitwise shift operators, that can lead to undesirable results. First, as hinted at by their mathematical equivalents, all numbers are floored (meaning the decimal values are removed). Also, unsigned 32-bit integers have a maximum value of 4,294,967,295 and cannot cope with negative numbers. Attempting to right shift negative numbers will lead to unexpected results, due to the way negative signed 32-bit numbers have their bits reversed, so -9 >>> 1 will return 2,147,483,643. See Figure 5-7 for this illustration.

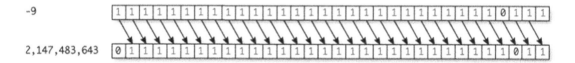

Figure 5-7. *Illustration of a zero-fill bitwise right shift of 1 against -9*

The whole notion of bit shifting can become quite complex because of all of the caveats. You may see the zero-fill right shift bitwise operator in real-world code, where people attempt to coerce numbers into unsigned 32-bit integers, using a >>> 0. This does not actually shift any bits, but instead simply coerces a number to 32-bit. This can be useful when dealing with the limitations of other systems or APIs, or binary buffers in Node.JS, but should be used with great caution because of the caveats listed.

Using the Bitwise NOT (~) Operator to Swap All Binary Bits in a 32-Bit Integer

Problem

You have a number that you'd like to coerce into a 32-bit integer, and swap every positive bit into a negative one, and every negative one into a positive. You might want to do this to toggle a flag value or get the Two's Complement binary opposite of a number.

Solution

The bitwise NOT (~) operator can be used to swap all of the binary bits in a number. Because of the Two's Complement, it does not simply just flip the sign of a number, but instead does the equivalent of -(n + 1).

The Code

Listing 5-5. Use the Bitwise NOT (~) Operator to Round Floating-Point Numbers

```
~0; // -1, the same as ⌊ -(0 + 1) ⌋
~1; // -2, the same as ⌊ -(1 + 1) ⌋
~2; // -3, the same as ⌊ -(2 + 1) ⌋
~3; // -4, the same as ⌊ -(3 + 1) ⌋
~4; // -5, the same as ⌊ -(4 + 1) ⌋
~5; // -6, the same as ⌊ -(5 + 1) ⌋
~6; // -7, the same as ⌊ -(6 + 1) ⌋
~7; // -8, the same as ⌊ -(7 + 1) ⌋
~8; // -9, the same as ⌊ -(8 + 1) ⌋
~2147483648; // 2147483647, reaches the integer overflow limit
~-1; // 0, the same as ⌊ -(-1 + 1) ⌋
~-27; // 26, the same as ⌊ -(-27 + 1) ⌋
~-2423; // 2422, the same as ⌊ -(-2423 + 1) ⌋
~-2147483648;  // 2147483647, the same as ⌊ -(-2147483648 + 1) ⌋
```

How It Works

The bitwise NOT operator first coerces the operand into a *signed* 32-bit binary integer. The bitwise NOT operator simply takes each bit and flips it to be the opposing value, so a 1 becomes a 0 and a 0 becomes a 1. Take a look at Figure 5-8 to see how the number +9 can be shifted right by 1 bit to become +4.

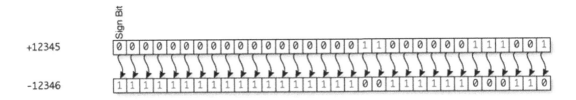

Figure 5-8. Illustration of a bitwise NOT operation against +12345

There are some fairly major caveats with using the bitwise NOT operators, that can lead to undesirable results. Just like the shift operators, as hinted at by their mathematical equivalents, all numbers are floored (meaning the decimal values are removed). Also, signed 32-bit integers have a maximum value of 2,147,483,647, so attempting to use numbers of a greater value leads to integer overflows. For example ~2147483648 will return 2147483647, where you would expect this to be -2147483649. See Figure 5-9 for this illustration.

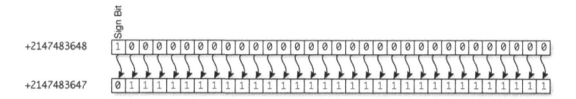

Figure 5-9. *Illustration of a bitwise NOT operation against +2147483648*

In reality, the bitwise NOT operator has a limited application, but like most of JavaScript, it does have some real-world misuses.

You may see real-world uses of the NOT operator in indexOf() operations, for example ~array. indexOf(4). This is an abuse of the bitwise NOT operator, as indexOf() will return -1 for a negative match, and values of 0 and above for a positive match. -1 and +1 and above coerce to the Boolean true, while 0 coerces to the Boolean false. However, using the bitwise NOT operator turns a 0 into -1 (true) and -1 to 0 (false), any other positive numbers still remain true (any number that isn't ±0 will coerce to true). This complex shifting means that a negative match will end up coercing to false, while a positive match will end up coercing to true. Unfortunately, this reads quite badly and the logic is very complex to explain to beginners and in the (somewhat unlikely) event you have an array or string with a greater than 32-bit length, you'll hit integer overflow problems as described previously! It is always preferable to use the more explicit array.indexOf(4) !== -1.

Another popular but misguided use case is the so-called "double NOT" operator, which is a concatenation of two bitwise NOT operators against a number, for example ~~3.141. In the case of ~~3.141, the first bitwise NOT will flip the number as usual, but also floor it, so it becomes -4; the second bitwise NOT will flip it *again* so it becomes +3. This gives the *appearance* of the number being floored, similar to Math.floor() and is supposedly "more performant" than its Math.floor() cousin. However, this pattern comes with all the baggage that the bitwise NOT operator comes with; the number is coerced to a 32-bit signed integer and the "flooring" mechanism does not operate the same way as Math.floor(). The flooring mechanism of coercing a number to a 32-bit Integer simply removes the decimal place, so ~~3.141 becomes 3, while ~~-3.141 becomes -3. The *real* Math.floor() function, however, behaves differently, in that 3.141 becomes 3, but -3.141 becomes -4.

Because of the caveats around this bitwise operator, avoid using it outside of its intended context— dealing with binary data, such as for turning off flags.

Using Bitwise AND (&) Operator to Get a Value of All Equal Bits in a 32-Bit Integer

Problem

You have a number that you'd like to coerce into a 32-bit integer and compare against another coerced 32-bit integer, where every positive bit in both integers creates a new integer with matching positive bits. This can be very useful for checking for a flag's existence in bit fields or bit masks.

Solution

The bitwise AND operator (&) compares 32-bit integers for their bit values and returns a new 32-bit integer that's a summation of all of the 1 or "On" bits in both of the numbers in the expression.

The Code

Listing 5-6. Check If a Number Is Even Using Bitwise AND (&)

```
14 & 9; // 8
92 & 46; // 12
92 & 0; // 0
0 & 0; // 0
96 & -1; // 96
```

How It Works

The bitwise AND operator first coerces the left and right hand operands into *signed* 32-bit binary integers (read more about signed 32-bit integers in the first section of this chapter). It then looks at each bit between the left and right hand operands and sets each bit in the resulting integer based on the results. The resulting bit in each position is 1 if the left hand and right hand bits in that position equal 1; otherwise, the resulting bit in that position is 0. Take a look at Figure 5-10 for a visual representation of this.

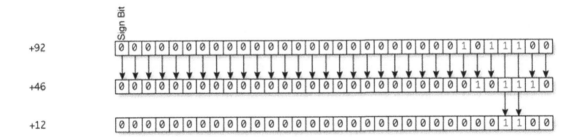

Figure 5-10. *Illustration of a bitwise AND operation of +92 against +46*

Because the resulting integer is a combination of all 1 or "on" bits in both operands, there are certain sets of integers that will have set values; for example, using 0 as either operand will result in the number being 0, as illustrated in Figure 5-11. Similarly if one of the operands is -1, then the resulting integer will be the other operand, as illustrated in Figure 5-12.

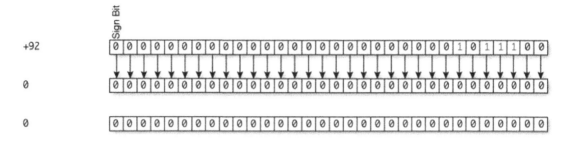

Figure 5-11. *Illustration of a bitwise AND operation of +92 against 0*

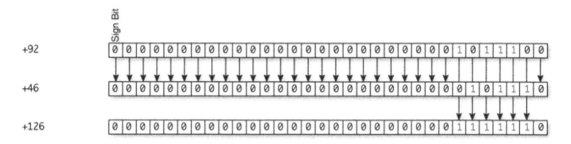

Figure 5-12. *Illustration of a bitwise AND operation of +92 against -1*

Just like most bitwise operators, there is a small set of use cases for the bitwise AND operator, and it can frequently be misused, for example to check if a number is even, you might consider using `(x & 1)` `===` `0` of course that would come with all of the caveats of bitwise operators, including the conversion to 32-bit, meaning you could not use this for large numbers. It works best when checking values in bit fields or bit masks.

Using Bitwise OR (|) Operator to Get a Value Positive Bits on One or Both Operands

Problem

You have a number that you'd like to coerce into a 32-bit integer and compare against another coerced 32-bit integer, where every positive bit in either operand creates a new integer with matching positive bits. This can be very useful for checking assigning a flag to a bit field or bit mask.

Solution

The bitwise OR operator (|) does just this—it compares 32-bit Integers for their bit values and returns a new 32-bit integer which is a summation of all of the 1 or "On" bits in either of the numbers' operands.

The Code

Listing 5-7. Check If a Number Is Even Using Bitwise AND (&)

```
14 | 9; // 15
92 | 46; // 126
92 | 0; // 92
0 | 0; // 0
96 | -1; // -1
```

How It Works

The bitwise OR operator first coerces the left and right hand operands into *signed* 32-bit binary integers (read more about signed 32-bit Integers in in the first section of this chapter). It then looks at each bit between the left and right hand operands and sets each bit in the resulting integer based on the results. The resulting bit in each position is 1 if the left hand *or* right hand operand's bits in that position equal 1; otherwise, the resulting bit in that position is 0. Take a look at Figure 5-13 for a visual representation of this.

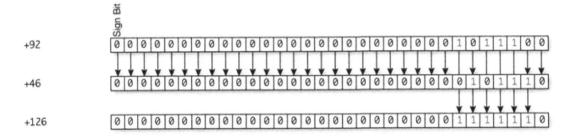

Figure 5-13. *Illustration of a bitwise OR operation of +92 against +46*

Because the resulting integer is a combination of all 1 or "on" bits in either operand, there are certain sets of integers that will have set values; for example, using 0 as either operand will result in the number being equal to the other operand, as illustrated in Figure 5-14. Similarly, if one of the operands is -1, then the resulting integer will be -1, as illustrated in Figure 5-15.

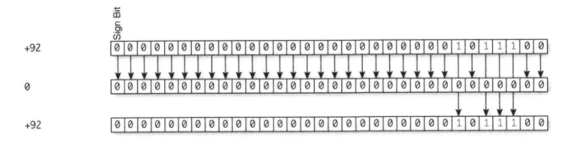

Figure 5-14. *Illustration of a bitwise OR operation of +92 against 0*

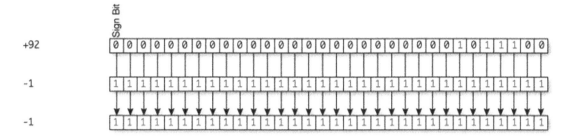

Figure 5-15. *Illustration of a bitwise OR operation of +92 against -1*

just like most bitwise operators, there is a small set of use cases for the bitwise OR operator, and it can frequently be misused. You may find code that rounds numbers using | 0, for example 293.3 | 0, which of course comes with all the caveats that bitwise operators provide. For example, this will not work with large numbers and does not use the same flooring mechanism as Math.floor(). For example using -3.141 | 0 results in 3, while Math.floor(-3.141) results in -4. It works best when combining values in bit fields or bit masks.

Using the Bitwise XOR (^) Operator to Get a Value of Differing Bits in Each Operand

Problem

You have a number that you'd like to coerce into a 32-bit integer and compare against another coerced 32-bit integer, where every differing bit in either operand creates a new integer with matching positive bits. This can be very useful for checking assigning a flag to a bit field or bit mask.

Solution

The bitwise XOR operator (^) compares 32-bit integers for their bit values and returns a new 32-bit integer, which is a summation of all of the differing bits (where one operand has a 0 and the other a 1) in the expression.

The Code

Listing 5-8. Check If a Number Is Even Using Bitwise AND (&)

```
14 ^ 9; // 7
92 ^ 46; // 114
92 ^ 0; // 92
0 ^ 0; // 0
96 ^ -1; // -97
```

How It Works

The bitwise XOR operator first coerces the left and right hand operands into *signed* 32-bit binary integers (read more about Signed 32-bit Integers in the first section of this chapter). It then looks at each bit between the left and right hand operands and sets each bit in the resulting integer based on the results. The resulting bit in each position is 1 if the left hand or right hand bits in that position equal 1. If they are both 1 or both 0, then the resulting bit will be 0. Take a look at Figure 5-16 for a visual representation of this.

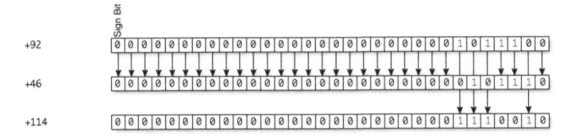

Figure 5-16. *Illustration of a bitwise XOR operation of +92 against +46*

Because the resulting integer is a combination of all differing bits in both operands, there are certain sets of integers that will have set values; for example, using 0 as either operand will result in the number equaling the other operand, just like in a bitwise OR, as illustrated in Figure 5-17. Interestingly if one of the operands is -1 then the operation is the equivalent act of using the bitwise NOT (~) on the other operand; see Figure 5-18.

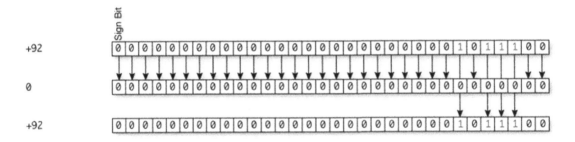

Figure 5-17. *Illustration of a bitwise XOR operation of +92 against 0*

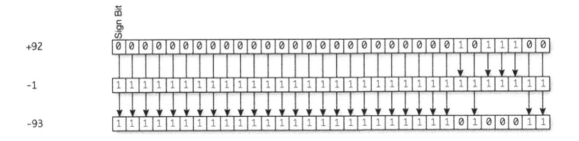

Figure 5-18. *Illustration of a bitwise XOR operation of +92 against -1*

Just like most bitwise operators, there is a small set of use cases for the bitwise XOR operator, and it can frequently be misused. It works best when checking values in bit fields or bit masks.

Converting RGB Color to Hexadecimal and Back Using the Bitwise Signed Shift (>>, <<) Operators and the Bitwise AND (&) Operator

Problem

You want to be able to convert hexadecimal colors into an RGB notation or take an RGB notation and convert that into a hexadecimal color.

Solution

This is a great application of bitwise operators, as the numbers required (0 - 255) fit inside a 32-bit integer, and shifting can be used quite elegantly to extract the right number components.

The Code

Listing 5-9. Convert RGB Color to Hexadecimal Using the Bitwise AND (&) Operator

```
function hex2rgb(hex) {
    return {
        r: hex >> 16,
        g: hex >> 8 & 255,
        b: hex & 255,
    };
}
function rgb2hex(r, g, b) {
    return ((1 << 24) + (r << 16) + (g << 8) + b).toString(16).slice(1);
}
console.log(hex2rgb(0xFFFFFF));
console.log(hex2rgb(0xFF69B4));
console.log(hex2rgb(0xDAA520));
console.log(rgb2hex(255, 255, 255));
console.log(rgb2hex(255, 105, 180));
console.log(rgb2hex(218, 165, 32));
```

The output is:

```
{r: 255, g: 255, b: 255}
{r: 255, g: 105, b: 180}
{r: 218, g: 165, b: 32}
Ffffff
ff69b4
daa520
```

How It Works

We have two functions, hex2rgb and rgb2hex. Each one takes the respective value (hex2rgb takes a hex and rgb2hex takes red, green, and blue values). Each one uses bit shifting to take their value and shifts them to the right binary positions. This can seem pretty daunting at first, but let's see what happens, line by line.

Hex2RGB

```
function hex2rgb(hex) {
```

This is a function declaration (you can read more about functions in Chapter 12). The function requires one argument named hex. You pass it hexadecimal numbers. In this example, we'll pass it the hexadecimal 0xFF69B4 (the CSS color "hot pink" which has an RGB value of 255, 105, 180). If the hex were to be coerced into a number, it would be 16738740. This number is the R, G, and B values combined.

```
r: hex >> 16,
```

Here, we take our hex value and shift the number 16 bits to the right—assuming our hex was 0xFF69B4, and therefore our parsed hex (16738740), shifting right 16 bits, or ⌊16738740 ÷ 2¹⁶⌋ returns 255. This removes the "green" and "blue" portions of this integer; see Figure 5-19 for an illustration of this.

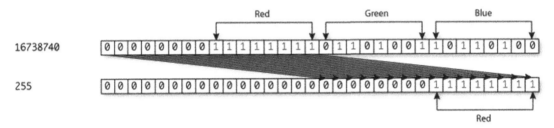

Figure 5-19. *Illustration of a bitwise sign-propagating right shift of 16 against 16738740*

```
g: hex >> 8 & 255,
```

This line takes the hex value and shift the number 8 bits to the right—assuming our hex was 0xFF69B4 (16738740), shifting right 16 bits, or ⌊16738740 ÷ 2⁸⌋ gives us 65385. This removes the "blue" section from the hex; see Figure 5-20 for an illustration of this. The next part of the operation, & 255, uses a bitwise AND to create a new integer which is capped to 255 (the first 8 bits). This effectively truncates the "red" part of the remaining color resulting in 105 - the green part of our color; see Figure 5-21 for an illustration of this operation.

```
b: hex & 255
```

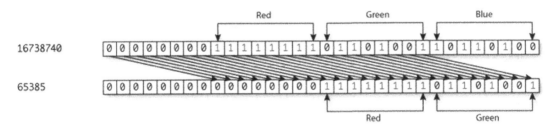

Figure 5-20. *Illustration of a Bitwise Sign-Propagating Right Shift of 8 against 16738740*

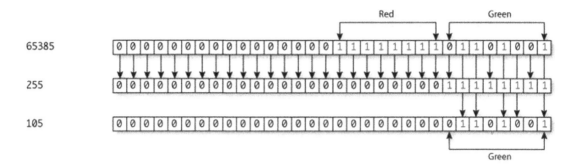

Figure 5-21. *Illustration of a Bitwise AND Operation of 65535 against 255*

To get the blue value, you can simply use the bitwise AND operator to extract the first 8 bits (225). The bitwise AND operator would effectively truncate the "red" and "green" parts of the remaining color. So assuming the hex was 0xFF69B4 (16738740), the result would be 180, the blue color. See Figure 5-22 for an illustration of this operation.

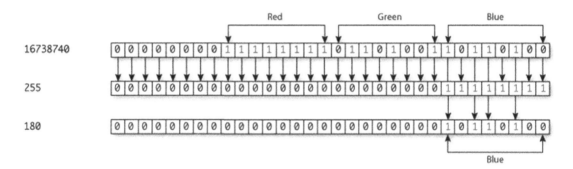

Figure 5-22. *Illustration of a Bitwise AND Operation of 16738740 against 255*

So, by using a mixture of the bitwise sign-propagating right shift operator (you could alternatively use the zero-fill right shift operator, it would be the same result as RGB colors are positive integers) and the bitwise AND operator with 255 as the operand, you can extract each color component and separate out the hexadecimal value into three distinct color values.

RGB2Hex

```
function rgb2hex(r, g, b) {
```

rgb2hex is a more complex function, but uses the same techniques as hex2rgb. The function declaration (you can read more about functions in Chapter 12) requires three arguments named r, g, and b, respectively. We will pass it three numbers for each call—a red, a green, and a blue value. In this example, we'll pass it the RGB of 255, 105, and 180 (the CSS color "hot pink" has a hex value of 0xFF69B4).

```
return ((1 << 24) + (r << 16) + (g << 8) + b).toString(16).slice(1);
```

This line looks complex, but is actually reasonably simple and is much simpler than Hex2RGB. The first part, (1 << 24) is a bit of a trick: it sets up the resulting integer to be a 25-bit integer. Each color section (red, green, and blue) is 8 bits, and 8 x 3 = 24, which means a full RGB color code is 24-bits, but it is calculated here to be 25 bits long because if the red value was 0 it would be truncated in the resulting integer (evaluated numbers in JavaScript have no leading 0s). By making the integer 25 bits (with a leading 1), we can truncate the MSB later but still maintain the six remaining hexadecimal colors. To give you an example of this, if the color was black (0,0,0), then the resulting Integer would be 0 (all leading 0s are removed), which would result in a hex of 0 when it should be 000000. The resulting value of (1 << 24) is 16777216, or a binary value of 0b1000000000000000000000000.

The next part, + (r << 16) shifts the red value by 16 bits to the left and adds this to the resulting integer. See Figure 5-23 for an illustration of this. Then + (g << 8) shifts the green value by 8 bits to the left, adding it to the integer as illustrated in Figure 5-24. Finally, as part of this integer operation, the blue value (b) is added. This whole integer—assuming an RGB of 255, 105, 180—would total 33515956 (0b1111111110110100110110100 in binary notation).

This entire integer is not converted to a 16-bit string using the toString(16) function, which converts the Base10 integer to a Base16 integer (this functionality is discussed in Chapter 4). Assuming our 255, 105, 180 values, this hex at this point would equal "1FF69B4".

The final.slice(1) function call slices off the string's first character (slice is discussed in more detail in Chapter 3), which makes the resulting string "FF69B4" in our example.

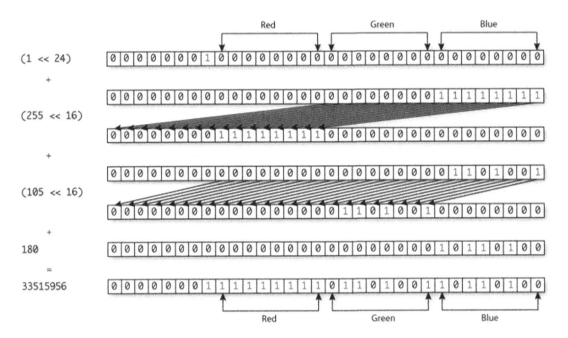

Figure 5-23. *Illustration of a bitwise sign-propagating right shift of 16 against 16777215*

Creating, Editing, and Testing a Bit Field Flag Set Using Bitwise Operators

Problem

You want to create or alter a *bit field* (which is a binary integer made up of a set of smaller integers, known as flags; popular examples are CHMOD permissions) using bitwise operators to accurately toggle or check values.

Solution

Bit fields make extensive use of bitwise operators to add, remove, toggle, and check flags in the field.

The Code

Listing 5-10. Creating, Editing, and Testing a Bit Field Flag Set Using Bitwise Operators

```
var execute = 1 << 0,   // 001 or 1
    write       = 1 << 1,   // 010 or 2
    read        = 1 << 2;   // 100 or 4

function removePermission(permission, flag) {
    return permission & ~flag;
}
function addPermission(permission, flag) {
    return permission | flag;
}
function togglePermission (permission, flag) {
    return permission ^ flag;
}
function permissionToString(permission) {
    var stringPermission = '';
    stringPermission += (permission & read) ? 'r' : '-';
    stringPermission += (permission & write) ? 'w' : '-';
    stringPermission += (permission & execute) ? 'x' : '-';
    return stringPermission;
}

var writeExecute = write | execute,          // 011 or 3
    readExecute   = read | execute,          // 101 or 5
    readWrite     = read | write,            // 110 or 6
    full          = read | write | execute;  // 111 or 7

console.log( permissionToString(1) ); // —x
console.log( permissionToString(2) ); // -w-
console.log( permissionToString(3) ); // -wx
console.log( permissionToString(4) ); // r—
console.log( permissionToString(5) ); // r-x
console.log( permissionToString(6) ); // rw-
```

```
console.log( permissionToString(7) ); // rwx
console.log( permissionToString( removePermission(7, read) ) ); // -wx
console.log( permissionToString( removePermission(7, write) ) ); // r-x
console.log( permissionToString( removePermission(7, execute) ) ); // rw-
console.log( permissionToString( addPermission(6, execute) ) ); // rwx
console.log( permissionToString( removePermission(7, execute) ) ); // rw-
console.log( permissionToString( togglePermission(6, execute) ) ); // rwx
console.log( permissionToString( togglePermission(7, execute) ) ); // rw-
```

The output is:

```
--x
-w-
-wx
r--
r-x
rw-
rwx
-wx
r-x
rw-
rwx
rw-
rwx
rw-
```

How It Works

Bit fields are a popular way to establish a command set for low-level protocols. They exist in transport protocols, binary files, and even file systems, and quite rightly so—they are an elegant and compact way to express a great deal of information in a short manner.

By using a combination of many of the bitwise operators, flags can be used to alter a bit field or check existing values. This section shows nothing new, just a combination and application of techniques throughout this chapter, applied to a well-known and commonly used bit field—a CHMOD permissions table. The CHMOD permissions table uses three flags for Read, Write, and Execute access on a file in Linux/UNIX (including Mac OSX) file systems. In these file systems, permission for a file is made of three octets (0-7)—one for the user, one for the Group, and one for "other" (everyone else). Each of these octets represents a bit field of Read, Write, and Execute values; see Table 5-3 for how this works.

Table 5-3. *Bitwise Operator Functions on Bit Fields*

Permission	Bit Indicator	Numerical Equivalent
Read	X00	4
Write	0X0	2
Execute	00X	1

Because of the way binary integers work, this bit field can only have a maximum number of values, and there are no ambiguous values. This means any combination can be used and none overlap. See Table 5-4 for all possible values.

Table 5-4. *Bitwise Operator Functions on Bit Fields*

Numerical Equivalent	Binary	Permission
0	0b000	None
1	0b001	Execute
2	0b010	Write
3	0b011	Write + Execute
4	0b100	Read
5	0b101	Read + Execute
6	0b110	Read + Write
7	0b111	Read + Write + Execute

This effectively means we can do low-level bit manipulation to check or alter the flags inside the bit field, as demonstrated in the code. Primarily the operators in use are the binary left-shift, NOT, XOR, AND, and OR operators. Each operator has its own purpose in bit fields, as illustrated in Table 5-5.

Table 5-5. *Bitwise Operator Functions on Bit Fields*

Bitwise Operator	Bit Field Function
Bitwise Shift (<<, >>)	Creating flag values
Bitwise OR operator	Adding flag values to a bit field
Bitwise NOT operator	Removing flag values from a bit field
Bitwise XOR operator	Toggling flag values on a bit field
Bitwise AND operator	Checking flag existence on a bit field

Refer to the previous sections of this chapter to learn more about each of these bitwise operators, in combination they can be used to perform powerful low-level operations on numerical or binary data.

CHAPTER 6

▦ ▦ ▦

Dates and Times

Using the Date Object

Problem

You need to get date and time information.

Solution

You need to create an instance of the Date object. Depending on if you need the current time or some other time in the past or future, you may need to pass parameters to the constructor.

The Code

Listing 6-1. Creating Instances of the Date Object

```
var now = new Date(); //returns todays date and time
console.log(now);

var fluxCapacitorDate = new Date('November 5, 1955');
console.log(fluxCapacitorDate); //returns the date with time being all 0' meaning midnight
of that day.

var infinityWarDate = new Date(2018, 4, 4);  //returns date at midnight
console.log(infinityWarDate);
var unixTimestamp = Date.now(); // returns numbers representing the current date in milliseconds
console.log(unixTimestamp);
```

How It Works

In order to work with dates, you need to make an instance of the Date object. Unlike the Math object, it is not static. If you want to work with the current date, you don't need to pass any parameters. If you need a certain date, there are a few ways of passing what you need over.

The quickest way is to pass a string representing the date. The value should be able to be in a format that the Date.parse() can recognize. You could spell out the date like in the previous example. You can also pass over the date as a string without spelling out the month. In this case, it would look like "1955-5-5". In either case, you can also pass the time inside the string. For example, adding hour, minutes, seconds, and milliseconds like this: 'November 5, 1955 03:24:00:00'.

You can also add each item as a number directly, comma-separated, including time. All time is based on the number of milliseconds since January 1, 1970 UTC.

JavaScript does not always format the date exactly the same in every browser. Some recommendations would be:

- If you add hours, also add minutes, because not all browsers will parse with just hours.

- Milliseconds seem to only get parsed in Chrome.

- If possible, use the YYYY/MM/DD format.

- Hyphens (-) work best in WebKit browsers but are trouble in Firefox and IE; use slashes (/) as an alternative.

- Make sure the year is four numbers. For example, passing '1/1/16' returns 1916-01-01 as the date in Firefox and IE.

- Using UTC time works in more recent browsers, but may not be supported in older browsers. IE 9, for example, would not parse it correctly.

Getting Date and Time Information

Problem

Now that you have an instance of the Date object, you need to get date and time information.

Solution

A good portion of what you will need is built into the Date object. In a few instances, the results are zero-based, similar to getting the length from an array.

The Code

Listing 6-2. Getting Date Information then Time Information

```
var now = new Date(); //returns todays date and time
 console.log(now.getDate()); //returns the day of the month from 1 to 31
 console.log(now.getDay()); //returns the day of the week its zero based like an array 0 - 6;
 console.log(now.getFullYear()); //returns the current year
 console.log(now.getHours()); //returns hours from 0-23
 console.log(now.getMonth()); //return month from 0-11
 //time information
 console.log(now.getSeconds()); //returns seconds from 0-59
 console.log(now.getTime()); //returns the amount of milliseconds since the first of January 1970
```

How It Works

There are a lot of methods that will give you most of the date or time information you need. In some cases, the values are treated similar to an array, being zero based. For example, running getMonth() if it's January results in 0.

These methods can be put together to give your users things like the current date and time. Now you can do interesting things with this information.

Calculating User Age

Problem

You need to figure out a user's age in years.

Solution

Create two date objects and subtract the current year if the birthday has not happened yet. This is also good for figuring out years from a certain date.

The Code

Listing 6-3. Create Two Date Objects and Subtract the Current Year if the Day Has Not Happed yet in a for Loop

```
var dob = new Date("12/3/1979");
var today = new Date();
var years = today.getFullYear() - dob.getFullYear();
dob.setFullYear(today.getFullYear());
if(today < dob){
        years--;
}
console.log(years);
```

How It Works

The first instance has the birthday you want to use. The second is the current date. The third variable calculates the current year from the year in question. This will give you the total amount of years. The reason for the `if` statement is in the case the birthday has not yet happened. If that's the case, it will remove a year.

Using the HTML5 Date Input Field to Make a Date Object

Problem

You need to create a date object based on the HTML5 date input form field.

Solution

HTML5 offers a lot of new input field types. One type is date. Unfortunately, at the time of this writing it is not supported in Firefox, Safari, or IE 11, but there is date support in Microsoft Edge and Opera. Since it is part of HTML5, it is not unreasonable to expect it to work in these browsers soon. There are other ways of creating this effect. For our example, we still stick with what is native to the browser.

When you select a date and submit the form, JavaScript will create a date object and print out the date in a text field.

The Code

Listing 6-4. Getting the Date from the HTML5 Date Input

```
//HTML form
<form>
<label for="dateComponent">Choose a date:
      <input type="date" id="dateComponent">
</label>
<label for="dateResult">You picked:
      <input type="text" id="dateResult">
</label>
      <input type="submit" value="Choose a date" id="subtmitBtn">
</form>
//JavaScript
var submitBtn = document.getElementById('subtmitBtn');
    submitBtn.addEventListener('click', function(e){
       e.preventDefault();

var dateSelected = document.getElementById('dateComponent');
var dateArray = [];
if(dateSelected.value != ''){
      console.log(typeof dateSelected.value); //result is a string
      dateArray = dateSelected.value.split('');

       for(var i = 0; i < dateArray.length; i++){
              if(dateArray[i] === '-'){
                     dateArray[i] = '/';
       }
        }
var formatedDate = new Date(dateArray.join(''));
document.getElementById('dateResult').value = (formatedDate.getMonth() + 1) + '-' +
formatedDate.getDate() + '-' + formatedDate.getFullYear();
    }
});
```

How It Works

In this example, you add an event listener to the Submit button. When the button is clicked, the first thing you do is run the `preventDefault()` method so the browser does not leave the current page.

An empty array called `dateArray` is created that will be used when a value is returned. After that, you check the value of the component `dateSelected` to see if it returned a value. If the user does not select a date, then it will return a blank string. If that is not the case, take the string and use the split method to turn it into an array and assign that array to `dateArray`. The reason for this is that the result that you get back (year-month-day) does not parse correctly when used as part of the date constructor. So here we just change the format by looping though the array and changing the format to (year/month/day). Our new array then is joined back into a string and used in the date constructor.

Finally, we take the date object and put the results into a text field. The `getMonth` method is zero based (0 is January), so we add 1 for display purposes.

Checking If Two Dates Are the Same

Problem

You need to compare two different date objects.

Solution

In this case, you are checking if they are equal, but it will return `false` if the times are different.

The Code

Listing 6-5. Determining If Two Dates Are Equal

```
var date1 = new Date("March 19, 1990 03:30:00");
var date2 = new Date("March 19, 1990 04:30:00");

if(date1.getTime() == date2.getTime()){
    console.log('date are the same');
}else{
    console.log('dates are different');
}
```

How It Works

Use the `getTime()` method to convert the time to numeric values that represent the amount of milliseconds since January 1, 1970. If these numbers match, then the time is the same. If you create a date object without specifying the time, by default the time will be midnight of that day. The time will show up as all 0s. In this case, even if the days are the same, you will not get a match. If the time does not matter, you can use the `setHours()` method and set hours, minutes, seconds, and milliseconds to 0 the make the comparison. This does not account for different time zones or daylight savings time.

Working with getTimezoneOffset

Problem

You need to figure out the offset between UTC and local time.

Solution

The `date` object has some built-in ways to convert date and time into different formats. It does not handle time zones or daylight savings time. There are ways of figuring out the difference or offset between the UTC and the local time zone. There are also libraries that specifically deal with date and time zone problems.

The Code

Listing 6-6. Working with UTC and Local Time

```
//Want to know what the offset between UTC time and my local time
var currentDate = new Date();
var offSet = currentDate.getTimezoneOffset() / 60; converts minutes to hours
console.log(offSet);

//check if we are on daylight savings time
var today = new Date();
function isDST(){
        var jan = new Date(today.getFullYear(), 0, 1);
        var jul = new Date(today.getFullYear(), 6, 1);
        return Math.max(jan.getTimezoneOffset(), jul.getTimezoneOffset());
}
if(isDST() != today.getTimezoneOffset()){
        console.log('On DST');
}else{
        console.log('Not On DST');
}
```

How It Works

The first example gives you the difference between UTC time and your local time in minutes. When you divide the number by 60, you then get the amount of hours the offset is. For example, if you live on the east cost of the United States the off set is 4 because of daylight savings time. Meaning that Coordinated Universal Time (UTC) is 4 hours ahead of Eastern Time in the United States. The result of the getTimezoneOffset() method could be positive if you are west of UTC or negative if you are east of UTC. This method does not account for daylight savings time.

With this information, you can figure out if your user is currently on daylight savings time. The second example creates two date objects. The first of the year and the first of July. These two dates should return different offsets. For example, New York returns -5 normally and -4 during daylight savings time. To figure out if you are currently on daylight savings time, you can compare the current local time offset with the larger of the two date objects by returning the larger number using the max() method. This is why it returns the larger of the two offsets. If the function returns the local offset and the number and they are different, then you are on daylight savings time.

Formatting Date and Time

Problem

You want to format dates, including language and time zone.

Solution

The date can be formatted not only by using methods like the getDate() method. It can also be formatted to use different languages. You can use toLocaleDateString, toLocaleDateSting, or the internationalization API. The locales, options, and internationalization API work with the latest desktop browsers and with Safari's nightly build. Mobile support is only for Chrome for Android 26.

The Code

Listing 6-7. Using toLocaleDateString and ECMAScript Internationalization API

```
//format the date using toLocaleTimeString
console.log(currentDate.toLocaleDateString('ja-JP'));
console.log(currentDate.toLocaleDateString('ja-JP', {weekday: 'long', year:'numeric',
month:'short', day:'numeric', hour:'2-digit', minute:'2-digit'}))

new Intl.DateTimeFormat('ja-JP', { weekday: 'long', year:'numeric', month:'short',
day:'numeric', hour:'2-digit', minute:'2-digit', timeZone:'Asia/Tokyo', timeZoneName:
'short'}).format(new Date(1975, 07, 19)); //returns 1975年8月19日火曜日 13:00 JST
new Intl.DateTimeFormat('en-US', { weekday: 'long', year: 'numeric', month: 'long', day:
'numeric' }).format(new Date(1975, 07, 19)); // returns Tuesday, August 19, 1975
```

How It Works

Using toLocaleDateString or toLocaleTimeString, the first parameter is the locales that can be used. Some examples are en-GB for British English or ko-KR for Korean.

The second parameter outlines the format details. This parameter is optional. Here you can set things like the time zone that you want to use. The times zones must recognize UTC and it uses the runtime as the default. It also understands names from the IANA time zone database like Asia/Tokyo or America/New_York.

Other options include weekday, era, year, month, day, hour minute, second, and timeZoneName.

Using the internationalization API, you can format the date the same way as using the toLocale methods. In the constructor, you can set the local as the first parameter. The second parameter uses the same options object. After that, you can use the format method and pass the date object.

Calculating Days from a Certain Date

Problem

You need to figure out how much time has passed since a certain date.

Solution

Use the getTime() method and check if your date is greater than the start date and less than the end date.

The Code

Listing 6-8. Calculating the How Many Days from a Certain Date

```
var date1 = new Date('6/15/2016');
var date2 = new Date('6/19/2016');

// 86,400,000 milliseconds is the number of milliseconds in one day
var oneDayInMS = 1000 * 60 * 60 * 24;

// Calculate the difference in milliseconds
var differenceInMS = Math.abs(date1.getTime() - date2.getTime());
var days = Math.round(differenceInMS/oneDayInMS);
console.log(days);
```

How It Works

You create two date objects like in similar examples. In this case, we also subtract the first date from the second by milliseconds. The result on its own would be a negative new number, which is why the equation is done inside the `Math.abs()` method. It will turn the number into a positive integer.

We also have a variable that is the amount of milliseconds in a day. It is expressed by 1000 milliseconds times 60 seconds, times 60 minutes, times 24 hours. This will give you 86,400,000 milliseconds. Divide the difference between the two days by the amount of milliseconds in a whole day and round to the next highest integer.

Checking If Your Date Is in a Range of Dates

Problem

You need to know if the date selected is within a specific range.

Solution

The abs method of the `Math` object will give you the non-negative number.

The Code

Listing 6-9. Check If the Selected Date Is Within the Range of the Start Date and End Date

```
var startDate = new Date('2/5/1990');
var endDate = new Date('3/25/2013');

var selectedDate = new Date('12/3/2000');

if(selectedDate.getTime() > startDate.getTime() && selectedDate.getTime() < endDate.getTime()){
        console.log('In the range');
        }else{
        console.log('Not in the range');
}
```

How It Works

The `getTime()` method returns time in milliseconds in UTC time (number of milliseconds since January 1, 1970). In this case, we are just testing If the date chosen is higher than the start time in milliseconds and lower than the end time in milliseconds. Both parts of the `if` statement need to be `true` for this example to work.

CHAPTER 7

Working with Arrays

What Is an Array?

Problem

You want to hold on to information in sequence without creating multiple variables.

Solution

Use an array to store your data. An *array* is an object where you can store information in a list-like order.

The Code

Listing 7-1. Creating Array Literals and Instances of an Array Object

```
var arrayLit = []; //Array Literal
var arrayObj = new Array(); //Array instance using a constructor
```

How It Works

In all instances, you get an array with all the properties and methods of an array. Using the array literal is a quick way of building an array and is considered an easy-to-read way of generating an array. Using the array constructor gives you the option of either setting the length of the array or passing values to it. Items in the array are not of any specific type.

Unlike with other languages, an array is not fixed. It can grow or shrink depending on your needs. If you pass a number to the constructor, you can set the length of an array; however, you can continue to add items past that original number. Arrays can be created using a constructor or you can create an array literal using the bracket syntax.

JavaScript refers to each value in an array as an element. Elements are zero-based, meaning that the first element in the array uses the index number of zero to access it. You will see how this is done in the next section.

How Do You Access Elements in an Array?

Problem

You need to access elements in the array and get their values.

Solution

You access each element of the array by its index number using the bracket syntax.

The Code

Listing 7-2. Returning the Value of an Element in the Array

```
var dayArray = new Array('monday', 'tuesday', 'wednesday'];
dayArray[0] //returns monday
dayArray[3] //returns undefined
```

How It Works

Elements in an array are zero-based. To access them, you need to use bracket syntax with a number. This number must not exceed the amount of items in the array. If you ask for a value that is not defined in the array, it will return undefined.

How Do You Create a Multi-Dimensional Array?

Problem

You want to keep track of the contents of a table, whereby one dimension represents rows and the other columns.

Solution

There isn't any special syntax to create a multi-dimensional array. You do this by adding a new array inside an element of another array. You can also create a multi-dimensional array with array literals.

The Code

Listing 7-3. Creating a Multi-Dimensional Array

```
var multiArray = new Array();
    multiArray[0] = new Array();

var litMultiArray = [[1,2], 3, 4];
```

How It Works

Multi-dimensional arrays are very similar to regular arrays. Accessing an element would mean first accessing the outer array, then the element in the inner array. For example, multiArray[0][1] would be the first item on the outer array and the second item in the inner array.

How Do You Initialize an Array with Values?

Problem

You need to create an array with values set upon initialization.

Solution

Using either array literals or a constructor, you can pass values into the array.

The Code

Listing 7-4. Creating Arrays with Values

```
var itemArray = new Array('item 1', 'item 2', 'items 3');
var itamArrayLit = ['item 1', 'item 2', 'item 3'];
```

How It Works

When using a constructor, make sure to pass more than one value. If you pass a single number into the constructor, it will think that you want to set the length of the array. A comma-separated list of numbers would be treated as values that would go into the array. If creating an array literal, you do not have this problem. All values will become elements in the array.

What Is the Size of the Array?

Problem

You want to know how many elements are in the array.

Solution

Use the length property.

The Code

Listing 7-5. Determining the Size of an Array Using the Length Property

```
var weekArray = ['Sunday', 'Monday', 'Tuesday', 'Wednesday', 'Thursday', 'Friday',
'Saturday'];
 console.log(weekArray.length);
```

How It Works

The length property gives the number of items in an array. Since arrays are zero-based, the first item in the array is zero. This is important to remember because, if the length is seven, like in Listing 7-5, that means there are seven items total, starting from zero to six.

How Do You Convert an Array to a String?

Problem

You want to take the values of an array and convert it to a string.

Solution

There are multiple ways to convert an array to a string. Two ways are the toString() method and the join() method.

The Code

Listing 7-6. Converting an Array to a String Using toString and Join

```
numberArray = [1, 2, 3, 4, 5, 5, 6, 7, 8, 9];  // returns [1, 2, 3, 4, 5, 5, 6, 7, 8, 9]
console.log( numberArray.toString() ); //returns 1,2,3,4,5,5,6,7,8,9
console.log( numberArray.join('') );   //returns 123456789
console.log( numberArray[0].toString() );  //returns 1
```

How It Works

The toString() method will create a comma-separated string based on all the elements in the array. You can also take a single element and convert that into a string.

The join method will convert all the elements in the array into a single string without commas.

How Do You Add an Element to the End of an Array?

Problem

You want to add an extra element to the end of an array.

Solution

The push() method will automatically add an element to the end of an array. It is also important to note that it does not account for gaps in the array. For example, if you create an element with no value, then use the push method, it will create a new element after the blank one.

The Code

Listing 7-7. Using the push() Method to Add to an Existing Array

```
var weekArray = ['Sunday', 'Monday', 'Tuesday'];
    weekArray.push('Wednesday');
    weekArray[4] = 'Thursday';
//result is now ['Sunday', 'Monday', 'Tuesday', 'Wednesday', 'Thursday']
```

How It Works

Using the push() method, you can add one or more elements to the current array. This method will return the new length of the array. Mixing the push method and naming an element specifically can create gaps in the array by accident. If you consistently use the push method, you will always add one more value to the array without the possibility of creating gaps.

How Do You Add Items to an Array Within a Range?

Problem

You want to give the array values in a certain range.

Solution

Using the fill() method, you can add a value with a start and end index number.

The Code

Listing 7-8. The Fill Method Will Add a Value Based on the Start and Ending Index Numbers

```
var numberArray = [1,2,3,4];
    numberArray.fill(5, 0, 1);
console.log(numberArray); //result [5, 2, 3, 4]
```

How It Works

The fill() method will add a value given to your array. Two optional parameters are the start and end indexes. When given these parameters, you can update values based on the index number.

How Do You Append an Array to the End of Another Array?

Problem

You need to combine the values of two arrays into one single array.

Solution

Use the concat() method to combine one array to the end of the other.

The Code

Listing 7-9. Appending the Values of an Array to Another Array

```
var numberArray = [1,2,3,4];
var numberArray2 = [5,6,7,8];
```

```
var resultArray = numberArray.concat(numberArray2);

console.log(resultArray);
```

How It Works

The concat() method returns a new array with the elements of the original array and the elements of the array being used in the argument as long as the argument is an array. This does not alter the original arrays. What this method does is make a shallow copy that contains references to the original arrays. This is important because if the reference or copy object is modified, the original array will also be modified.

How Do You Reverse the Order of the Items in an Array?

Problem

You want to reverse the order of the elements in your array.

Solution

Use the reverse() method to combine one array to the end of the other.

The Code

Listing 7-10. Reversing Elements in the Array Using the Reverse Method

```
var numberArray = [1, 2, 3, 4, 5, 6, 7, 8, 9];
    numberArray.reverse();

console.log(numberArray);  //returns [9,8,7,6,5,4,3,2,1]
```

How It Works

In this example, the reverse method returns an array in place. The first element in the array becomes the last and the list will be the first element. This method mutates the array and returns a reference to the array.

How Do You Copy Elements Based on Their Position Inside an Array?

Problem

You have an array where you want to copy only the elements in a range to other elements in the same array.

Solution

Use the copyWithin() method to copy a rage of elements and use those values to replace other elements in the same array.

The Code

Listing 7-11. Copying and Updating Elements in the Same Array

```
var numberArray = [1, 2, 3, 4, 5, 6];
console.log(numberArray.copyWithin(3, 0));  //returns [1, 2, 3, 1, 2, 3]
```

How It Works

Understanding the copyWithin() method can be a little confusing. This method takes three arguments—target, start, and end. All of these arguments are numbers. The end argument is optional; in that case, the browser will use the length of the array as the end value.

When discussing these parameters, target tells the browser which element in the array it should update. The start argument defines which element it should start copying. In Listing 7-11, the target element would be 3 (4 because arrays are zero-based) and then it will start copying from 0 (the first element). Since this example does not have an ending argument, it will copy the rest of the array and replace the elements in the array. This method does not have support in Internet Explorer, Opera, or Safari.

How Do You Add Multiple Items to the Beginning of an Array?

Problem

You need to add elements to the beginning of an array.

Solution

Use the unshift() method to push the elements back to make room for new elements in the front.

The Code

Listing 7-12. The unshift() Method Pushes All Elements Back to Make Room for New Ones

```
var numberArray = [4, 5, 6];
numberArray.unshift(1, 2, 3)
console.log(numberArray); //returns [1, 2, 3, 4, 5, 6]
```

How It Works

The unshift() method will shift elements in array-like objects and place new elements in the front of the current elements. This method will return the new length of the array when finished.

How Do You Change the Contents of an Array by Adding or Removing Elements?

Problem

You need a quick way to change the elements in the array by adding or removing elements .

Solution

Use the splice() method to change the contents of an array.

The Code

Listing 7-13. The splice() Method Allows You To Add or Remove Elements of the Current Array

```
var marxBros = ['Groucho', 'Harpo', 'Chico'];
marxBros.splice(2, 0, 'Zeppo');
console.log(marxBros); //returns ['Groucho', 'Harpo', 'Chico', 'Zeppo']
marxBros.splice(1, 3);
console.log(marxBros); //returns ['Groucho']
```

How It Works

When using splice, you need to pass over at least two arguments. The first argument, start, tells the browser where to start modifying the array. The next value describes how many items you would like to delete, called the deleteCount. The third optional argument would be a comma-separated list of items you would like to add to the array.

In Listing 7-13, we are deleting no items after the second element in the array, and then adding Zeppo to the array. After that, another splice call is made removing three elements after the first element, only leaving Groucho.

How Can You Simulate First-In First-Out Behavior?

Problem

You want to treat your array like a stack and get the first element in the array .

Solution

The shift() method will return the first item in the array.

The Code

Listing 7-14. The shift() Method Will Remove the First Element from the Array

```
var marxBros = ['Groucho', 'Harpo', 'Chico'];
var shiftedItem = marxBros.shift();
console.log(shiftedItem); //returns ['Groucho']
```

How It Works

The shift() method will remove the first item in the array (the item at index 0). It will then shift the rest of the items forward. This method changes the length of the array.

How Can You Simulate Last-In First-Out Behavior?

Problem

You want to treat your array like a stack and get the last element in the array.

Solution

The pop() method will return the first item in the array.

The Code

Listing 7-15. The pop() Method Will Remove the Last Element from the Array

```
var marxBros = ['Groucho', 'Harpo', 'Chico'];
marxBros.pop();
console.log(marxBros); //returns ['Groucho',  'Harpo']
```

How It Works

The pop() method will remove the last item in the array and return the value to the caller. Similar to the previous example, you can simulate a stack and, with this method, perform last in, first out (LIFO) operations.

How Do You Create a Smaller Array Based on the Values in a Range?

Problem

You want to create a variable that contains a portion of the current array.

Solution

The slice() method will return a shallow copy of the array based on the range you give it.

The Code

Listing 7-16. The slice() Method Returns Only the Elements in the Given Range

```
var albumNames = ['Hack', 'Violator', 'Designation', 'Wild', 'Surrender'];
console.log(ablumNames.slice(0,2)); //returns ["Hack", "Violator"]
```

How It Works

This method returns a shallow copy of the array. That means that the copy is done by reference. The slice() method take two arguments, The first is the start index number, where the browser should start editing the array. The second argument is the end index number. In Listing 7-16, the slice starts with the first element and ends with element 2. The array returns all elements up to the end number.

How Do You Get the Index Number of a Value?

Problem

You have a value that belongs to an array but need the index number.

Solution

Using the indexOf() method will give you the first index of a value you pass to it. Or using lastIndexOf() will return the last index of the value you pass to it.

The Code

Listing 7-17. Examples of indexOf() and lastIndexOf()

```
var albumNames = ['Hack', 'Violator', 'Designation', 'Wild', 'Surrender', 'Hack'];
console.log(ablumNames.indexOf('Hack')); //returns 0
console.log(ablumNames.lastIndexOf('Hack')); //returns 5
```

How It Works

These methods are useful if you know a value is being used more than once. For example, you may get results back from the server and lastIndexOf() can quickly give you the latest data. The reverse is also true. The indexOf() method would give you the first instance of the value given to it. If you do not get a result, these methods return -1.

How Do You Return the Index or Object Based on a Value in an Array?

Problem

You need either the value of an array or the index.

Solution

Use the find() method to get the value from an array and findIndex() to get the index number.

The Code

Listing 7-18. The Difference Between Find and FindIndex

```
var albumCollection = [{album: 'Hack', artist: 'Information Society'}, {album: 'Violator',
artist: 'Depeche Mode'}, {album: 'Designation', artist: 'The Cure'}];
var foundAlbum = albumCollection.find( function(element, index, array){
        return element.album == 'Violator' })
console.log(foundAlbum); //returns Object {album: "Violator", artist: "Depeche Mode"}
var foundIndex = albumCollection.findIndex( function(element, index, array){
        return element.album == 'Violator'
});

console.log(foundIndex); //returns 1
```

How It Works

These methods work in a similar way that the map method works. You can assign a callback function to the method or use an anonymous function. In either case, you can run the function on each element of the array and evaluate it. If the test passes, you return the value or the index number from the array.

The callback function will receive the element, index number, and the array each time it's called. There is an optional parameter that lets you set the value of this. These methods are not supported in Internet Explorer or Opera.

What Is a Spread Operator and How Does It Work?

Problem

You need to allow an undefined amount of arguments (for functions), elements (for arrays), or variables (for destructuring assignment).

Solution

The spread operator allows you to assign an unspecified amount of values.

The Code

Listing 7-19. Using the Spread Operator on Functions, Arrays, and Variables

```
function myValues(...values){
        return values
}
console.log(myValues(1,2,3)); // returns [1, 2, 3]
console.log(myValues(1,2,3,4,5,6)); // returns [1, 2, 3, 4, 5, 6]
var firstThree = ['One', 'Two', 'Three'];
var myArray = [...firstThree, 4, 5, 6];
console.log(myArray); // returns  ["One", "Two", "Three", 4, 5, 6]
[a ,b, ...otherShips] = ['Tardis', 'X-Wing', 'B-Wing', 'Enterprise', 'Moya']
console.log(otherShips); // returns ["B-Wing", "Enterprise", "Moya"]
```

How It Works

The spread operator works in a similar way to the rest parameter. The main difference is the spread operator will let you express multiple values inside a single variable, whereas the rest parameter takes all values after the first one and expresses each value as an element in an array.

In these examples, there is a function that can take multiple arguments. The second takes the values of the first array and adds them to the second array. It is important to note that, without the dots (...), we would be creating a multi-dimensional array. In the third example, without the dots, the browser would just map the next value. The spread operator is available in Chrome, Firefox, and Microsoft Edge.

How Do You Take an Iterable Object and Convert It to an Array?

Problem

You have an object that you can iterate through and you want to convert into an array.

Solution

The Array.from() method can take an iterable object and convert it into an array.

The Code

Listing 7-20. Returning an Array When Arguments Are Passed to the Function

```
function myValues(){
      return Array.from(arguments)
}

console.log( myValues('one', 'two', 'three')); // returns ["one", "two", "three"]
```

How It Works

The from() method is a static method. Using it is similar to using a method of the Math class. This method can take three arguments, the second and third are optional. The first is the array-like object; the second is a map function.

This function works the same way as the map method. The function is executed on each element of the array. The third optional argument is the value that will set the value of this while the function is being executed. This method does not have support in Internet Explorer or Opera.

How Do Typed Arrays Work and What Makes Them Different from Regular Arrays?

Problem

You need to decide to use either a regular array or a typed array.

Solution

If you are working with raw binary data, use a type array.

The Code

Listing 7-21. Loading a File Using the File API and Passing the ArrayBuffer to a Typed Array

```
document.querySelector('#fileInput').addEventListener('change', getFileInfo);
var fileReader = new FileReader();
    fileReader.addEventListener('load', showBuffer);
function getFileInfo(e){
fileReader.readAsArrayBuffer(e.target.files[0]); //creating the arrayBuffer based on the
loaded file
};
function showBuffer(e){
    var bytes = new Uint8Array(e.target.result); //creating a typed array using the
    arrayBuffer
    console.log(bytes.length);
    console.log(bytes[0]);
    console.log(bytes[1]);
}
```

How It Works

Typed arrays are designed to work with binary data. Unlike regular arrays that can hold multiple types of data, typed arrays only have the same type. In addition, typed arrays cannot have any empty values making them contiguous. Typed arrays do not have all the methods that normal arrays have, like push or pop, and the isArray() method will return false.

There are several APIs that support typed arrays. Web Workers, Media Source API, File API, Canvas, and XMLHttpRequest are just some of the APIs that provide support.

Typed arrays are one of two different types of views for an ArrayBuffer, the other being DataView. In this two-step process, the ArrayBuffer holds the binary data with no way to access its contents. Then the data gets passed into either a typed array or a DataView object. Once there, it can be read or changed. There is a list of different type array views. Based on the data you are working with, they come in the 8 ,16, 32, and 64 numeric types. For the full list, look at Mozilla's site at `https://developer.mozilla.org/en-US/docs/Web/JavaScript/Typed_arrays`.

In Listing 7-21, we load a file based on the File API. When the file is loaded, it is passed over to the `fileReader` object. There the file is read as an `arrayBuffer`. The `arrayBuffer` is then used in creating a `Unit8Array`. This typed array then can use some of the syntax of a regular array.

CHAPTER 8

Working with Arrays in Loops

How Do You Use a for Loop on an Array?

Problem

You want to iterate through all the values of an array-like object where order is important.

Solution

A for loop lets you iterate through the values of an array in numeric order.

The Code

Listing 8-1. Iterating Through an Array-Like Object with a For Loop

```
var alphaArray = ['a', 'b', 'c', 'e', 'd', 'e', 'f', 'g'];
var arrayLength = alphaArray.length;
for (let i = 0; i < arrayLength; i++){
    console.log(alphaArray[i]); //returns a,b,c,d,e,f,g
}
```

How It Works

For loops are often used when iterating through array-like objects. In Listing 8-1, we are using let to set a block level variable. This variable is available in the block and its sub-blocks. The variable is compared to the length of the array. If the current value, which starts at 0, is less than the length of the array (the number of elements in the array), then add 1 to the value. While the loop is happening, we log the value of the array. One of the important things to remember about using a for loop is you can control the range of elements you want to work with in order.

How Do You Use a for...in Loop with an Array?

Problem

You want to iterate through an array-like object using a for..in loop.

© Russ Ferguson and Keith Cirkel 2017
R. Ferguson and K. Cirkel, *JavaScript Recipes*, DOI 10.1007/978-1-4302-6107-0_8

Solution

If you want to see all the enumerable properties of an array-like object, use a for..in loop.

The Code

Listing 8-2. Looping Through an Array-Like Object with a for..in Loop

```
var alphaArray = ['a', 'b', 'c', 'e', 'd', 'e', 'f', 'g'];
for (prop in alphaArray){
    console.log("alphaArray." + prop + " = " + alphaArray[prop]);
}
```

How It Works

For..in loops allow you to loop only over enumerable properties of array-like objects. This loop works in an arbitrary order. If order is important, use a for loop from the previous example. Built-in objects like arrays and objects have non-enumerable properties from Object.prototype and String.prototype.

How Do You Use a for...of Loop with an Array?

Problem

You want to loop over iterable objects that include Array, Map, Set, String, and TypedArray.

Solution

A for...of loop allows you to loop over collections. Over each iteration, the value of each property is assigned to a variable.

The Code

Listing 8-3. Using a for..of Loop on an Array

```
var alphaArray = ['a', 'b', 'c', 'e', 'd', 'e', 'f', 'g'];
for (let value of alphaArray) {
    console.log(value);   //returns a,b,c,d,e,f,g
}
```

How It Works

The for..of loop allows you to work on each element of the array. Each iteration of the loop will assign the value of each property to the variable that you set in the loop. This variable is set using the let statement, which creates a block-level variable. It also can be set using the var statement. The second argument is the object that you are iterating over.

How Do You Loop Through an Array Using do...while?

Problem

You want to set conditions of a loop and iterate as long as the conditions are not met.

Solution

Using do...while loops allow you to loop based on a condition.

The Code

Listing 8-4. Do...while Lets You Loop Over an Object Based on Conditions

```
var planetExpressCrew = ['Fry', 'Bender', 'Amy', 'Lela' ];
var indexNum = 0;

do {
    console.log(planetExpressCrew[indexNum]);
    indexNum++;
}while(planetExpressCrew[indexNum] != 'Amy');
```

How It Works

The do...while loop will continue to execute until the condition evaluates a false value. This condition is evaluated after executing statements set up in the do block. Because of this, the statement is executed at least one time.

How Do You Use a while Loop on an Array?

Problem

You want to loop based on a condition, but have that condition evaluate to true.

Solution

The while loop is similar to a do..while but will stop if the condition results in a true value.

The Code

Listing 8-5. The While Loop Will Iterate until the Condition Results in a True Statement

```
var planetExpressCrew = ['Fry', 'Bender', 'Amy', 'Lela' ];
var indexNum = 0;
while(indexNum < planetExpressCrew.length){
    console.log(planetExpressCrew[indexNum]);
    indexNum++;
}
```

How It Works

Similar to the do...while in Listing 8-4, the while loop will continue until the condition results in a true value. The condition is evaluated before executing the statements.

If you want to first check a position before performing an action, the while loop would be appropriate. On the other hand, if you want the action to be performed at least once, a do/while loop would work.

How Do You Sort an Array?

Problem

You want to take the values of an array and convert them to a string.

Solution

To sort the contents of an array, you can use the sort method.

The Code

Listing 8-6. Using the sort() Method to Sort the Contents of an Array

```
var planetExpressCrew = ['Fry', 'Bender', 'Amy', 'Lela' ];
console.log(planetExpressCrew.sort()); //returns  ["Amy", "Bender", "Fry", "Lela"];
```

How It Works

The Array object has a built-in sort method. This method will sort all the elements of the array in place. This type of sorting is not considered stable (See Wikipedia's article on sorting algorithms at https://en.wikipedia.org/wiki/Sorting_algorithm#Stability). This method can also accept a function to make custom comparisons. If it is not supplied to the method, it will sort elements based on the Unicode point value.

How Do You Sort a Multidimensional Array?

Problem

You have a multidimensional array that needs to be sorted.

Solution

The sort() method can be customized using a function.

The Code

Listing 8-7. Sorting a Multidimensional Array

```
var multiDArray = [[7,8], [3,4], [1,2], [5,6]];

multiDArray.sort(function(a,b){
    return a[0] - b[0];
});
console.log(multiDArray); //returns [[1,2], [3,4], [5,6], [7,8]];
```

How It Works

Adding a function to the sort() method gives you the ability create a custom sort. Using this function, you can evaluate the elements and make comparisons. When making comparisons, the array is sorted based on the value returned from the function. In Listing 8-7, we compare the first two numbers in the subarray. If the value of a is less than b then return a. This will return an array in ascending order.

How Do You Run a Function for Each Element in Ascending Order?

Problem

You want to perform an operation on each element inside an array, in ascending order.

Solution

The forEach() method allows you to perform a callback function on each element of the array, in ascending order.

The Code

Listing 8-8. forEach Allows You to Perform a Function on Every Element of an Array, But Passes Undefined if There Is No Value

```
var myArray = [9, 2, 7, 6, 8, 5, 3];

myArray.forEach(function(element, index, array){
    console.log(element + ' element'); //returns 9, 2, 7, 6, 8, 5, 3
    console.log(element + ' index '); //returns 0 ,1, 2, 3, 4, 5, 6
    console.log(element + ' array '); //returns the entire array
});
```

How It Works

The forEach() method will execute a function once for every method in ascending order. This function will not run on elements that have been deleted or are missing. This method works similar to other methods used on the array prototype. It will receive the element value, the index, and the array.

How Do You Test for a False Condition in an Array?

Problem

You need to check the elements for a value that does not meet the conditions you set up.

Solution

The every() method allows you to have a function that runs a test. The method stops when a false value is returned.

The Code

Listing 8-9. Appending the Values of an Array to Another Array

```
var myArray = [9, 2, 7, 6, 8, 5, 3];
myArray.every(function(element){
    console.log(element >= 1); //returns true
});
```

How It Works

The every() method will run on every element similar to Listing 8-8. The important difference is that the callback function will evaluate the element and return true only if every element meets the conditions. Otherwise, it will stop evaluating and return false. This function is only called on indexes with a value.

How Do You Test for a True Condition in an Array?

Problem

You want to check the elements for a value that meets the conditions you set up.

Solution

The some() method will evaluate all elements until a true value has been returned.

The Code

Listing 8-10. Reversing Elements in the Array Using the Reverse Method

```
var myArray = [9, 2, 7, 6, 8, 5, 3];
    myArray.some(function(element){
        console.log(element == 9); //returns true then false for all the other values
    });
```

How It Works

The some() method works very much like the example in Listing 8-9. The some() method returns true for the element that meets the condition. It will return false for everything else. Just like the every() method, it will not execute on indexes that do not contain a value or have been deleted.

How Do You Filter the Elements in an Array?

Problem

You need an array of only the elements that meet some certain criteria.

Solution

The filter() method will return a new array of only the elements that pass the test in the callback function.

The Code

Listing 8-11. Creating a New Array Using the filter() Method

```
var myArray = [9, 2, 7, 6, 8, 5, 3];
var elementsOver5 = myArray.filter(function(element){
    return element > 5;
});
console.log(elementsOver5); //returns [9, 7, 6, 8]
```

How It Works

This method runs a callback function on every element. Similar to Listing 8-8, it will return a new array based on the current one using only the elements that either return true or coerces to true. Also like some of other examples, it will not run the callback function on indexes that do not have a value or were deleted from the array. Any elements that do not pass the test set up on the callback function are ignored and not included in the new array. The callback function receives the same parameters each time—the value of the element, the index number, and the array itself.

How Can You Reverse Each Word in a String in Place?

Problem

You want to reverse each word, but not change the order of the words.

Solution

Using map() on an array will allow you to run a callback function on every element of the array. This gives you the opportunity to perform work on the element and return a new array.

The Code

Listing 8-12. Using map() to Reverse Each Element in the Array Like Object in Place

```
var phrase = 'It\'s the information age brother!';
var phraseArray = phrase.split(' ');
var reverseArray =  phraseArray.map(function(element){
        return element.split('').reverse().join('');
})
console.log(reverseArray); //returns ["s'tI", "eht", "noitamrofni", "ega", "!rehtorb"]
```

How It Works

Array.prototype.map() will run a callback function on every index in the array, including indexes whose value is *undefined*. It will not run the callback on indexes that are missing or were previously deleted. Like most methods on the array prototype, the callback can accept three values—the value of the element, its index, and the array that is being transversed. This method will return a new array based on the results returned from the callback function. If you are testing for a palindrome, you can compare the results to the original string using triple equals sign (===).

How Do You Combine the Elements in an Array into a Single Value?

Problem

You want to reduce the elements into a single value.

Solution

The reduce() method will allow you to run a callback function on each element. This gives you the opportunity to return a single value based on all the values in the array.

The Code

Listing 8-13. The reduce() Method Can Return a Single Value Based on All the Values in an Array

```
var numArray = [1,2,3,4,5,6];
var reducedValue = numArray.reduce(function(prev, current){
        return prev + current;
});
console.log(reducedValue); //returns 21
```

How It Works

If you ever heard the term *MapReduce,* this is the reduce part of that programming model. This method, like others, takes parameters. In this case, the callback function will receive the previousValue, the currentValue, the currentIndex, and the array.

The first time the callback is executed an initialValue can be provided in the reduce method: reduce(function, initialValue).

If this is the case, the value used in the reduce call will be used as the previousValue. The currentValue will be the value of the first element in the array. If the initialValue is not provided, everything will shift over one position. The previousValue will be the first value in the array and the currentValue will be the second.

If the initialValue has been provided but the array is empty, the initialValue is returned without running the callback function. This is also true if the initialValue was not provided and the array has only one element.

If a initialValue has not been provided and the array is empty, the browser will return a TypeError.

What Is the Difference Between reduce and reduceRight?

Problem

How do you perform a reduce method starting from the right?

Solution

The reduceRight() method functions similar to reduce, but transverses the array from right to left.

The Code

Listing 8-14. The shift() Method Will Remove the First Element in the Array

```
var numArray = [1,2,3,4,5,6];
var reducedValue = numArray.reduceRight(function(prev, current){
        return prev + current;
});
console.log(reducedValue); //returns 21
```

How It Works

The reduceRight() method works the same way as reduce does in Listing 8-13. The important difference is that you are traversing the array from right to left. ReduceRight uses the same rules as the reduce() method. This includes the callback function receiving previousValue, currentValue, the current index number, and the array being transversed.

How Do You Find Unique Values in an Array?

Problem

You want to remove duplicate values from an array.

Solution

Use the filter and indexOf methods to create an array of unique values.

The Code

Listing 8-15. Looping Through the Array Using the Filter Method and Creating a New Array of Unique Values

```
var  numArray = [2,2,3,6,7,7,7,7,8,9];

var uniqueArray = numArray.filter(function(element, index, arrayObj){
        return arrayObj.indexOf(element) == index;
});
console.log(uniqueArray); //returns [2, 3, 6, 7, 8, 9]
```

How It Works

Using the filter method, you can set the callback method and check the index of the element you are currently looking at. The indexOf method will return the first index number it can find using the element provided and will ignore the duplicate elements.

How Do You Keep Count of Values in an Array?

Problem

You want to know how many times a value is used in an array.

Solution

Use the forEach() method and save the count to another object.

The Code

Listing 8-16. Looping Through and Keeping Count of Each Element

```
var  numArray = [2,2,3,6,7,7,7,7,8,9];
var countObj = {};
var uniqueArray = numArray.forEach(function(element, index, arrayObj){
      if(countObj[element]){
              countObj[element] = countObj[element] + 1;
                    }else{
                 countObj[element] = 1;
              }
      });

console.log(countObj); //returns Object {2: 2, 3: 1, 6: 1, 7: 4, 8: 1, 9: 1}
```

How It Works

Using the forEach() method, we loop through every element in the array. Inside the callback function, we run an if statement to see if the property exists in the object we are calling countObj. If the property exists, then take the value and add 1; if not, then create the property on the object and give it a value of 1. Once the loop is finished the countObj will then have a count of every value in the array.

How Do You Get the Max or Min Value in an Array?

Problem

You need to find either the largest or smallest number in an array.

Solution

The Math object has a Max and Min method. Pass the array to either of these methods.

The Code

Listing 8-17. Find the Largest Number in the Array or the Smallest

```
var  numArray = [2,2,3,6,7,7,7,7,8,9];
console.log(Math.max.apply(null, numArray)); //returns 9
console.log(Math.min.apply(null, numArray)); //returns 2
```

How It Works

The Math object contains a max or min method that will give you either the largest number in the array or the smallest. The call method allows an unlimited amount of parameters. This gives you the ability to pass the entire array to be processed.

CHAPTER 9

Working with Objects

What Is the Difference Between an Object Constructor and an Object Literal?

Problem

You want to know what the difference is between creating an object using the new operator or an object literal.

Solution

Object literals are usually easer to read. When creating an object literal, you can assign properties at the same time. Using a object constructor can create an object but will require extra lines to define properties.

The Code

Listing 9-1. Objects Can Be Created Using Either the Object Constructor or by Creating an Object Literal

```
var R2D2 = new Object();
    R2D2.class = 'Astromech Droid';

var R2D2 = {
        class:'Astromech Droid';
        manufacturer: 'Industrial Automaton';
};
```

How It Works

Objects can be created both ways. When creating an object literal, you can set all the properties and methods of the object in one statement. This is usually considered easier to read. When creating properties and methods to an object, they are available in every instance of that object.

R. Ferguson and K. Cirkel, *JavaScript Recipes*, DOI 10.1007/978-1-4302-6107-0_9

How Do You Access and Set Properties of an Object?

Problem

You want to know how to access properties of an object.

Solution

Properties can be accessed in two ways—using dot notation or bracket notation.

The Code

Listing 9-2. Accessing Properties of an Object Using Dot Notation and Bracket Syntax

```
var R2D2  = {
};
R2D2['class'] = 'Astromech Droid'

console.log(R2D2['class']);   //returns Astromech Droid

R2D2.manufacturer = 'Industrial Automaton';

console.log(R2D2.manufacturer);   //returns Industrial Automaton
```

How It Works

The term properties are sometimes used when talking about variables assigned to an object and functions assigned to an object. When accessing variables, dot notation is used more often. However you can also use array-like bracket notation. In that case, property names are in quotes. Other languages call this a hash, lookup table, dictionary, or map.

When giving properties names using dot syntax, the same rules apply that you would use for variables. Property names can have numbers, underscores, and dollar signs. However, they cannot start with a number. If you're using bracket notation, property names must be a string. In this case, the names are not formatted in the same way as if you created properties using dot notation.

What Is the Difference Between Objects and Arrays?

Problem

You want to know when you should you use an object versus an array.

Solution

Because arrays are indexed, they are iterated in order, whereas with objects, order is not guaranteed. Arrays also have helper methods for adding and removing values. Objects are good at representing groups of data at the cost of order.

The Code

Listing 9-3. Some of the Differences Between Objects and Arrays

```
Object.prototype.good = "stuff";
var ship  = {
        type:40,
        name:'tardis',
        color:'blue'
};

for(var prop in ship){
    console.log(prop + ': ' + ship[prop]);
}
var numArray = [1, 2, 3, 4, 5, 6, 7, 8, 9];
for(var prop in numArray){
    console.log(prop + ': ' + numArray[prop]);
}

for(var i = 0; i <numArray.length; i++){
    console.log(numArray[i]);
}
```

How It Works

Since almost everything you work with in JavaScript is an object, arrays also inherent properties of objects. Depending on how you loop through the object or array, you access any enumerable property on the object or its prototype. If you're using a for...in loop, both the array and the object will access the "good" property.

When using a for loop on the array, only the indexed elements are accessed.

Can You Use Variables to Represent Object Properties?

Problem

You want to know if it's possible to use variables as properties of an object.

Solution

You can use variables. Objects in JavaScript can use the bracket notation similar to an array when using a variable.

The Code

Listing 9-4. Using Variables to Access Properties of an Object

```
var ship = {};
var type = 'spaceShip';
ship[type] = 'X-Wing';
```

```
console.log(ship[type]); //returns X-Wing
console.log(ship.spaceShip);  //returns X-Wing
console.log(ship.type);  //returns undefined
```

How It Works

Objects in JavaScript are sometimes called associated arrays. Instead of having a indexed value, it uses properties. In Listing 9-4, the variable is referencing an object. Next is a variable that is referencing a value. The third line combines the two, and we create a property of the object. Since JavaScript passes objects by reference, you can see from the logs that the property can be used using the square brackets. Since it's a variable, you do not need to put the property in quotes. However, if you're accessing the property using dot notation, you would need to access the value and not the variable.

What Does It Mean to Assign Properties of an Object with Metadata?

Problem

You want to create customized properties of an object.

Solution

The defineProperty method of an object will allow you to create custom properties for your object.

The Code

Listing 9-5. Using the defineProperty Method Inside a Class

```
function SuperHeroTeam() {
    this.name = 'The Avengers';
    var _numberOfMembers; // private member

Object.defineProperty(this,"numberOfMemebers",{
    get: function() { return _numberOfMembers; },
    set: function(value) { _numberOfMembers = value; }
});

Object.defineProperty(this,"tagline",{
    value: 'Earth\'s Mightiest Heroes',
    configurable: false
  });
}

var team = new SuperHeroTeam();
team.numberOfMembers = 8;
console.log(team.numberOfMembers);

team.tagline = 'The Amazing'; //not editable
console.log(team.tagline);  // returns Earth's Mightiest Heroes
```

How It Works

The defineProperty method allows you to create a custom property and the rules that govern that property. In the first example, we create a getter/setter function called numberOfMembers. You can see in the code the defineProperty method refers to the variable _numberOfMembers. Since functions are objects, this variable is not exposed to the outside. Using the defineProperty method, we can access this variable and give it a value.

We have a similar situation with the second example. The tagline property is set but in this case we set the properties confirmation setting to false. This will make our property read-only. If you try to delete the property, the browser will ignore the request.

There is another option, called enumerable. By default this property is set to false, which means the properties are accessible but you cannot iterate through them. If it's true, you can iterate through the properties of the object.

In this example, we define two properties, each using the defineProperty method. If you wanted to define them using one method call, use defineProperties.

How Do You Get All the Properties from an Object?

Problem

You want to know both the enumerable and non-enumerable properties of an object.

Solution

The getOwnPropertyNames method of the Object object will return an array of all properties.

The Code

Listing 9-6. getOwnPropertyNames Returns an Array of All Properties

```
function SuperHeroTeam() {
  this.name = 'The Avengers';
  var _numberOfMembers; // private member
  Object.defineProperty(this,"numberOfMemebers",{
    get: function() { return _numberOfMembers; },
    set: function(value) { _numberOfMembers = value; }
  });

  Object.defineProperty(this,"tagline",{
        value: 'Earth\'s Mightiest Heroes',
        configurable: false
  });
}

var team = new SuperHeroTeam();
Object.getOwnPropertyNames(team).forEach(function(val){
        console.log(val); // returns name. numberOfNames, tagline
});
```

How It Works

The getOwnPropertyNames method will return an array of both enumerable and non-enumerable properties found in the object. In the case of the enumerable properties, they would return in the same order that they would in a for...in loop.

How Do You Get Just the Enumerable Properties of an Object?

Problem

You want an array of just the enumerable properties.

Solution

The keys() method will return an array of an object's enumerable properties.

The Code

Listing 9-7. Returning Only the Enumerable Properties of an Object

```
var myObj = {a:1, b:2, c:3};
console.log(Object.keys(myObj)); //returns ["a", "b", "c"]
```

How It Works

This method will return an array of the object's enumerable properties, in the same order as if you performed a for..in loop. If you are using ES5 and pass over a primitive (for example, a string), you will receive a type error. If you are using ES6, each letter in the string will return as its index number.

How Do You Know If a Property Is Enumerable?

Problem

You want to check if a property of an object is enumerable.

Solution

The IsEnumerable() method will return true if the property is enumerable.

The Code

Listing 9-8. forEach Allows You to Perform a Function on Every Element of an Array, but Passes Undefined If There Is No Value

```
var myObj = {a:1, b:2, c:3};
console.log(myObj.propertyIsEnumerable('a')); //returns true
console.log(myObj.propertyIsEnumerable('length')); //returns false
```

How It Works

Every object has a propertyIsEnumerable method. It will return true if the property could be enumerated similar to the results of a for..in loop. Properties that are inherited by way of the prototype chain are not checked. If the property is not enumerable, the method will return false.

How Can You Check If an Object Is a Child or Descendant of Another Object?

Problem

You want to know if the current object has a parent object.

Solution

Object.isPrototypeOf() will return true if one object is the prototype of another object.

The Code

Listing 9-9. Checking If an Object Is the Prototype of Another

```
var Person = function(){
    this.firstName = 'Peter',
    this.lastName = 'Parker';
    this.location = 'Queens/New York';
}

var Hero = function(){
    Person.call(this);
    this.heroName = 'Spider-Man';
    this.powers = 'Climb Walls/Shoots Webs';
}

Hero.prototype = Object.create(Person.prototype);
Hero.prototype.constructor = Hero;

var superHero = new Hero();
console.log(Person.prototype.isPrototypeOf(superHero)); //returns true
console.log(superHero instanceof Person); //returns true
```

How It Works

To understand this method, it helps to think of it in these terms: "Is this object in the prototype chain of another object?". If that is the case, then the method will return true.

This works in a similar way to instanceOf, although an important difference is that the isPrototypeOf method is part of the Prototype object. In this way, it is available to all objects. Using instanceOf requires two operands, the first being an object, the second being a Constructor function. There it will test if the constructor's prototype chain exists on the object you are working with.

How Can You Tell If a Property Is on the Current Instance or on the Prototype of an Object?

Problem

JavaScript slows down if it needs to go too far up the prototype chain.

Solution

Use the hasOwnProperty method to check if the property is on the instance or on the prototype chain.

The Code

Listing 9-10. The firstName Property Is on the Instance, Whereas the toString Property Is Not

```
var Person = function(){
    this.firstName = 'Peter',
    this.lastName = 'Parker';
    this.location = 'Queens/New York';
}

var Hero = function(){
    Person.call(this);
    this.heroName = 'Spider-Man';
    this.powers = 'Climb Walls/Shoots Webs';
}

Hero.prototype = Object.create(Person.prototype);
Hero.prototype.constructor = Hero;

var superHero = new Hero();
console.log(superHero.hasOwnProperty('firstName')); //returns true
console.log(superHero.hasOwnProperty('toString')); //returns false
```

How It Works

This method will check if the property is directly on the object. It will not go up the prototype chain. All objects that descend from Object will have access to the hasOwnProperty method. This could also be used inside for..in loops to retrieve only the properties associated with the current object.

How Do You Copy All Enumerable Values from One or More Objects?

Problem

You need an array of only the elements that meet some criteria.

Solution

Object.assign will copy all enumerable and own properties from one or more objects.

The Code

Listing 9-11. The Character Object Has All the Properties of the First Two Objects

```
var person = {firstName: 'Rick Hunter', born:'October 22, 1990'};
var creature = {species: 'Human', gender:'Male', eyes:'Blue', hair:'Black'};

var character = Object.assign(person, creature);
console.log(character);
//returns Object {firstName: "Rick Hunter", born: "October 22, 1990", species: "Human",
gender: "Male", eyes: "Blue"...}
```

How It Works

This method will copy all enumerable and own properties from target objects and assign them to a target object. If a property is non-writeable, the browser will throw a TypeError and not update the object.

What Is the Difference Between Object.create and Using the New Operator?

Problem

When would you use the new operator over the Object.create method?

Solution

With Object.create you can assign the prototype of the object that you are creating. When using the new operator the methods and properties are not part of the object's prototype.

The Code

Listing 9-12. Using the Create Method and Assigning a Prototype Object to It

```
var Human = {
    name: 'Luke Skywalker'
}
var person = Object.create(Human, { droid: {value: 'R2-D2'}});
console.log(person.name);  //returns Luke Skywalker from the prototype
console.log(person.droid); //returns R2-D2
```

How It Works

The create method gives you the ability to specify the prototype of the object you are creating. Since a prototype is an object, we pass an object as the first parameter. The second contains all the properties and methods that you want the object to have. If you do not want your object to have a prototype, you can pass null as the first parameter.

Can You Change the Prototype of an Object After the Object Has Been Created?

Problem

You want to change the value of the current prototype object.

Solution

Object.setPrototypeOf will reset the prototype of an object that you created.

The Code

Listing 9-13. Updating the Value of the Prototype Object, After Setting It Using Object.create

```
var Human = {
    name: 'Luke Skywalker'
}
var person = Object.create(Human, { droid: {value: 'R2-D2'}});
var person = Object.setPrototypeOf(person, null);
console.log(person.name);  //returns undefined
console.log(person.droid); //returns R2-D2
```

How It Works

Before using the setPrototypeOf method, you should be aware that updating the prototype is a very slow operation and will affect the performance of every browser. The effect of changing the prototype of an object can have unintended consequences.

If the prototype of the object is extensible, it will be replaced with the object being passed as the second parameter. Otherwise, a TypeError will be thrown. Using this method is part of ECMAScript 6 and considered a better way of updating the prototype object over using the prototype._proto_ property.

How Many Ways Can You Prevent an Object from Being Modified?

Problem

You want to know which methods prevent modification of objects.

Solution

Use the freeze, seal, and preventExtensions methods.

The Code

Listing 9-14. Showing the Difference Between the Freeze, Seal, and preventExtensions Methods

```
var robot1 = {
    type: 'Autobot',
    vehicle: 'Truck'
}

var robot2 = {
    type: 'Autobot',
    vehicle: 'Truck'
}

var robot3 = {
    type: 'Autobot',
    vehicle: 'Truck',
    likes: 'Music'
}

var optimusPrime = Object.freeze(robot1);
    optimusPrime.type = 'Decepticon'; //silently fails
    console.log(optimusPrime.type);   //returns Autobot
var hotRod = Object.seal(robot2);
    hotRod.vehicle = 'Car'; //value is updated
    console.log('vehicle = ' + hotRod.vehicle); //returns Car
var jazz = Object.preventExtensions(robot3);
    console.log(jazz.likes); //returns Music
    delete jazz.likes;
    console.log(jazz.likes); //returns undefined
```

How It Works

The freeze() method prevents properties to be added, modified, or removed. An object in this state is considered immutable.

Seal works similar to the freeze method. Objects by default are extensible, meaning that new properties can be added, modified, and deleted. When sealing an object, new properties cannot be added to the object. Existing properties cannot be modified. One difference with the seal method is that the values of properties can be updated.

Using the preventExtensions method will make an object no longer extensible, meaning that properties that exist at the time the method is being used will still exist, but new ones cannot be created. However, properties of this object *can be deleted*. Attempting to add new properties will either fail silently or result in a TypeError.

Can You Check If an Object Is Immutable?

Problem

You need to check the mutability of an object.

Solution

The isFrozen, isSealed, and isExtensible methods will check the mutability of an object.

The Code

Listing 9-15. Testing If Objects Are Immutable

```
var optimusPrime = Object.freeze(robot1);
    console.log(Object.isFrozen(optimusPrime));  //returns true
var hotRod = Object.seal(robot2);
    console.log(Object.isSealed(hotRod)); //returns true

var jazz = Object.preventExtensions(robot3);
    console.log(Object.isExtensible(jazz)); //returns false
```

How It Works

Expanding on text examples in the previous sections, when an object is frozen it is not extensible. The isFrozen method will return true if all properties that are not getter or setters are non-writable.

isSealed will return true if properties are not configurable.

The isExtensible method will check if new properties can be added to it.

Can You Tell If Two Values Are the Same?

Problem

You want to compare two different values for equality.

Solution

The Object.is method can be used to check if two values are the same.

The Code

Listing 9-16. Using the Object.is Method to Compare Two Values

```
var robot1 = {
    type: 'Autobot',
    vehicle: 'Truck'
}
console.log(Object.is(robot1, robot1)); //returns true
console.log(Object.is(0, false)); //returns false
console.log(Object.is(-0, +0)); //returns false
console.log(Object.is(NaN, NaN)); //returns true
```

How It Works

When thinking abut this method, it is important to note that is it not the same as using either the equals operator (==) or strict equality (===). The first of these two operators performs coercions if the values are not the same type. The second is considered equal if they are not NaN (not a number) and the same value or if one is +0 and the other -0.

There are some rules to how this method works that separate it from the other ways of testing equality:

- Both must be undefined

- Both must be null

- Both must be either true or false

- If they are strings, they need the same length and the same characters

- Both objects must be the same

- If using numbers, both must be +0, -0, NaN, or have the same value

It is also important to note that browser support is is lacking in Internet Explorer and Safari 7 and 8 (but is supported in Microsoft Edge).

What Is Object Destructuring?

Problem

You want to extract data from arrays or objects and turn them into distinct values.

Solution

Destructuring objects and arrays, is the ability to bind properties to variables.

The Code

Listing 9-17. An Example of Destructing an Array and an Object

```
var spaceShip = ['1701-A', '1701-B', '1701-C', '1701-D'];
var [A, B, C, D] = spaceShip;
console.log(D); //returns 1701-D
var timeMachine = {type: 40, color: 'blue', desguise: 'Police Box'};
var {type, color, desguise} = timeMachine;
console.log(desguise);  //returns Police Box
```

How It Works

Destructing objects and arrays allows you to assign the values of either variables, then reference those variables directly. In Listing 9-7, the values of the array spaceShip are mapped to an array running A through D. Similarly, the values of the object timeMachine is mapped to an object.

To keep the example simple, the names are the same for the objects and arrays that the values are being mapped to. This does not need to be the case. Once the values have been assigned, they can be used as variables independent of the object or array they originate from.

How Do You Loop Through Objects Using a for…in Loop?

Problem

You want use a for...in loop to iterate through the properties of an object.

Solution

A for...in loop will loop over all enumerable properties. However, if you only want the properties of the object and not its prototype, include the hasOwnProperty method.

The Code

Listing 9-18. Looping Through an Object's Own Properties and Not Properties from Its Prototype

```
var Hero = function(){
    this.heroName = 'Spider-Man';
    this.powers = 'Climb Walls/Shoots Webs';
}
Hero.prototype.firstName = 'Peter';
Hero.prototype.lastName = 'Parker';
Hero.prototype.location = 'Queens/New York';

var superHero = new Hero();
for(var key in superHero){
    console.log(key + ' = ' + superHero[key]); //returns all properties including what is
    in the prototype
}
```

```
for(var key in superHero){
    if(superHero.hasOwnProperty(key)){
        console.log(key + ' = ' + superHero[key]); //only returns properties directly
        from the object
      }
}
```

How It Works

By default the for..in loop will display all the properties, including properties included in the prototype chain. If you only are interested in the properties directly associated with the object itself, use the hasOwnProperty method. This will only return objects that are not part of the prototype.

How Do You Loop Through Objects Using a for…of Loop?

Problem

You want to use a for…of loop to iterate through the properties of an object.

Solution

The for...of loop is useful for looping through iterable objects. For example, TypedArrays, arguments, maps, and strings are some of the objects that can be used.

The Code

Listing 9-19. The for..of Loop Will Loop Through Collections

```
var myArray = [10, 20, 30];
for (let value of myArray) {
    console.log(value);  //returns 10, 20, 30
}

var myObj = new Object();
    myObj.name = "Rodd";
    myObj.address = "Brooklyn";
for(let value of myObj){
    console.log(value); //returns Uncaught TypeError: myObj[Symbol.iterator] is not a
function
}
```

How It Works

The for...of loop works with iterable objects. This allows JavaScript to define or customize how the values are looped over. Some types like arrays or maps have built-in iterables with a default behavior. Objects however do not have such a feature, resulting in an [Symbol.iterator] error.

How Do You Loop Through Objects Using a do...while loop?

Problem

You want to loop through an object at least one time.

Solution

The `do..while` loop will loop until a condition returns `false`. This will execute the statement at least one time.

The Code

Listing 9-20. *A do...while loop Will Execute until the Statement Returns a False Value*

```
var i = 0;

var nameArray = ['Cameron', 'Greyson', 'Vanessa', 'Emily', 'Cate'];
do{
   console.log(nameArray[i]); //returns  Cameron, Greyson Vanessa
   i++;
}while(nameArray[i] != 'Emily');
```

How It Works

While looping, the condition is evaluated at the end of executing the loop. Because of this, the loop will happen at least one time. If multiple statements need to be evaluated, use a block {} to group statements together.

How Do You Loop Through Objects Using a while Loop?

Problem

You want to loop through an object as long as the test condition is true.

Solution

The `while` loop will continue to execute the given statement as long as it evaluates to `true`.

The Code

Listing 9-21. As Long as the Condition Returns True a While Loop Will Continue to Execute It

```
var i = 0;
var nameArray = ['Cameron', 'Greyson', 'Vanessa', 'Emily', 'Cate'];
while(i < 2){
     console.log(nameArray[i]); //returns Cameron Greyson
     i++;
}
```

How It Works

Similar to the last example, this will loop based on a condition. The exception is that this will loop as long as the condition evaluates to true.

CHAPTER 10

Working with Sets

What Is the Difference Between a Set and an Array?

Problem

In what situation would you use a set object over an array?

Solution

There are some similarities between the two objects. They can both hold on to data of different types. What separates a set is that the values all need to be unique.

The Code

Listing 10-1. Showing the Difference Between Sets and Arrays

```
var numberSet = new Set();
    numberSet.add(1);
    numberSet.add(2);
    numberSet.add(3);
    numberSet.add(3); //does not get added
    console.log(numberSet.entries()); //returns SetIterator {[1, 1], [2, 2], [3, 3]}

var numArray = new Array();
    numArray.push(1);
    numArray.push(2);
    numArray.push(3);
    numArray.push(3);
    console.log(numArray); //returns [1, 2, 3, 3]
```

How It Works

Some of the properties and methods associated with a set are very similar to what you would find with an array. For example, the `size` property is like using the `length` property in an array. Where arrays can have multiple elements with the same value, sets are made to contain unique values for each element.

© Russ Ferguson and Keith Cirkel 2017
R. Ferguson and K. Cirkel, *JavaScript Recipes*, DOI 10.1007/978-1-4302-6107-0_10

How Do You Add and Remove Elements of a Set?

Problem

You need to manage elements of a set.

Solution

An array uses push to add elements, whereas sets use the add method. To remove elements, use the delete method.

The Code

Listing 10-2. Adding and Removing Elements from a Set Object

```
var numberSet = new Set();
    numberSet.add(1);
    numberSet.add(2);
    numberSet.add(3);
    numberSet.add('things');
    console.log(numberSet.size);   //returns 4
    numberSet.delete('things');
    console.log(numberSet.size); //returns 3
```

How It Works

If you wanted to remove the last element of an array, you can use the pop method. If you know the index number, you can use the splice method. With sets, you can use the delete method and pass the value of the element you want to delete. Use the add method like in Listing 10-2 to add elements.

How Do You Remove All the Elements of a Set?

Problem

You need to remove all elements of a set object.

Solution

The clear method will remove all elements from a set, whereas delete will only remove one.

The Code

Listing 10-3. Removing All Elements from a Set Object

```
var numberSet = new Set();
    numberSet.add(1);
    numberSet.add(2);
```

```
numberSet.add(3);
numberSet.add('things');
console.log(numberSet.size);   //returns 4
numberSet.clear();

console.log(numberSet.size); //returns 0
```

How It Works

There are a few ways of removing items from an array. Sets make it easy with the clear method. In the example in Listing 10-3, clear will remove all existing elements from the set.

What Is the Difference Between the Keys and Values Methods?

Problem

You need to know when to use the keys method over the values method.

Solution

Both methods return an iterator object that contains values for each element. The keys method is an alias for the values method.

The Code

Listing 10-4. Checking If a Value Exists in a Set

```
var numberSet = new Set();
    numberSet.add(1);
    numberSet.add(2);
    numberSet.add(3);
    numberSet.add('things');
    console.log(numberSet.keys());   //returns SetIterator {1, 2, 3, "things"}
    console.log(numberSet.values());   //returns SetIterator {1, 2, 3, "things"}

    var elements = numberSet.values();
    console.log(elements.next().value);   //returns 1
    console.log(elements.next().value);   //returns 2
```

How It Works

The values and keys methods both return an iterator object. If you want to manually see the next element, you can use the next method.

How Many Elements Are in the Current Set?

Problem

You want to know the number of elements in a current set.

Solution

Use the `size` property to determine how many elements are in a set object.

The Code

Listing 10-5. Using Size to Determine How Many Elements Are in a Set

```
var numberSet = new Set();
numberSet.add(1);
numberSet.add(2);
numberSet.add(3);
numberSet.add('things');
console.log(numberSet.size);  //returns 4
```

How It Works

The size property returns an integer letting you know how many elements are in the set. Unlike with an array, this property cannot be set.

What Is a WeakSet?

Problem

You need to know the difference between a set and a WeakSet.

Solution

WeakSets only hold on to objects, where a set can hold on to items of any type. References to objects in the collection are garbage collected if there are no references to them.

The Code

Listing 10-6. WeakSets Work in a Similar Way to Sets

```
var weakSet = new WeakSet();
var obj1 = {};

weakSet.add(obj1);
console.log(weakSet.has(obj1)); //returns true just like a Set
```

How It Works

The methods of a weakSet are the same as a set object. The main difference between the two is that only objects can be saved as elements. WeakSets are also not enumerable and are garbage collected if there are no references to objects in the weakSet.

How Does a forEach Method Work with a Set Object?

Problem

You need to know if there a difference using a forEach method on a set versus an array.

Solution

The forEach method works the same when using a set as when using an array. The method is called for each value in the set.

The Code

Listing 10-7. Looping Through a Set Using the forEach Method

```
var numberSet = new Set();
    numberSet.add(1);
    numberSet.add(2);
    numberSet.add(3);
numberSet.forEach(function(value){
    console.log(value);   //returns 1,2,3
});
```

How It Works

In order to be consistent with the map and array versions, the forEach method will be called once for each element in a set. When the function is called, three arguments are sent over. The first two will be the value of the element. The third would have been the set object that is being transversed.

Can You Check If an Element Exists in a Set?

Problem

You want to know if an element with a certain value exists in the set.

Solution

The has method will return a Boolean based on if there is an element with the given value inside the set.

The Code

Listing 10-8. Determining If Any Element in the Set Has a Certain Value

```
var bandSet = new Set();
    bandSet.add('Dave');
    bandSet.add('Martin');
    bandSet.add('Fletch');

console.log(bandSet.has('vince')); //returns false
console.log(bandSet.has('Dave')); //returns true
```

How It Works

The has method is similar to the find method in an array, in that you can search for the value in an array. The has method does not require a callback function. It simply returns a value of true or false if there is any element in the set that contains the given value.

Can a Set Generate Iterator Objects?

Problem

You want to customize how you iterate through a set.

Solution

The entries method will return an array of each element in the order of insertion.

The Code

Listing 10-9. Creating a Custom Iterator with a Set

```
var bandSet = new Set();
    bandSet.add('Dave');
    bandSet.add('Martin');
    bandSet.add('Fletch');
    bandSet.add('Jim');
    bandSet.add('Paul');
    bandSet.add('Kurt');
    bandSet.add('Andy');
    bandSet.add('Vince');

var entry = bandSet.entries();
console.log(entry.next().value); //returns ["Dave", "Dave"]

console.log(entry.next()); //returns Object {value: Array[2], done: false}

while(entry.next().done == false){  //as long as the current item returns false then keep going
    console.log(entry.next().value)
}
```

How It Works

When using the entries method, you can create a custom iterator for the set. (For more information about iterators, see Chapter 13.) The iterator object contains two properties, done and value. Sets do not have keys in the same way that a map does. Because of this, it returns the same value as both the key and the value. This keeps the API similar to the Map object.

The done property returns a Boolean letting you know if you have reached the last item in sequence. The value is false until the last item has been reached.

The value property returns an array. Because set objects do not have a key, the value of both items in the array are the same. This keeps it consistent with the Map object.

CHAPTER 11

Working with Maps

What Are the Advantages of Using a Map over an Object?

Problem

When is it better to use a map rather than an object?

Solution

While there are similarities to maps and objects, maps can contain both objects and primitives as keys or values.

The Code

Listing 11-1. Maps Can Use Different Types as Keys, Whereas Objects Use Strings

```
var mapObj = new Map();
    mapObj.set('myString', 'myString is a string key');
    console.log(mapObj.get('myString')); //myString is a string key

var myObj = {};
    mapObj.set(myObj, 'Object is a used as a key');
    console.log(mapObj.get(myObj)); //Object is a used as a key
```

How It Works

Maps are similar to objects in that they have name/value pairs. Some of the methods associated with maps resemble the Set object (for more information on sets, see Chapter 10). One instance where maps are different than plain objects, is that map keys can be any value. In addition, the size of a map does not need to to be manually counted.

How Do You Add and Remove Elements of a Map?

Problem

You need to manage elements of a map.

Solution

Maps use the set method to set keys and values. Similar to the set object, it uses the delete method to remove a key.

The Code

Listing 11-2. Adding and Removing Elements from a Map Object

```
var mapObj = new Map();
    mapObj.set('myString', 'myString is a string key');
    mapObj.delete('myString');
    console.log(mapObj.get('myString')); //undefined
```

How It Works

In Listings 11-1 and 11-2, the set method is used to create a key and its value. With the Map object, keys can be of any type. When using the set method, both keys and values are required properties. Keys can be updated by using the set method with the same key. The delete method will expect a key to delete the key/value pair from the object. If the element exists and has been deleted, the delete method will return true; otherwise it will return false.

How Do You Remove All the Elements of a Map?

Problem

You need to remove all elements of a Map object .

Solution

The clear method will remove all elements from a map, whereas delete will only remove one.

The Code

Listing 11-3. Removing All Elements from a Set Object

```
var mapObj = new Map();
    mapObj.set('myString', 'myString is a string key');
    mapObj.clear();
    console.log(mapObj.size); //returns 0
```

How It Works

The Map object uses the same method name as a set. Using the clear method will remove all the elements from a Map object.

How Do You Determine If a Key Exists in a Map?

Problem

You need to find a key in the Map object.

Solution

Use the has key to check the existence of a key in the Map object.

The Code

Listing 11-4. The Has Method Will Return True if an Element Exists

```
var numberSet = new Set();
    numberSet.add(1);
    numberSet.add(2);
    numberSet.add(3);
    numberSet.add('things');
    console.log(numberSet.keys());  //returns SetIterator {1, 2, 3, "things"}
    console.log(numberSet.values());  //returns SetIterator {1, 2, 3, "things"}

    var elements = numberSet.values();
    console.log(elements.next().value);  //returns 1
    console.log(elements.next().value);  //returns 2
```

How It Works

The has method will return true only if the key exists as an element of the Map object.

How Do You Get All the Keys of a Map Object?

Problem

You want access to all the elements of a Map object.

Solution

The keys method will return a MapIterator object, which can be used to access all the elements of the Map object.

The Code

Listing 11-5. The Keys Method Will Return a MapIterator Object That Lets You Access the Keys of Each Element

```
var mapObj = new Map();
    mapObj.set('1st value', '1st key');
    mapObj.set('2nd value', '2nd key');
    mapObj.set('3rd value', '3rd key');
    console.log(mapObj.keys()); //returns MapIterator object
var mapIterator = mapObj.keys();
    console.log(mapIterator.next().value); //1st value
    console.log(mapIterator.next().value); //2nd value
```

How It Works

The `MapIterator` object is returned from the keys method. In this example, it is saved as a separate variable. With the `MapIterator` saved as a separate variable, the next method lets you access each key that is in the Map object. There is no support for this method in Internet Explorer.

How Do You Get Access to the Value of Each Key Using the Values Method?

Problem

You want to use the values method of the `Map` object.

Solution

The `values` method works just like the `keys` method. The only difference is that you are returning the values of each element and not the key.

The Code

Listing 11-6. The Values Method Returns an Iterator Object Just Like the Keys Method

```
var mapObj = new Map();
    mapObj.set('1st value', '1st key');
    mapObj.set('2nd value', '2nd key');
    mapObj.set('3rd value', '3rd key');
    console.log(mapObj.values()); //returns MapIterator object

var mapIterator = mapObj.values();
    console.log(mapIterator.next().value); //1st key
    console.log(mapIterator.next().value); //2nd key
```

How It Works

The results of calling the `values` method is the same as calling the `keys` method of a map. An iterator object is returned that can then be used to look at each value used in the Map object. In the previous example, the key of each element is being returned. Just like with the key element, there is no support for this in Internet Explorer.

How Can You Return Both the Key and Value from a Map Object?

Problem

You want to return both the key and value of an element from the Map object.

Solution

Using the `entries` method will return an array of a single key and value from the Map object using an `Iterator` object.

The Code

Listing 11-7. Looping Through a Set Using the forEach Method

```
var mapObj = new Map();
    mapObj.set('1st value', '1st key');
    mapObj.set('2nd value', '2nd key');
    mapObj.set('3rd value', '3rd key');
    console.log(mapObj.entries()); //returns MapIterator object

var mapIterator = mapObj.entries();
    console.log(mapIterator.next().value); //["1st value", "1st key"]
    console.log(mapIterator.next().value); //["2nd value", "2nd key"]
```

How It Works

Using the last two examples as a base, the `entries` method will return an iterator object that can be used to access the elements of the Map object. In this case, it will return an array containing the key and value of each element. To access the next element in the object, the next method needs to be used. As with the other methods, this does not have support in Internet Explorer.

How Many Elements Are Currently in the Map Object?

Problem

You want to know the number of elements currently being used in the Map object.

Solution

The size property is similar to an array's length property because it returns the number of elements being used in the Map object.

The Code

Listing 11-8. The Size Property Returns the Number of Elements in a Map

```
var mapObj = new Map();
    mapObj.set('1st value', '1st key');
    mapObj.set('2nd value', '2nd key');
    mapObj.set('3rd value', '3rd key');
    console.log(mapObj.size); //returns 3
```

How It Works

Just like the length property of an array, the size property will return the number of elements that currently exist in a Map object.

How Do You Iterate Over a Map Using forEach?

Problem

You want to loop through each key in the map using forEach.

Solution

The forEach method works the same way as it does for the Set object. It will give you the ability to execute a callback once for each key.

The Code

Listing 11-9. The forEach Method Will Run a Function on Every Key on a Map

```
var mapObj = new Map();
    mapObj.set('1st value', '1st key');
    mapObj.set('2nd value', '2nd key');
    mapObj.set('3rd value', '3rd key');
mapObj.forEach(function(value, key){
    console.log('mapObj['+key+'] = ' + value); //returns mapObj[N value] = N key
});
```

How It Works

Using forEach will ensure that a function will be called on every key that currently exists. The function can take the current value, its key, and the map as a whole as parameters each time the function is called.

■ ■ ■

CHAPTER 12

Working with Functions

How Do You Create a Function?

Problem

You want to know how many ways there are to create a function.

Solution

There are three ways to create a function, using a constructor, declaration, or expression.

The Code

Listing 12-1. Creating a Function

```
//function constructor
var fun1 = new Function('name', 'return name;');
fun1('Jessica');

//function declaration
function myFun(name){
    var greeting = 'Hello ' + name;
    return greeting;
}
myFun('Danny');

//function expression
var fun3 = function(name) {
    return name;
}
fun3('Mami');
```

How It Works

There are the main ways to create functions. Using a constructor, a function decollation, or using a function expression. According to the ECMAScript specification, adding an identifier to a function is optional. In short, you do not need to give your function a name. This would create an anonymous function. In most cases, function declaration and function expressions are used.

© Russ Ferguson and Keith Cirkel 2017
R. Ferguson and K. Cirkel, *JavaScript Recipes*, DOI 10.1007/978-1-4302-6107-0_12

When using function declaration you would provide the function name, a comma-separated list of parameters to use inside parentheses. The curly brackets {} are used to hold all the statements that are required by the function.

Function expressions can be anonymous, this is often used where functions can be passed as an argument for another function. Take a look at Chapter 11's use of the Map function.

Functions by default return a value. If you want to return a specific value, use the return keyword. In JavaScript, every function is really a function object.

How Do You Call a Function?

Problem

Once a function has been created, you want to know how to execute it.

Solution

Executing or calling a function requires the name of the function and, if necessary, any parameters needed for the function to work.

The Code

Listing 12-2. Calling a Function

```
//if a function called login was already defined
login(username, password);

console.log(sayHello('Peter')); //returns Hello Peter
function sayHello(name){
    return 'Hello ' + name;
}
```

How It Works

When functions are created, as you saw in Listing 12-1, they are not executed. Instead they wait until called upon to execute all the commands listed inside the function. The function itself must be in the same scope when it is called. The arguments that are passed over to the function can be objects including other functions.

What Are Anonymous Functions?

Problem

You want to create and execute an anonymous function.

Solution

Anonymous functions are function expressions. These expressions do not need to have a name to identify them.

The Code

Listing 12-3. Examples of Anonymous Functions

```
document.addEventListener('DOMContentLoaded', function(){
    console.log('content loaded');
});

(function(){
    console.log('running closure');
})();

var greeting = function(name){
    return 'Hello ' + name;
};
greeting('Jenny');
```

How It Works

Anonymous functions do not have a named identifier applied to them. Because of this, the function is usually not accessible after it is created. Since functions are objects, and they can be assigned to variables and executed. If the function in that case has a name, the name of the function will not change if the function is reassigned to a new variable.

Immediately-invoked function expressions or IFFE (pronounced 'iffy') are functions that will automatically execute. One of the reasons for using an IFFE is to keep variables from reaching the global scope. You can also create publicly accessible methods that use privately held variables. Most use cases for anonymous functions are for closures or using a function as a argument for another function.

How Do You Create Functions Inside an Object?

Problem

You want to control the scope of your functions.

Solution

Creating functions inside an object will control the scope of the function so that it is in the scope of the object and does not fall into the global scope.

The Code

Listing 12-4. Creating Functions Inside an Object Literal

```
var spiderMan = {
    powers: function(){
        return 'Super Strength, Sticks to walls, Spider Sense';
    },
    realName: function(){
        return 'Peter Parker';
```

```
        }
}
//call the function
spiderMan.powers() //returns 'Super Strength, Sticks to walls, Spider Sense
```

How It Works

Functions inside an object are assigned to a property of the object. This relationship is how object methods are created. When used inside a method, the property name is given first followed by a colon, then the function follows with any needed properties.

The scope that a function can then have is limited to the object scope. This will prevent the function from being part of the global scope. In order to call the function, the object is referenced first then the property that contains the function is referenced.

How Do You Return a Value from a Function?

Problem

You want a function to return a value.

Solution

The return statement will return values from a function.

The Code

Listing 12-5. Returning Values from Functions

```
function sayGoodnight1(name){
    return //function stops executing here
    'Goodnight ' + name;
}

function sayGoodnight2(name){
    return 'Goodnight ' + name;   //returns full statement
}

console.log(sayGoodnight1('Gracie'));
console.log(sayGoodnight2('Gracie'));
```

How It Works

The return statement stops executing any of the statement inside a function and specifies what value to return. The default value is undefined if no other value is returned. Return is also subject to automatic semicolon insertion (ASI); there cannot be any line termination after a return statement. The browser will not execute any command after the return statement and will return undefined.

How Are Parameters Defined in a Function?

Problem

You need to know if the parameters defined in the function have values when executed.

Solution

Prior to ES6, parameters had a value of undefined. Parameters can now have default values.

The Code

Listing 12-6. Checking If a Parameter Has a Value in Before ES6 and After

```
//before ES6, checking if a property has a value
function doMath(num1, num2){
    var num2 = typeof num2 !== 'undefined' ? num2: 10;
    return num1 + num2;
}
console.log(doMath(1)); //returns 11
console.log(doMath(1,4)); //returns 5
//using ES6 default properties
function ES6DoMath(num1, num2 = 10){
    return num1 + num2;
}
console.log(ES6DoMath(1)); //returns 11
console.log(ES6DoMath(1,4)); //returns 5
function doCount(first, second = first + 1, third = second + 1){
    return [first, second, third];
}
console.log(doCount(1)); //returns [1,2,3]
```

How It Works

Up until ES6 properties, had a value of undefined if a value was not passed when the function was called. Default properties are not restricted to strings or numbers. Objects, arrays, and functions can be used as default values. One of the values that could be passed over is undefined the result would be the same as not passing a value. This would be different than passing null. Using the previous example, the browser will return 1 and not 11 if null was passed.

Properties can also be evaluated at call time. This would give you the ability to assign a function as the default property and return the result.

Properties can also be chained together. In the last example, the value of the second property is a combination of the first property and the second's default value. The value of the third property follows the same pattern. When returned as an array, the values are in sequence.

How Does Using Rest Parameters Allow Unlimited Number of Parameters in a Function?

Problem

You want to pass parameters to a function but don't know how many you will need.

Solution

If the last parameter of a function is prefixed with …, all values that are passed to it will be part of an array.

The Code

Listing 12-7. Using Rest Parameters on a Function

```
function daysOfTheWeek(...weekdays){
    return weekdays[2];
}

console.log(daysOfTheWeek('Monday', 'Tuesday', 'Wednesday'));  //returns Wednesday
```

How It Works

Using rest parameters is similar to using the `arguments` object. However, there are some important differences. The `arguments` object is not a real array. This means that methods like `map`, `sort`, and `pop` will not work. The values of the arguments object would have to be converted into a real array first. The `arguments` object also returns all arguments sent to a function. Rest parameters only handle arguments that are not mapped to a name in the function. The rest parameters do not have the same methods that the arguments object does; for example `callee` is not available.

Can You Use Object Destructuring with Parameters of a Function?

Problem

You want to use object destructuring to extract properties of an object.

Solution

ES6 does support object destructuring with parameters.

The Code

Listing 12-8. Using Object Destructuring with a Function

```
function es5GetName(myObj){
    var name = myObj.name;
    console.log(name);
}

es5GetName({name: 'Bruce Banner'});

function getName({name}){
    console.log(name);
}
getName({name: 'Bruce Banner'}); //returns Bruce Banner
```

How It Works

Object destructuring allows you to map variable to properties of an object. Most examples show the values of arrays being mapped to variables. Both examples in this section produce the same results. The main difference with the second one is that you can explicitly access the property then use it a variable within the function. If curly braces were wrapped around the variable, an object would return with the same name/value pair and not just the value.

How Do You Call Methods from an Object's Parent?

Problem

You want to use a method that is not defined in the current object but in the object's parent.

Solution

The super keyword can be used to call a function on an object's parent.

The Code

Listing 12-9. Using the Super Keyword to Call Methods Defined in the Parent Object

```
class Ship{
      constructor(name, type, color){
      this.name = name;
      this.type = type;
      this.color = color;
      }
```

```
    shipName(){
        return 'I am ' + this.name;
    }

    shipType(){
        return  'I am type: ' + this.type;
    }

    shipColor(){
        return  'My color is ' + this.color;
    }
}

class SpaceShip extends Ship{
    constructor(type, name, color){
        super(type, name, color)
    }

    spaceShipName(){
        return super.shipName();
    }

    spaceShipType(){
        return super.shipType();
    }

    spaceShipColor(){
        return super.shipColor();
    }
}

var planetExpress = new SpaceShip('Planet Express Ship', 'Delivery Ship' ,'Green');

console.log(planetExpress.spaceShipName()); //returns I am Planet Express Ship
console.log(planetExpress.shipType());  //return I am type: 'Delivery Ship
console.log(planetExpress.spaceShipColor()); // returns My color is Green
```

How It Works

The super keyword gives you the ability to reference properties or methods that have been created in the parent object. In the previous example, the parent class is called Ship and the other class SpaceShip extends Ship to that make it the parent class. At this point if you were to try to access elements of the parent class you would generate a ReferenceError.

In order to access properties and methods of the parent class, the super keyword must be called first. When the call is made it will execute the parent's constructor. This also gives you the ability to pass any parameters to the parent class that may be necessary. After that, all properties can be referenced using the this keyword.

How Does the Keyword This Work Inside a Function?

Problem

How does the keyword this behave compared to other languages?

Solution

The behavior of the keyword this is generally set by the context in which it is called.

The Code

Listing 12-10. The Different Ways This Can Be Used in JavaScript

```
console.log(this); //returns Window
function globalFunction(){
    return this;
}
console.log(globalFunction()); //returns Window
console.log(window.globalFunction());
function globalStrictFunction(){
    'use strict'
return this;
}
console.log(globalStrictFunction());
console.log(window.globalStrictFunction());
function saySomething(){
    return this.something;
}
var phrase = saySomething.bind({something: 'Brothers! Sisters!'});
console.log(saySomething()); //returns undefined
console.log(phrase());  //returns Brothers! Sisters!
function useCallFunction(){
    return this.greeting;
}
var greetingObj = {greeting: 'Hello, Mr. Robot'};

console.log(useCallFunction.call(greetingObj));
console.log(useCallFunction.apply(greetingObj));
document.getElementById('myButton').addEventListener('click', function(e){
    console.log(this); //<button id="myButton">Click Me</button>
});
var globalArrayFunction = () => this;
console.log(globalArrayFunction());  //returns Window
var micCheck = {
    isThisOn: function(){
    return (() => this);
    }
}
```

```
var returnedFunction = micCheck.isThisOn();
console.log(returnedFunction()); //returns Object
var theNumber = {p: 42};
    function magicNumber(){
        return this.p;
 }

theNumber.theMagicNumber = magicNumber;
console.log(theNumber.theMagicNumber()) //returns 42
```

How It Works

In order to understand all the different ways this can change, let's look at it step by step. The value of the keyword this is assigned during a function call. So depending on the how the function is called, the value may be different.

First let's talk about the global context. If you were to just print out the value of this in the console in an otherwise blank JavaScript file, it would refer to the Window object.

When returning this from a function call, its value is also Window. In this instance, the function is part of the global scope, which means you can also call this same function this way: window.globalFunction(). In either case the result would be the same.

In the earlier examples we are not using *strict* mode. Strict mode is a more restricted version of JavaScript that is designed to have different semantics. If you were to use strict mode at the top of the page, the first and second results would return undefined.

Strict mode can also be defined on the function level. Before all other statements add use strict to run the function in strict mode. When using the globalStrictFunction the result of this is undefined. The reason you receive undefined is that this keeps the value of whatever it was set to when the function is being executed.

Using the Bind Method on a Function

Using this method on a function creates a new function called a bound function (BF). The value of this is set to the value that is provided in the first argument. In the following example, the function saySomething returns a property called something. On its own it would return undefined since there isn't a variable in the function called something. When using the bind method, we provide an object with the property something. So the object becomes bound to the function and the property something now has a value.

Using Call and Apply on a Function

Using the call and apply methods on a function is similar to using bind, where you define the object that the keyword this is bound to. In the previous example, the call method passes an object over and the function uses the properties of that object to return some values. If you're using the apply method, you would get the same results.

Using an Event Handler

If the function that is being executed is from an event handler, the value of this is set to the element that fired the event. The same is true if the event is fired from a inline event.

Using Arrow Functions

Arrow function expressions give you the ability to create functions just like a function expression but with less code. They start with the list of parameters, the arrow pointing to the statement that needs to be executed. If using this in a global context, the Window object would return. It is also the case if the function were to be called as the method of another object, or if the call or bind methods were used. This lets you know that the value of this will be set to the execution context. For example, if arrow functions were used inside an object, the result of this would be the object that *this* was defined in.

Using Object Methods

Object methods make using this much simpler. The value is always set to the object the method is called on, no matter how the method is defined.

What Is the Spread Syntax?

Problem

You want a quick way of passing multiple arguments.

Solution

The spread syntax allows functions, arrays, or variables to accept multiple arguments.

The Code

Listing 12-11. Using the Spread Syntax

```
function showSpread(one, two, three, four){
    console.log(one);
    console.log(two);
    console.log(three);
    console.log(four);
}

var myArray = [1,2,3,4];
//showSprcad(myArray[0], myArray[1], myArray[2], myArray[3]) //without using spread
//showSpread(...myArray); //using the spread syntax

var dayInfo = [1975, 7, 19];
var dateObj = new Date(...dayInfo);
console.log(dateObj); //returns Tue Aug 19 1975 00:00:00 GMT-0400 (EDT)

var numArray2 = [ 2, 3, 4, 5, 6, 7]
var numArray = [1, ...numArray2, 8, 9, 10];

console.log(numArray); //returns 1, 2, 3, 4, 5, 6, 7, 8, 9, 10
```

```
var part1 = [1,2,3];
var part2 = [4,5,6];

var part3 = [...part1, ...part2];

console.log(part3); //returns 1,2,3,4,5,6
```

How It Works

The spread syntax can be used in multiple ways. The first example has a function that is expecting four different values. When the function is called, the spread syntax is being used to collect all the values at one time. The browser understands the syntax and splits the values into individual variables. This syntax can also be used in other function calls.

In a similar example, passing an array with date information over to the Date constructor can produce the correct date. The date contractor uses the spread syntax to take all the elements of the array and return a date object.

The next example shows how you can add elements to an array literal without using for loops. The spread syntax is used in the place of an element. This merges the two arrays. The result is a combined array with all of the elements present.

The spread syntax can be used with other functions like apply, and it can also be used more than once. The last example has two arrays. These two are merged into a third array using the spread syntax.

The ability to use the spread syntax more than once is available in any instance where you normally would use a spread.

What Are Rest Parameters?

Problem

You want a quick way of passing multiple arguments.

Solution

Similar to the spread syntax, the rest parameters allow for an indefinite amount of arguments to be passed to a function as an array.

The Code

Listing 12-12. Using the Spread Syntax

```
function showSpread(one, two, three, four){
    console.log(one);
    console.log(two);
    console.log(three);
    console.log(four);
}
```

```
var myArray = [1,2,3,4];
//showSpread(myArray[0], myArray[1], myArray[2], myArray[3]) //without using spread
//showSpread(...myArray); //using the spread syntax

var dayInfo = [1975, 7, 19];
var dateObj = new Date(...dayInfo);
console.log(dateObj); //returns Tue Aug 19 1975 00:00:00 GMT-0400 (EDT)

var numArray2 = [ 2, 3, 4, 5, 6, 7]
var numArray = [1, ...numArray2, 8, 9, 10];

console.log(numArray); //returns 1, 2, 3, 4, 5, 6, 7, 8, 9, 10

var part1 = [1,2,3];
var part2 = [4,5,6];

var part3 = [...part1, ...part2];

console.log(part3); //returns 1,2,3,4,5,6
```

How It Works

Rest parameters are similar to using the spread syntax. Both start with three dots (...). One way of thinking about what makes them different is that a spread will take an object and "spread" the properties to work within a function. Rest will consolidate the properties into one array that can be used in the function.

Rest properties are also different from the arguments object. Both rest and arguments will allow you to access arguments that were passed to the function using an array-like syntax. The arguments object is not a true array, because of this, other methods that are part of the array object like map are not available.

The arguments object does have an object called callee. This method can refer to the function that is currently running inside another function. It is useful for referring to anonymous functions. However, it is not available when working in strict mode.

The first example shows how rest parameters can be added anywhere in an array. The first two properties are mapped with the last property using rest. When executed, the last property everyThingElse is an array containing all the values passed to the function. This can be tested by accessing the properties using the square brackets ([]).

The second example expands on the idea that the rest property is an array. Here we can use the forEach method. This method would not be available to the arguments object.

How Do Arrow Functions Work?

Problem

You want to create a function with a short syntax.

Solution

Arrow functions are shorter than the highly used function expressions. They are always anonymous and cannot be used as constructors.

The Code

Listing 12-13. Using Arrow Functions

```
//ES 5
document.getElementById('myButton').addEventListener('click', function(){
       var self = this;
       self.currentInterval = 0;
       setInterval(function myInterval(){
               self.currentInterval++;
       }, 1000);
});

//ES 6
document.getElementById('myButton').addEventListener('click', () => {
       this.currentInterval = 0;
       setInterval(() => {this.currentInterval++;}, 1000);
});

//retuning object literals
var myObj = () => ({name:'June'}) ;
console.log(myObj()); //returns Object {name: "June"}
```

How It Works

Arrow functions give you a shorter way of creating functions. Using this syntax removes some of the features you would be used to having when using a function expression. Arrow functions are not named; they can be assigned to a variable but are always anonymous. The basic syntax has a set of parentheses that will hold all the parameters like a function expression. Next the arrow, then curly braces ({}) that will have the body of the function inside.

Parentheses are optional only when one parameter is being passed. If no parameters are being passed, parentheses are required.

Rest and default parameters are supported with arrow functions as well as with object destructuring.

When using arrow functions, keep in mind that the keyword this is not available. It inherits that property from the enclosing scope.

The first example first shows how the keyword this has different context between the callback function and the function associated with setInterval. The only way to bridge the gap is the create a new variable. The inner function (closure) can access the outer variable without using the keyword this.

The second example done with ES6 shows a similar version that is less verbose using the arrow functions. Because arrow functions inherit the property this (due to lexical scoping), you do not need to define another variable to reference the outer context.

If the arrow function needs to return an object literal, the object must be surrounded by parentheses. The reason for this is because if the block were to start with the curly braces ({}), the JavaScript engine does not know the difference between an object literal and the code block. Therefore, by surrounding the object with parentheses the object will be returned, even if the return keyword is not explicitly used.

What Are Parameter Defaults?

Problem

You want a default value for a parameter in case a value has not been passed.

Solution

Default parameters ensure that there is a value in case undefined or no value is passed.

The Code

Listing 12-14. Using Argument Defaults

```
function multiParams(one, two, three, four){
    if(typeof three == 'undefined'){
        console.log('three is undefined') //returns three is undefined
    }
    console.log(one); //returns 1
    console.log(two); //returns 2
    console.log(three);   //returns undefined
    console.log(four); // returns undefined

}
multiParams(1,2);

function playList(song = 'Seek 200'){
    console.log('Playing ' + song);
}

playList('Think'); //returns Playing Think
playList('Hack 1'); //returns Playing Hack 1
playList() //returns Playing Seek 200
```

How It Works

In JavaScript when the function contains more parameters than what was passed to it, by default the remaining parameters have a value of undefined. In the past undefined can be checked by using the typeof operator.

Default parameters allow you to make sure a value is provided in any situation. If a value is passed, the function will accept that value; if not, then the default value takes over.

CHAPTER 13

Working with Generators

How Do You Create a Generator?

Problem

You want to know what a generator is and how you make one.

Solution

Generators are functions that do not immediately execute when called on. They return an iterator object that lets you call and pass parameters at another time. You can continue to call this function until the first yield expression is executed.

The Code

Listing 13-1. Creating a Generator

```
function * helloGenerator(){
        yield 'HELLOFRIEND';
}

var sayHello- = helloGenerator();
        console.log(sayHello) //returns generator
        //console.log(sayHello.next()) //returns Object
        console.log(sayHello.next().value)  //yield returns HELLOFRIEND
        console.log(sayHello.next().value) //returns undefined
```

How It Works

Generators are functions that do not execute immediately. When executing a function, instead of returning a value, an iterator object is returned. Iterators execute the function by using the next method. What is returned is an object that has two values—done and value. The first done will have a value of true if the iterator has reached the end and there are no more results to return. It will be false if it can produce more values. The second value called value returns any value from the iterator until undefined is returned.

© Russ Ferguson and Keith Cirkel 2017
R. Ferguson and K. Cirkel, *JavaScript Recipes*, DOI 10.1007/978-1-4302-6107-0_13

How Exactly Does Yield Work with a Generator?

Problem

You want to know how the yield keyword works inside a generator?

Solution

Yield will pause a generator or resume a generator function.

The Code

Listing 13-2. Working with Iterators

```
function fun1(){
    console.log('function 1');
}
function fun2(){
    console.log('function 2');
}

function *runFun(){
    yield;
    yield fun1();
    yield fun2();
}
var iterator = runFun();
console.log(iterator.next()); //pauses function  Object {value: undefined, done: false}
console.log(iterator.next()); //returns 'function1' Object {value: undefined, done: false}
console.log(iterator.next()); //returns 'function 2' Object {value: undefined, done: false}
console.log(iterator.next()); //done = true Object {value: undefined, done: true}
```

How It Works

The yield keyword is used to pause a function as it is running. This is very similar to the return keyword. One of the main differences is with return, the function is executed and the final value is returned to the caller. Here, the function can be executed again. When the function is paused using yield it cannot be restarted on its own. In order to restart the function, the iterator method next() must be called. In every instance, an object is returned with two properties. The done property will have a value of false, letting you know that you can run the next() method and continue using that function. The value property will return whatever value is being returned from the yield keyword.

How Do You Set Up a Generator Function?

Problem

How can you create a generator object?

Solution

Generator functions are defined using the `function` keyword with an * (asterisk) or using a `GeneratorFunction` constructor.

The Code

Listing 13-3. Different Ways of Creating a Generator Function

```
function *myGen(){
    yield 'generator function'
}
var iterator = myGen();
console.log(iterator.next()); //Object {value: "generator function", done: false}
console.log(iterator.next()); //Object {value: undefined, done: true}
var GeneratorFunction = Object.getPrototypeOf(function*(){}).constructor
var myGenFunction = new GeneratorFunction('value',  'yield value');
var myGenIterator = myGenFunction();
console.log(myGenIterator.next()); //Object {value: undefined, done: false}
console.log(myGenIterator.next()); //Object {value: undefined, done: true}
```

How It Works

There are two ways to create a generator function. Using the `function` keyword with the * (asterisk) is the best way to create one. The other way is to use the `Object.getPrototypeOf` method. This will return the constructor of the `GeneratorFunction`. This second way is less efficient and a little harder to understand.

When using the `GeneratorFunction` constructor, you can pass parameters; however, these parameters must be a list of comma-separated strings. The last parameter defines what the function does.

How Do You Create a Function that Maintains State?

Problem

You want to create an iterative function that maintains state.

Solution

When a generator reaches the `yield` keyword, it pauses and returns the current value. The next time the `next()` method is called, the generator will continue to run, thereby creating a new value.

The Code

Listing 13-4. Creating a Function that Maintains State

```
function *numCount(){
    var count = 0;
      while(count < 5)
      yield count++;
}
```

```
var irt = numCount();
console.log(irt.next()); //Object {value: 0, done: false}
console.log(irt.next()); //Object {value: 1, done: false}
console.log(irt.next()); //Object {value: 2, done: false}
console.log(irt.next()); //Object {value: 3, done: false}
console.log(irt.next()); //Object {value: 4, done: false}
console.log(irt.next()); //Object {value: undefined, done: true}
```

How It Works

Because the yield keyword pauses the generator, the current values of the variables or *state* of the function is then frozen. The current value is then returned to the caller and can be updated when the next() method is called. This will run the generator and update the value until another yield keyword is reached, which would pause the generator again. Other options would be for the generator to throw an exception. You can reach the end of the function where the IteratorResult object is returned with the value property being undefined. The last option would be if a return statement is reached. This would end the generator and also return an IteratorResult, with the value property having the value of what is being returned and the done property having the value of true.

How Do You Send Values to a Generator Using the next() Method?

Problem

You want to pass properties to a generator function.

Solution

Use the next() method that is part of the iterator object to pass properties to the generator.

The Code

Listing 13-5. Passing a Parameter Using the next() Method

```
function *returnMSG(){
    var value = yield value
    return value;

}

var it = returnMSG();
console.log(it.next()); //Object {value: undefined, done: false}
console.log(it.next('things')); //Object {value: "things", done: true}
```

How It Works

The next() method can let you pass properties to the generator function. The first time you run the next() method, yield does not have a value. The second time next() is called, you can push a parameter to the generator.

Can You Use Throw Inside a Generator?

Problem

You want to know if you can use a try...catch block inside a generator.

Solution

Generators can let you run a throw function, either inside the generator or outside of it.

The Code

Listing 13-6. Using Throw...Catch Inside and Outside a Generator

```
function *insideThrow(){
    while(true){
            try{
yield 'inside try block';
    }catch(e){
            console.log('inside catch')
        }
    }
}
var it = insideThrow();
console.log(it.next());  //Object {value: "inside try block", done: false}
console.log(it.throw(new Error('this is an error'))) //catch runs and returns last yield
value Object {value: "inside try block", done: false}
function *outsideThrow(){
    var value = yield value;
    return value;
}

var it2 = outsideThrow();
console.log(it2.next());  //Object {value: undefined, done: false}
    try{
        console.log(it2.next('outside try block'));  //Object {value: "outside try block",
        done: true}
        console.log(it2.throw(new Error('this is an error')));  //catch runs
    }catch(e){
      console.log('outside catch')
}
```

How It Works

The first example shows that you can use try...catch blocks inside a generator and use them as expected.

Properties can also be evaluated at call time. This would give you the ability to assign a function as the default property and return the result.

Properties can also be chained together. In the last example, the value of the second property is a combination of the first property and the second property's default value. The value of the third property follows the same pattern. When returned as an array, the values are in sequence.

Can You Create a Custom Iterator Inside an Object?

Problem

You want to create a custom iterator for an object.

Solution

Custom iterators can be created by providing a next method inside the object while keeping track of its current position.

The Code

Listing 13-7. Creating an Object with a Custom Iterator

```
var countdown = {
    max: 3,
    [Symbol.iterator]() {
        return this;
},
   next() {
    if(this.max == undefined){
        this.max = max;
      }else if(this.max > -1){
        return {value: this.max --};
      }else{
        return {done: true};
      }
    }
};

for (let i of countdown) {
    console.log(i);
}
```

How It Works

In order to make an object an iterator, it needs to know how to access items one at a time. This is done by having a next method in the object. ES6 provides some shorthand in defining properties and methods of an object. Here we can add Symbol.iterator as a property using square brackets. After that, the next method has been defined without using the word function. This is also valid JavaScript as of ES6. This method will check the current value, change it, and return an object with the property's value and done. Now that this object has an iterator, you can use it within a for..of loop. It is important to note as of this writing that Symbol.iterator does not have support in Internet Explorer or Safari.

How Do You Use a Custom Iterator to Make a Fibonacci Sequence of Numbers?

Problem

You want to create a Fibonacci sequence using iterators.

Solution

Very similar to Listing 13-7, the object keeps track of the values and returns the result.

The Code

Listing 13-8. Using a Custom Iterator to Make a Fibonacci Sequence

```
var fibObj = {

    one: 0,
    two: 1,
    temp: 0,

     [Symbol.iterator](){
        return this;
     },

    next(){
        this.temp = this.two;
        this.two = this.temp + this.one;
        this.one = this.temp;
        return {value: this.two}
    }
}

for(var I = 0 ; I < 1000; I++){
        consolel.log(fibObj.next().value) //1,2,3,5,8.....
}
```

How It Works

Recall that a Fibonacci sequence is the sum of the previous two numbers. Knowing that, our object needs to take two numbers, add them, return the value, and remember the new sum.

In our object we have three properties—one, two, and temp. Similar to the previous exercise, we add both the Symbol.iterator and next methods. Inside our next method, we use the properties of the object to keep track of the values. This exercise assigns the value of property two to temp. Then it takes temp and one adds them together and assigns the new value. Then it reassigns the value of one. Finally, it returns an object with the property value and the next number in our Fibonacci sequence.

CHAPTER 14

Working with Template Literals

How Do You Use Template Literals?

Problem

You want to know how to use a template literal in a project.

Solution

Template literals are very similar to template systems like *Handlebars*. Template literals give you the ability to set placeholders for values and render them at runtime.

The Code

Listing 14-1. Using Template Literals

```
var characterName = 'Pinky'
var quote = `Same thing we do every night ${characterName}!`;
console.log(quote) //Same thing we do every night Pinky!
```

How It Works

Template literals work in a similar way to using a template system like Handlebars. Instead of using single or double quotes, template literals use *backticks*. This is similar to using quotes to work with a string; however, if you use single or double quotes you cannot add expressions to the template literal.

Expressions are placeholders that will display a value when rendered. Expressions are defined by using a dollar sign and curly braces (${expression}). In Listing 14-1, there is a variable called characterName. When the variable quote is rendered to the browser, it will also display the value of characterName. If single or double quotes are used, then everything will be rendered as is, meaning that expressions will not be rendered. However, single and double quotes can be used inside template literals.

© Russ Ferguson and Keith Cirkel 2017
R. Ferguson and K. Cirkel, *JavaScript Recipes*, DOI 10.1007/978-1-4302-6107-0_14

Can You Use Template Literals with Functions ?

Problem

You want to call a function that will work with a template literal.

Solution

These are called *tagged* template literals. With these, you can modify a template literal using a function.

The Code

Listing 14-2. Using a Tagged Template Function

```
function countdown(stringLiteralArray, ...values){
      console.log(stringLiteralArray); //returns full array
      console.log(stringLiteralArray[1]); //returns Mississippi
      console.log(values); //returns array of values
      console.log(values[0]);   //returns 1
      console.log(values[1]);   //returns 2

  let fullSentance = values[0] + stringLiteralArray[1] + values[1] + stringLiteralArray[2];
  return fullSentance;
}
let one = 1;
let two = 2;
let results = countdown `${one} Mississippi ${two} Mississippi`;
console.log(results); //returns 1 Mississippi 2 Mississippi
```

How It Works

Tagged template functions allow you to take a template literal and its values as its parmeters. The template literal comes over as an array, where each word is an element of that array. The values come over using ...rest by way of the spread operator. Passing values this way also gives you an array and avoids the arguments object. Inside the function's body, the parameters can be arranged in any order you like and then returned to the caller.

Can You Create Line Breaks with Template Literals?

Problem

You want to have line breaks inside the generated string.

Solution

Line breaks can be created in a much more intuitive way than concatenating strings.

The Code

Listing 14-3. Using Line Breaks with Template Literals

```
var seriesOfWords = ' this is line one\n this is line two\n this is line three';
console.log(seriesOfWords);

var temp = `
          one

          two

          three
`
console.log(temp);
```

How It Works

When adding line breaks using strings, most of the time you use a linefeed character, by using the backward slash and n (as in \n). The JavaScript engine will see it and render everything after that on the next line. Template literals give you a more natural way of handing this. It will render everything as it is represented in the backticks.

When using the GeneratorFunction constructor, you can pass parameters; however, these parameters must be a list of comma-separated strings. The last parameter defines what the function does.

How Do You Use the Raw Property with a Template Literal?

Problem

You want to know how to use the raw property when using a template literal in a function.

Solution

The raw property gives you raw strings as they are passed in to the function.

The Code

Listing 14-4. Returning a String with the Raw Property

```
function rawWithVars(stringArray, ...values){
      console.log(stringArray.raw)
      console.log(stringArray.raw[2])  //returns Jones\n
      console.log(stringArray[2]) //returns Jones
}

let name1 = 'Luke';
let name2 = 'Jessica';
let name3 = 'Danny';
let name4 = 'Matt';
rawWithVars `${name1} Cage\n ${name2} Jones\n ${name3} Rand\n ${name4} Murdock`;
```

How It Works

When using a tagged template function, the first parameter is the string that contains a raw property. Normally this property gives you an array of string literals. When using the raw property, you get an array with values exactly as they are in the template literal. In the example in Listing 14-4, a line break has been added to each name. When using the raw property, they are printed just as they were put into the template literal.

Can You Update Expressions Using a Function?

Problem

You have a template literal and want to update expressions dynamically.

Solution

Values returned from a function can be used in template literal expressions.

The Code

Listing 14-5. Using a Function to Give Expressions Values

```
var str = `Today is ${getToday()}`;

function getToday(){
        var myDate = new Date();
        return    myDate.getMonth() +'/' + myDate.getDate() + '/' + myDate.getFullYear();
}

console.log(str);
```

How It Works

Similar to using variables for expressions, the value returned from a function can be used in a template literal. When the template literal is rendered, the function will execute and return the value. In Listing 14-5, the getToday function is called when rendering the str template. When rendered, the function is called. It fills the expression and prints the result.

CHAPTER 15

Working with Symbols

What Are the Advantages of Using Symbols?

Problem

You want to know why and how to use symbols in a project.

Solution

Symbols give you the ability to create unique tokens that will never clash with other symbols. Similar to UUIDs (Universal Unique Identifiers), symbols can be used on objects to make unique properties.

The Code

Listing 15-1. Creating Symbols

```
let mySym1 = Symbol('This is my first Symbol');
let mySym2 = Symbol(); //returns false

console.log(mySym1 == mySym2);
console.log(mySym1.toString()) //returns  Symbol(This is my first Symbol)
```

How It Works

Symbols are unique objects that can be used as properties of an object. They are primitive datatypes, similar to `Number` or `String`. When creating a symbol, the syntax is similar to creating an object instance. The main difference is that you do this without the `new` operator. Using `new` when creating an object would result in a `TypeError`.

When creating a symbol, you can also create a label for that symbol. A label does not change the value of the symbol; it is mostly for debugging. To create a label, pass a string as the first parameter of the symbol constructor. If you wanted to see the label, for example in the browser's console, use the `toString` method. Symbols with the same label are not equal to each other.

© Russ Ferguson and Keith Cirkel 2017
R. Ferguson and K. Cirkel, *JavaScript Recipes*, DOI 10.1007/978-1-4302-6107-0_15

How Do You Create a Symbol?

Problem

You want to create a symbol to use as an object property.

Solution

Creating symbols is very similar to creating an object instance. One exception is you should *not* use the new operator. This would throw an TypeError. Each call of the Symbol function generates a unique value. Labels can be added to symbols for debugging purposes. These labels do not change the value generated by a symbol. Using bracket notation, you can use symbols as properties of an object, thereby creating unique values for each property.

The Code

Listing 15-2. Creating Symbols to Use as Object Properties

```
flet characterObj = {};
let dad = Symbol();

characterObj.name ='Elliot'
characterObj[dad] = 'Mr. Robot';

console.log(Object.keys(characterObj));
```

How It Works

Once a symbol has been created, you can use bracket notation to make it the property of an object. Because you are using a symbol, the property has a unique value that cannot clash with another symbol. The symbol can then be given a value. The unique values of symbols make them different from using strings or numbers as property keys.

Can You Access a Symbol by its String Name?

Problem

The symbol global registry contains many symbols. How do you access the one you want?

Solution

Using the Symbol.for() method will allow you to access a symbol from the registry. If the symbol does not exist, one will be created.

The Code

Listing 15-3. Accessing a Symbol Using the Symbol.for() Method

```
let player1 = Symbol.for('player1'); //creates the symbol and puts it in the registry

console.log(Symbol.for('player1') == player1); //returns true
```

How It Works

The global symbol registry constrains multiple symbols. It is very similar to having multiple global objects. Using the `Symbol.for()` method allows you to retrieve a symbol if it currently exists. If the symbol is not currently in the registry, the symbol will be created. Moving forward every time there is a request for that symbol the same one will be returned. Symbols in the registry can be accessed from different realms. For example, Iframes and service workers can share symbols.

Can You Return a Key Based on a Symbol?

Problem

You want to return a key based on a symbol.

Solution

The `Symbol.keyFor()` method returns a key based on its symbol.

The Code

Listing 15-4. Using the forKey() Method You Can Return the Key of a Symbol

```
let firstPlayer = Symbol.for('player1'); //creates the symbol and puts it in the registry

console.log(Symbol.keyFor(firstPlayer)) //returns player1
```

How It Works

When using the `keyFor()` method, it will return the key for any given symbol that is in the registry. If this key does not exist, the method will return `undefined`.

Can You Use a Symbol as Part of a Function or Method in an Object?

Problem

You want to know if symbols can be used to define functions.

Solution

Because of computed property names, symbols can be used as part of a function definition.

The Code

Listing 15-5. Computed Property Names Enable You to Use Symbols as Part of a Function Definition

```
let helloSymbol = Symbol('Hello World Function');

let myObj = {
        [helloSymbol] () {
                return 'Hello World';
        }
}

console.log(myObj[helloSymbol]());

let iterableObj = {
        Symbol.iterator]() {
            let dataArray = ['this', 'that', 'other'];
            let currentIndex = 0;
                return {
                    next(){
                        if(currentIndex < dataArray.length){
                            return {value: dataArray[currentIndex++]};
                            }else{
                                return {done: true};
                            }
                    }
                }
            }
        }

for(let x of iterableObj){
    console.log(x); //returns this, that, other
}
```

How It Works

Computed property names is a ES6 feature that allows you to create a property for an object literal or class using bracket ([ ]) notation. By first creating a public symbol, then using it as a property, this property will always be unique.

Another example is if the symbol was an iterator. This would make the object iteratable. In the second example the object has properties stored in an array. Using Chapter 13 as a reference on iterators, we can use the next function to continue to move to the next property until currentIndex has the same value as the length of the array. Then use a for-of loop to iterate through the object.

How Can a Symbol Override the Constructor Function of Your Custom Class?

Problem

You have a situation where you want to return the constructor from a derived objet and not the current class.

Solution

The Symbol.species property will return the constructor function of the main class and not a subclass.

The Code

Listing 15-6. The Property Species Used on the Symbol Object Returns the Constructor of a Derived Object

```
class ArraySubClass extends Array{
        static get [Symbol.species]() {return Array;}
}
var subClassInstance = new ArraySubClass(1,2,3,4,5,6);
var derivedObj = subClassInstance.filter(function(value){
    if(value % 2){
    return value
    }
});

console.log(derivedObj) //returns 1,3,5
console.log(derivedObj instanceof Array); //returns true
console.log(derivedObj instanceof ArraySubClass); //returns false
```

How It Works

To fully understand what Symbol.species does, you must first understand what a derived object is.

*Derived object*s are created when an operation is called on the original object. In our example, ArraySubClass extends Array. Because of this ArraySubClass on its own it does not have a filter() method. By calling the filter() method, the original Array object is used to fulfill the request.

The object that returns as the result of the filter has a constructor of the parent Array object and not that of the ArraySubClass. Using the instanceof operator shows that the derived object does not have the same constructor of the ArraySubClass but that of the Array object.

Can a Constructor Object Recognize an Object as its Instance?

Problem

You need to know if an object is an instance of a certain type.

271

Solution

Creating a custom instanceof operator with the hasInstance property will allow you to check for type.

The Code

Listing 15-7. The hasInstance Property Will Check if the Constructor Object Recognizes Another Object as Instance

```
class CheckArrayInstance {

    static [Symbol.hasInstance](instance){
        return Array.isArray(instance)
    }
}

var myArray = new Array();

console.log(myArray instanceof CheckArrayInstance); //returns true
```

How It Works

Usually when using the instanceof operator, you can check the prototype of an object. However, you can customize the instanceof operator to get more specific and check the type of an object.

In Listing 15-7, we create the static method that checks if the instance is an array. If true, the method returns a value of true.

Can You Convert an Object to a Primitive Value?

Problem

You want to determine the primitive value of an object.

Solution

When used as a method of an object, Symbol.toPrimitive can convert an object to its primitive type.

The Code

Listing 15-8. The toPrimitive Method Converts an Object to its Primitive Type

```
var  PrimitiveObj = {
         [Symbol.toPrimitive](hint){
    if(hint == 'number'){
        return 100 ;
                }else if (hint == 'string'){
                        return 'this is a string';
```

```
                    }else{
                        return 'this is the default;
                    }
            }
    }

    console.log(+PrimitiveObj) //returns 100
    console.log(`${PrimitiveObj}`) //returns this is a string
    console.log(PrimitiveObj + ' ')  //returns this is the default
```

How It Works

The toPrimitive method lets you create a function that will turn an object into a primitive. This method takes one property called hint. This property can have only one of three values—string, number, or default. In Listing 15-8, we call the function three different times.

The first time the plus (+) operator is used. Using this operator performs type conversion. Using this operator, the object will be converted into a number. Under normal circumstances, the result would be not a number (NaN). Using the toPrimitive function allows us to see that the conversion to number was trying to take place. The result is that hint then has the value of number.

The second example uses a template literal (discussed in detail in Chapter 14). Since template literals use string literals, the value of hint would be string.

The third call would by default return an object when making the conversion. Because of our toPrimitive method, it returns default.

How Can You Get the Class of the Object You Are Working With?

Problem

You want to know the type of object you are working with and not have [object object] as a return value.

Solution

Adding the toStringTag property to a custom class will allow you to return the type of object you are working with.

The Code

Listing 15-9. The toStringTag Property Used in a Class Will Return the Type

```
var myDate = new Date();
var myArray = new Array();
var myObj = new Object();
class myClass{};
var myClassObj = new myClass();
```

```
console.log(Object.prototype.toString.call(myDate));  //returns [object Date]
console.log(Object.prototype.toString.call(myArray)); // returns [object Array]
console.log(Object.prototype.toString.call(myObj));  //returns [object object]
console.log(Object.prototype.toString.call(myClassObj));  //returns [object object]
class WithToStringTag{
     get [Symbol.toStringTag](){
          return 'WithToStringTag';
     }
}

var withToStringTagObj = new WithToStringTag();
console.log(Object.prototype.toString.call(withToStringTagObj)); //returns [object
WithToStringTag]
```

How It Works

The built-in toString() method can be used in every object. This will allow you to get the class the object is based on. In order to access this method, we can use Object.prototype.toString.call. Using the call() method is important. Here it sets the value of this and has the result comes from the object that we are passing. For further understanding of the call() method, look at Chapter 12.

In Listing 15-9, all of the objects that are part of the JavaScript language return their class names. When you reach custom objects, the result is [object object]. By adding the Symbol.toStringTag method, you can return the name of the custom class and override the built-in toString method.

Can You Hide Properties of an Object?

Problem

You want certain properties not to show up when you're doing a with statement.

Solution

The well-known Symbol.unscopables symbol will exclude property names from being exposed using a with statement.

The Code

Listing 15-10. Symbol.unscopables Will Prevent Properties from Being Exposed Using a with Statement

```
class MyClass{
     firstProp() {return 'First Prop';}
}

with(MyClass.prototype){
     console.log(firstProp()) //returns First Prop
}
class MyClassWithUnscopables{
     firstProp(){return 'First Prop';}
```

```
        get[Symbol.unscopables](){
                return {firstProp : true}
        }
}
with(MyClassWithUnscopables.prototype){
        console.log(firstProp()); //ReferenceError: firstProp is not defined
}
```

How It Works

The Mozilla Developer Network (MDN) does not recommend using the with statement. However, when an expression is being used inside a with statement, methods could be called on that object. This brings us to Symbol.unscopables, which enables you to prevent certain properties from being exposed to the scope from inside the with statement.

Adding the unscopables symbol to the custom class protects the method from being executed within the with statement. In this instance, it returns a ReferenceError because it does not believe the method exists.

CHAPTER 16

Working with Proxies

When Should You Use a Proxy?

Problem

What is a proxy and when should you use one?

Solution

A proxy object allows you to customize the behavior of an object. Some of the ways you can use a proxy is for interception of an object, object virtualization, profiling, and contracts for object use.

The Code

Listing 16-1. Creating and Using a Proxy

```
var handler = {
        set (target, key, value){
                console.info(`property "${key} set on object "${target}" with a value of
                "${value}"`);
        }
}

var target = {};
var proxy = new Proxy(target, handler);

proxy.a = 'a' //outputs  property "a set on object "[object Object]" with a value of "a"
proxy.b = 'b' //outputs property "b set on object "[object Object]" with a value of "b"
proxy.c = 'c' //outputs  property "c set on object "[object Object]" with a value of "c"
```

How It Works

In a similar way, a proxy server is used as the intermediary between clients and other servers. A proxy object allows you to have code that is between the client and the target object. Proxies determine behavior whenever the properties of the target object are being accessed.

© Russ Ferguson and Keith Cirkel 2017
R. Ferguson and K. Cirkel, *JavaScript Recipes*, DOI 10.1007/978-1-4302-6107-0_16

This is an example of interception, and we have a generic objects called `target` and `handler`. While `target` does not do anything, `handler` will execute the `set` method anytime a property has be set on the target object.

What Are Traps?

Problem

When working with a `proxy` object, what is a trap and how do you use one?

Solution

Traps are methods that provide access to the object being proxied. This allows you to know things like when a property is being set or whether the object is extensible.

The Code

Listing 16-2. Setting Traps with the Handler Object

```
function trapMessage() {
    return "It's a Trap!!!"
}

var handler = {
    apply: function(target, thisArg) {
        return target.apply(thisArg);
    }
};

var proxy = new Proxy(trapMessage, handler);
console.log(proxy());   //returns It's a Trap!!
```

How It Works

Listing 16-1 showed how traps can work. The proxy is aware of when a property of the object is being set. Every time a property is set on the object, the `set` method in the proxy is called. This allows you to make judgments on what should happen.

Methods like these are called *traps*. They allows you to define custom behavior when operating on an object.

In this case, a function is the target for the proxy. When the function is being called through the proxy, it uses the `apply` method to make the function call. The `apply` function is the trap. The proxy calls the function instead of it being called directly. This gives your code a level of protection where you can do things like evaluate the results.

There is a long list of trap methods that you can use to evaluate what is going on with your object. Traps can be used in situations like when the `new` operator has been called. The full list can be found on the Mozilla Developer Network at `https://developer.mozilla.org/en-US/docs/Web/JavaScript/Reference/Global_Objects/Proxy`.

What Is the Difference Between Object.observe and a Proxy?

Problem

You need to know when you would use a proxy object rather than Object.observe.

Solution

Object.observe is now considered obsolete. Browsers will not support this feature in the future.

How It Works

The proxy object has more features than the now obsolete Object.observe method. If you are required to see any changes to an object, using a proxy object will allow your projects to work into the future without worrying about when or if a browser will no longer support Object.observe.

By setting a series of traps, you can see how an object changes over time. One advantage is that the trap is set as the object is being changed where the Object.observe method would notify you after the change has been made.

What Is a Revocable Proxy?

Problem

You need to find a key in the Map object.

Solution

Use the has key to check the existence of a key in the Map object.

The Code

Listing 16-3. Creating and Using a Revocable Proxy

```
var handler ={
        set (target, key, value){
                console.log('PROPERTY SET')
        }
}

var target = {};
var revocable = Proxy.revocable(target, handler);
var proxy = revocable.proxy;

proxy.prop1 = 'Prop1'; //returns PROPERTY SET
revocable.revoke();

proxy.prop2 = 'Prop 2'; //returns TypeError
```

How It Works

In all the examples in this chapter, the proxy object has been used to grant access to an object. It used traps to determine what is happening with the object. A revocable proxy takes away access to the object. This works in a similar way to a normal proxy; however, the new operator is not used. In this case, to access the revoke method, you must use the proxy object in a static fashion just like the Math object.

After the results of the Proxy.revocable method are stored in a variable, you can set the conditions for when the revoke() method can be called. When it is called, all access to the object by way of the proxy will result in a TypeError.

▮ ▮ ▮

CHAPTER 17

Working with Classes

How Do You Make a Class in JavaScript?

Problem

How do you create a class using either ECMAScript 5 or ECMAScript 6?

Solution

JavaScript is a prototype-based language, therefore its use of inheritance is also prototype-based. ECMAScript 5 uses functions to make classes. ECMAScript 6 introduces the class keyword as syntactical sugar for class creation in JavaScript.

The Code

Listing 17-1. Creating an ES5 Class and an ES6 Class

```
//ECMAScript 5 class
var Human = (
        function Human(name){
                this.name = name;
        }
)

Human.prototype.sayGoodNight = function(){
      return 'Say Goodnight ' + this.name;
}

var george = new Human('Gracie');

console.log(george.sayGoodNight());

//ECMAScript 6 class
class Greeting{
        constructor(name){
                this.name = name;
        }
```

© Russ Ferguson and Keith Cirkel 2017
R. Ferguson and K. Cirkel, *JavaScript Recipes*, DOI 10.1007/978-1-4302-6107-0_17

```
        sayHello(){
                return 'Hellooo ' + this.name;
        }
}

var yakko = new Greeting('Nurse!');

console.log(yakko.sayHello());
```

How It Works

If you come from a language like Java, Python, or any other language that is what we call *class-based,* then you will find that JavaScript works a little differently.

JavaScript uses what is called prototypical inheritance to provide access to methods and properties found in other objects. Each object contains a prototype object with a reference to another object up until an object's prototype has a null value. At this point, you have reached the end of the chain and there are no other objects to inherit from.

The first example shows how function objects can be used to create a class. Here we use a function expression and assign it to a variable; inside the function property names are created and given value based on the argument passed to the function.

The next section is where the prototypical inheritance comes in. Function objects like other JavaScript objects have a prototype property. However, the function's prototype does not link to another object. We then assign new functions to the object that can be used with other instances of that objects.

With functions assigned to the prototype, you can access internal properties to the object (in this case, the name property) and a separate instance can be developed by using the new operator.

The second example is the ECMAScript 6 version of how to create a class. The result is the same as the ES5 version, but this uses syntactical sugar to achieve similar results.

One if the things that may stick out is the use of a constructor function. In this class declaration, the constructor is a special method that can accept properties when initializing an object. If it's declared more than once, a SyntaxError will be thrown. Creating an instance is exactly the same as what someone would be used to. Because of the prototypical nature of JavaScript, if a method or property gets changed in the class, the instance is also updated.

Class declarations like in this example are not hoisted. Because of this, be sure to declare the class you want to use before trying to access it. Not doing so will return a ReferenceError.

How Does the ES6 Class Keyword Work with Prototypal Inheritance?

Problem

You want to know if JavaScript is using class-based inheritance now that it has the class keyword.

Solution

JavaScript is not a class-based language like Java. This can make the ES6 Class keyword confusing. This keyword hides the prototypical inheritance that JavaScript is based on and provides a way to create objects that would be familiar to developers coming from class-based languages.

The Code

Listing 17-2. In the ES5 and ES6 Examples, All the Methods Are Added to the Prototype

```
//ES5 Class Creation

function Show(name, network){
        this.name = name;
        this.network = network;
};

Show.prototype.getShowName = function getShowName(){
    return this.name;  //added to the Show prototype it now has access to it's
    properties.
};
Show.prototype.getShowNetwork = function getShowNetwork(){
    return this.network;
};

var gravityFalls = new Show('Gravity Falls', 'Disney XD');
console.log(gravityFalls.getShowName());  //returns Gravity Falls
console.log(gravityFalls.getShowNetwork()); //returns Disney XD
Show.prototype.getShowNetwork = function getShowNetwork(){
    return 'On My TV!';
};

console.log(gravityFalls.getShowNetwork()); //returns On My TV!

console.log(Show.prototype); //shows getShowName and getShowNetwork functions are now part
of the Show prototype

//ES6 Class Creation
class MyTVShow{
    constructor(name, network){
        this.name = name;
        this.network = network;
    }

  getShowName(){
        return this.show;
    }

  getShowNetwork(){
        return this.network;
    }
}

console.log(MyTVShow.prototype)
//shows getShowName and getShowNetwork functions are now part of the MyTVShow prototype.
```

How It Works

It is important to understand that class-based inheritance is very different from prototypical inheritance. In a class-based language like Java, a class will inherit or extend another class. This creates a a hierarchy between classes. The new class will be a subclass of the original or parent class. One of the benefits is that you now gain all the functionality of the parent class in addition to the functions of the child class.

With JavaScript inheritance is maintained by using the prototype property. Every object contains a prototype property that references another object. This is called the prototype chain. Even when using the keywords class, constructor, static, extends, and super, JavaScript remains prototype-based. Because the prototype can reference other objects, you can be more flexible than with the class-based approach.

Listing 17-2 is similar to Listing 17-1; however, we can get more into the details of how it works. The function Show at this moment does not have anything assigned to its prototype. The next two lines define functions that will now become methods to the class. When assigning functions to the prototype, every instance based on this class will now inherit these properties.

After retrieving the results in the log, we reassign the method getShowNetwork. Here, we can see that the result returned from the method is different than it was originally.

The last line of the first example shows the result of the Show class prototype. When looking at the console in your browser, you can see the both previous functions are part of the prototype object.

The ES6 example is a condensed version of the first example. Here we have less code to achieve the same result. To illustrate that the results are the same, the last line also shows the prototype object in the browser console. If you were to compare the results of both objects, they would both contain the methods needed in the prototype object.

How Do You Assign Getters and Setters to a ES6 Class?

Problem

You want to be able to quickly get and set properties using the ES6 syntax.

Solution

Similar to class-based languages, ES6 allows for the creation of getter and setters properties for objects.

The Code

Listing 17-3. Using Getters/Setters in an ES6 Class

```
class Cookies{
      constructor(){
            this._typeOfCookie;
      }

      set cookieType(typeOfCookie){
            this._typeOfCookie = typeOfCookie;
      }
      get cookieType(){
            return this._typeOfCookie;
      }
}
```

```
var myCookie = new Cookies();
        myCookie.cookieType = "Chocolate Chip";

        console.log(myCookie.cookieType); //returns Chocolate Chip;
        console.log(myCookie._typeOfCookie);
```

How It Works

Getters and setters allow you to access properties inside a class without talking to the property directly. The way that it works in ES6 is that the syntax is bound to a function that will look up the property when called. In Listing 17-3, we create a class and inside set up a get and set keyword that point to a function called cookieType. When assigning a value, we use the equals sign (=). This will be used by the set method since we are setting a value. When retrieving a result, we just point to the property and the get method will retrieve the inner value of _typeOfCookie.

It is important to note that, in this case, the underscore (_) is just the developer's way to signaling to other developers not to access this property directly. It does not really keep this property private.

What Do the Extend and Super Keywords Do?

Problem

You want to know what the purpose of extending a class is and why you need the keyword super.

Solution

The extends keyword is used to create a subclass or child class of an existing class.

The Code

Listing 17-4. Using the Extends Keyword to Make Child Classes

```
class Robot{
        constructor(){
                this.type;
        }
}

class BendingUnit extends Robot {
            constructor(){
              super();
              this.name;
              this.occupation = 'Industrial Robot';
              this.origin = 'Tijuana, Mexico';

            }
}
```

```
class AstromechDroid extends Robot{
      constructor(){
            super();
            this.name;
      }
}

var bender = new BendingUnit();
      bender.type = 'Bending Unit 22';
      bender.name = 'Bender Bending Rodriguez';

      console.log(bender.type);  //returns Bending Unit 22
      console.log(bender.name);  //returns Bender Bending Rodriguez

var r2d2 = new AstromechDroid();
      r2d2.type = 'Astromech Droid';
      r2d2.name = 'R2-D2';

      console.log(r2d2.type);  //returns Astromech Droid
      console.log(r2d2.name);  //returns R2-D2
```

How It Works

Like in other class-based languages, the extends keyword allows the current class to inherit properties and methods from another class. When declaring a class that will need properties from another class, the keyword extends is provided in the definition with the name of the class it is extending.

The child class must then use the super keyword to access any properties of the now *parent* class. If values need to be passed to the parent class to prevent any errors, they can be used as parameters of the super function call.

In Listing 17-4, we have two child classes, BendingUnit and AstromechDroid. Both of these classes extend Robot. Because of this, both instances of these classes have a property called type. This property is inherited because of using the extends keyword. After the instance has been created, a developer can use the type property as if it were native to the child class.

In each case with the child classes, the Robot class becomes the prototype object. This is because of the prototypical nature of JavaScript. Subclasses can also extend built-in objects like the Date object.

What Are Static Methods?

Problem

You want to know how static methods are different than regular methods in a class.

Solution

Static methods do not need the class to be instantiated in order to use them.

The Code

Listing 17-5. Static Methods Are Called Directly from the Class

```
class Human{
        constructor(){
        }

        static hasLegs(){
                return 'Person has legs';
        }

        static hasAmrs(){
                return 'Person has arms';
        }
}

console.log(Human.hasLegs())  //returns Person has legs
console.log(Human.hasAmrs())  //returns Person has arms
```

How It Works

Static methods can be used without instantiation of an instance of a class. A similar example would be the Math class. Instances cannot be made of the Math class. If an instance is created with a class that uses static methods, these methods cannot be called.

CHAPTER 18

Working with Events

How Do Events Work in JavaScript?

Problem

What are DOM events and how do you handle them?

Solution

DOM events notify you when something is happening in the browser, for example a mouse click. There is a long list of events that you as a developer can listen for. A function is then called to handle the event once it occurs.

The Code

Listing 18-1. Listening for the DOMContentLoaded Event

```
function loadedFunction(){
        console.log('The DOM has been loaded')  //returns The DOM has been loaded
}

document.addEventListener('DOMContentLoaded', loadedFunction, false);
```

How It Works

Events are attached to DOM elements and get executed when that type of event happens. This chapter uses the addEventListener method to register events. This method not only provides a way of listening for a certain type of event, but also allows you to register multiple events to the same object.

This method takes three properties—the *type* of event, which is a string that represents the event (click, DOMContentLoaded, and keypress), the *listener,* which a function that gets executed when the event type has occurred, and useCapture, which is a Boolean that will tell the browser how to send or *propagate* the event to other elements that have registered a handler for the same event.

© Russ Ferguson and Keith Cirkel 2017
R. Ferguson and K. Cirkel, *JavaScript Recipes*, DOI 10.1007/978-1-4302-6107-0_18

How Do Events Propagate Through a Browser?

Problem

You want to know how nested elements in the browser are alerted when an event occurs.

Solution

JavaScript goes through three phases—*capturing, target,* and *bubbling.* How the browser responds to these events is determined by the last of three parameters of the addEventListener function.

The Code

Listing 18-2. Event Propagation Based on the useCapture Property (the Default Value Is False)

```
function assignListeners(){
        var divs = document.getElementsByTagName('div');
        for(var i = 0; i < divs.length; i++){
            divs[i].addEventListener('click', showID, true);
            divs[i].addEventListener('click', showID, false);
    }
}

function showID(evt){
        alert(evt.currentTarget.id)
        //returns when clicking on div 3 it will return
        //3,2,1 for the capture phase, then 1,2,3 for the bubbling phase
}

document.addEventListener('DOMContentLoaded', assignListeners, false);
```

How It Works

Before an event is dispatched to its target, the browser determines what is called the *propagation path.* This path is the hierarchical tree-like structure of the document.

The first phase is the *capture phase,* and once the path has been set, the event travels down the path to the target's parent element. This phase usually starts at the window object.

The second phase is called the *target phase.* When the event reaches its target, the event can indicate if it should then bubble up to the top. If the preventDefault() method is used, it prevents bubbling from happening and the event stops at this phase.

The third is the *bubble phase,* where the event reverses order starting with the target's parent object and goes back up the path to the window. If, in the previous event, the preventDefault() method was executed, bubbling will not occur.

If multiple eventListeners are registered to the same object with the same properties, the duplicate instances are ignored. They do not cause the event to be handled more than once.

How Do You Create Custom Events in JavaScript?

Problem

You want to create events that are not part of the built-in events that JavaScript uses.

Solution

The Event constructor and the CustomEvent interface allow you to create custom events.

The Code

Listing 18-3. Dispatching Custom Events

```
var myEvent = new Event('finished');
var myOtherEvent = new CustomEvent('done', {'detail': 'done looping!'});

document.addEventListener('finished', function(e){
      console.log('finished event called');
});

document.addEventListener('done', function(e){
      console.log(e.detail);
})

for(var j = 0; j < 100; j++){
      if( j == 99){
              document.dispatchEvent(myEvent);
              document.dispatchEvent(myOtherEvent);
      }
}
```

How It Works

Custom events can be created by using either the Event constructor or the CustomEvent interface. The first lets you make an object that can be dispatched when needed and listened by any addEventListener() method. The event object passed to the function resembles an object that came from any other event.

The second method (using the CustomEvent interface) allows you to attach any custom data to the event that you would like and still be able to retrieve the data using a function handler.

In the first example, a custom event called finished is dispatched when the for loop reaches 99. This is then picked up by an event listener that triggers an anonymous function that will write to the console.

The second event called done has two parameters when using the CustomEvent interface—the name of the function and an object with a property called detail. This property will contain any extra information that needs to be passed to the event handler. It is exposed in the same way you would work with other event properties.

How Do You Remove Event Listeners When They Are No Longer Needed?

Problem

You want to remove event listeners when they are no longer necessary.

Solution

The removeEventListener() method removes registered events.

The Code

Listing 18-4. Removing Events with removeEventListener

```
var textField = document.getElementsByTagName('input');
var isListening = true;

function changeMessage(e){
        if(isListening){
                isListening = !isListening;
                document.removeEventListener('click', changeMessage);
                textField[0].value = 'eventListener = ' + isListening;
        }
}

function setupDoc(e){
        textField[0].value = 'eventListener = true';
        document.addEventListener('click', changeMessage);
}

document.addEventListener('DOMContentLoaded', setupDoc);
```

How It Works

When you no longer want an event attached to an object, the removeEventListener() method will remove the event so that when action is taken, the event handler will not react to it. The combination of add and remove event listeners can give you the ability to use events when needed and ignore them when they are not needed.

When removing events, the same arguments must be present. If the method is used and they do not match the arguments of the addEventListener, it will have no effect.

When removing events that use the useCapture argument, each event needs to be removed separately. For example, if an object has been registered twice, one with the capture and the second without, they would need separate removeEventListener calls to remove both events.

In this example, an event listener is added to the document. When the document is clicked it will run the changeMessage function that will change the text in the input field. The if statement inside this function will never become true a second time because the event listener has been removed from the document. If the removeEventListener() method is commented out, then the value of the input field would change on every click of the document.

What Is an Event Emitter in NodeJS?

Problem

You want to know what event emitters are in NodeJS and how they are similar to what is in the browser.

Solution

Event emitters are similar to addEventListener() in a browser. Objects will broadcast or emit an event and other objects will listen for them.

The Code

Listing 18-5. Sample Code for NodeJS Event Emitters.

```
//NODEJS CODE

const EventEmitter = require('event');

class EmitterClass extends EventEmitter{}

const emitterInstance = new EmitterClass();

emitterInstance.on('firstEvent', function(){
        console.log('firstEvent fired')
});

function secondEventHandler(data){
        console.log('secondEvent fired with data = ' + data)
}

emitterInstance.addEventListener('secondEvent', secondEventHandler);

emitterInstance.emit('firstEvent');
emitterInstance.emit('secondEvent', 'This is the data from the secondEvent');

emitterInstance.removeEventListener('secondEvent', secondEventHandler);
```

How It Works

NodeJS is a JavaScript runtime environment. When most people think of NodeJS, they think of it as a web server. Node uses the Google V8 JavaScript engine to compile JavaScript code to native machine code. Node's use of modules allows developers to handle functions like networking and cryptography.

In this example, Node is using the Event module. This process is similar to creating custom events in Listing 18-3. The module is assigned a variable called EventEmitter, which is then used to extend a the class EmitterClass.

Like with other JavaScript classes (classes are covered in Chapter 17), you can create an instance of this class. This new instance can now broadcast or emit events and listen for them.

The uses of on and addEventListener provide the same result. You can assign an anonymous function or a named function as the handler.

The emit function is similar to dispatchEvent at this point. The function contains two parameters, the name of the event and optionally any data associated with the event.

The last part of this example adds the removeEventListener method. Just like on the client side, it will remove events, making sure they are not handled in the future.

NodeJS has a long list of methods that can be used with the EventEmitter. Some of these will allow an event to be handled only once; others can set the maximum amount of listeners for an event or remove all listeners for an event.

CHAPTER 19

Debugging and Handling Exceptions

What Is an Error in JavaScript?

Problem

How do errors occur and can you create an error object?

Solution

Errors result when there is a problem with code execution in the runtime. When this happens, the runtime will generate an `Error` object with information about what just happened. There are instances where developers can create user-defined errors that can be useful when debugging.

The Code

Listing 19-1. Two Types of Errors, One During Runtime, the Other User-Defined

```
new Array(-1) //returns Uncaught RangeError: Invalid array length

//user defined error
console.log(new Error('this is a problem')); //returns Error: this is a problem(...)
```

How It Works

Errors usually happen when the runtime is faced with something unexpected. In Listing 19-1, trying to create an array with a new constructor and a negative number will result in an error.

The second example is a user-defined error object. You can define the error message as part of the object.

What Are the Different Types of Errors?

Problem

You want to know how many types of errors exist in JavaScript.

© Russ Ferguson and Keith Cirkel 2017
R. Ferguson and K. Cirkel, *JavaScript Recipes*, DOI 10.1007/978-1-4302-6107-0_19

Solution

There are a few types of error objects that JavaScript generates. The runtime will throw them depending on the code being executed.

The Code

Listing 19-2. Different Types of Errors that Can Happen in JavaScript

```
var evalMsg = new EvalError('This is an eval error');

console.log(evalMsg.message); //returns This is an eval error

new Array(-1);  //returns RangeError: Invalid array length
32.3333.toExponential(-1) //returns RangeError
434.2322.toFixed(-100) //return RangeError

var rangeMsg = new RangeError('This is a Range error');

console.log(rangeMsg.message); //returns This is a Range error

console.log(myVar); //returns Uncaught ReferenceError: myVar is not defined

window.alert( //return Uncaught SyntaxError: Unexpected end of input

var myObj = new Object();
console.log(myObj.causeError()) //returns Uncaught TypeError: myObj.causeError is not a
function

decodeURIComponent('a%AFc'); //returns Uncaught URIError: URI malformed
```

How It Works

EvalError: This is the result of an error with the eval() function. JavaScript does not throw this error anymore, but it retains it for compatibility.
RangeError: This object is the result of a value not in the range of allowed values.
ReferenceError: Happens when you try to use something like a variable that has not been defined yet.
SyntaxError: Sometimes called parsing errors, these happen when the runtime cannot parse the code.
TypeError: Happens when trying to access a method or property of an object that does not exist.
URIError: This error is thrown when the URI a function is using is malformed.

How Can Try/Catch/Finally Be Used for Debugging?

Problem

You want to know how a try/catch statement can be used for debugging.

Solution

Try/catch statements can execute code. If an error occurs, the code can catch the error and fix any problems.

The Code

Listing 19-3. An Example of a Try/Catch/Finally Block

```
function checkStarShip(shipName){
        try{
                if(shipName !== 'Enterprise'){
                        throw new Error('Wrong Ship');
                }
        }catch(e){
                console.log(e);
                console.log('Looking for Enterprise');
        }finally{
                console.log('Continue working with code');
        }
}

checkStarShip('TARDIS');
//returns
//Error: Wrong Ship
//Looking for Enterprise
//Continue working with code
```

How It Works

Try/Catch statements give developers a chance to recover if an error is thrown. You can also check if the error is of a certain type by using the instanceof keyword.

The try block contains a statement where you believe the code may throw an exception. Curly braces ({}) are required if a single statement is made. After the try block you can have a combination of either the catch block, the finally block, or both.

The catch block will give the developer the opportunity to handle when an exception has been thrown in the try block. The purpose is to try to fix any errors that happen within the try block. If no errors are thrown, then the catch block is ignored.

The finally block executes after the try and catch blocks. The finally block always executes even if no exception is thrown.

How Does Throw Work in a Try/Catch and Can You Rethrow?

Problem

The throw statement is used often with a try/catch, so you wonder how it can help debug the app.

Solution

If you have functions that call functions (what is called a *call stack*), the throw statement can return errors to the previous catch block in the call stack.

The Code

Listing 19-4. The Throw Statement Returns an Error to the Previous Catch Statement

```
function level1(){
        try{
                level2();
        }catch(e){
                console.log('Error in Level 1: ' + e.message); //returns Error in
                Level 1: Error started in Level 3
                console.log(e.stack);   // returns Error: Error started in Level 3
                                                        // also shows all the
                                                        stack information

        }
}

function level2(){
        try{
                level3();
        }catch(e){
                console.log('Error in Level 2: ' + e.message); //returns Error in
                Level 2: Error started in Level 3
                throw(e)
        }
}

function level3(){
        throw(new Error('Error started in Level 3'));
}

level1();
```

How It Works

The throw statement will stop execution of all code that is after it when a user-defined exception is found. It will pass the exception to the first catch block on the call stack.

In this example, we do what is called a *rethrow*. Even though the word itself is not part of the JavaScript language, the principle is the same. As functions call other functions, generating what is known as the *call stack*, exceptions are checked for using the try block.

When you're finding an error, preserving the stack trace information becomes important. This is what tells you where the problem lies. The throw statement gives you a bubble-like effect (see Chapter 18 about events and bubbling), where the error goes back up the stack trace.

When reaching the top of the stack, not only will the error be displayed in the console, but the stack property of the error object retains where the error originated from.

What Is the Callback Pattern?

Problem

You want to know what a callback pattern is and how you can use it to find errors.

Solution

Callbacks are used often in JavaScript. Functions are passed as properties of other functions. You can execute a particular function in case of error.

The Code

Listing 19-5. A Simple Example of the Callback Pattern

```
function onSuccess(){
        console.log('You are Correct');
}

function onError(e){
        console.log(e.message);
}

function isFirstOfficer(name, onError, onSuccess){
        if(name === 'Spock'){
                onSuccess();
        }else{
                onError(new Error('Sorry, Wrong Officer'));
        }
}

isFirstOfficer('Scotty', onError, onSuccess);
isFirstOfficer('Spock', onError, onSuccess);
```

How It Works

Callback functions are used often in JavaScript. The second argument in an addEventListener method is a function. Many of the methods used with objects like arrays like forEach have functions passed to them. Using functions as arguments of other functions is possible because functions are first-class objects in JavaScript.

Because functions are first-class objects, they can be executed inside other functions. This type of thinking is known as *functional programming*. Functions can get executed depending on what is happening in the container function.

This example starts with two functions—onSuccess and onError—one of these functions will be executed based on the outcome of the isFirstOfficer function.

To relate this to error handling, focus on the error. Imagine if an image did not load or the result from the server did not have the data you expected. Here you can throw an error and use it as an argument for your function. This will take the error and execute the function, thereby giving you some way to handle the result.

Can You Create Errors?

Problem

You wonder if you can create errors that suit your needs.

Solution

Error objects can be created and extended, thereby allowing developers to customize errors.

The Code

Listing 19-6. Creating Error Objects and a Custom Error Class

```
var rngError = new RangeError('The value is out of range');
        console.log(rngError.message);  //returns The value is out of range

var refError = new ReferenceError('This reference is not valid');
        console.log(refError.message); //returns This reference is not valid

class myCustomError extends Error{
        constructor(message){
                super(message)
        }
}

var myCustomErrorInstance = new myCustomError('This is a Custom Error');
        console.log(myCustomErrorInstance.message);  //returns This is a Custom Error
        console.log(myCustomErrorInstance.stack);     //returns stack trace

try{
        throw new myCustomError('There has been a mistake')
}catch(e){
        console.log(e.message);  //returns There has been a mistake
        console.log(e.stack); //returns stack trace
}
```

How It Works

Even though JavaScript can return runtime errors, it does give your a way of creating your own error objects. One way is to create an object based on existing error types. These errors work in the same way that runtime errors work. They can be used in try/catch statements and can use the throw keyword.

There may be other times where you'll need to make an error object that is totally unique. Here, you can create a *class* (see Chapter 17 about classes) and extend the error that you want to base the custom error on.

This class extends the Error object and passes a message from the constructor to its superclass. Now instances of this class can be used in a try/catch statement.

■ ■ ■

CHAPTER 20

Working with Regular Expressions

What Is a Regular Expression?

Problem

You want to know what a regular expression is and how to use one in JavaScript.

Solution

Regular expressions are patterns used to match characters. In JavaScript, they are also objects.

The Code

Listing 20-1. Creating a Simple Regular Expression

```
//regular expression literals
var companyBio = 'Twitter is an online social networking service that enables users to send
and read short 140-character messages called "tweets".';
var simplePattern = /(twitter)/gi;

var simplePatternConstructor = new RegExp(simplePattern);
console.log(simplePatternConstructor.exec(companyBio));  //returns ["Twitter", "Twitter",
index: 0, input: "Twitter is an online social networking service tha...ead short
140-character messages called "tweets"."]
```

How It Works

Regular expressions are objects that describe a pattern of characters in text. They are often used with search functions. You can create a pattern that will be used on a single line of text or an entire document.

Regular expressions can be created one of two ways. One simple way of creating a regular expression is to have a string inside a set of forward slashes (/). The other way of creating a regular expression is to use the constructor. This way is preferred if you think that the pattern may change or come from an outside source.

In both of these cases, you are looking for a direct match.

© Russ Ferguson and Keith Cirkel 2017
R. Ferguson and K. Cirkel, *JavaScript Recipes*, DOI 10.1007/978-1-4302-6107-0_20

How Do Regular Expression Flags Work?

Problem

You want to know how to take advantage of a flag when using regular expressions.

Solution

Flags in regular expressions give you extra functions when running the expression code.

The Code

Listing 20-2. Using Flags as Part of the Regular Expression

```
//regular expression with flags

var words = `Moff mon darth solo jabba yavin darth. Skywalker endor k-3po mon fett binks.`;/
       words += `\nMoff mon darth solo jabba yavin darth. skywalker endor k-3po mon fett binks.`;

var multiLineExpression = /(Skywalker)/gi; //a match group that is global and ignores case

 var multiLineResult = multiLineExpression.exec(words);

console.log(multiLineResult);
```

How It Works

Flags or modifiers customize a regular expression to give it extra functions while it is performing a search. If you need to search multiple lines or find a word regardless of its case, a flag will help you perform that type of search.

Global (g): This will tell the engine not to stop after the first match has been found.

Multiline (m): This will force the (^) hat or carrot and the dollar sign ($) to match the beginning and end of each line in a multiline document.

Case insensitive (i): This flag will have the search ignore the case of the string being searched.

Ignore whitespace (x): This flag will ignore all the whitespace inside a search.

Unicode (u): Strings are treated at UTF-16.

Sticky (y): This feature has a Boolean value where a search can begin not from the beginning, but from the last index that was found.

In this example, we have a multiline string with two regular expressions. The expression creates a *match group* to group a set of characters. The flags being used (gi) will make this a global search and will ignore the case. The search will result in two matches.

How Do You Match Literal and Special Characters?

Problem

In your regular expression, you want to find a certain phrase even if it has special characters.

Solution

Using the dot (.) can help you find certain characters and the backslash (\) escapes special characters.

The Code

Listing 20-3. Searching for Characters Even if There Are Special Characters in the Search

```
var words = "Moff mon darth solo jabba yavin darth. Skywalker endor k-3po mon fett binks.";
    words += "\nMoff mon darth solo jabba yavin darth. skywalker endor k-3po mon fett
    binks.";

var multiLineExpression = /(darth\.)/gi; //a match group that includes the period
var multiLineResult = multiLineExpression.exec(words);

console.log(multiLineResult); //returns ["darth.", "darth.", index: 32, input: "Moff mon darth
solo jabba yavin darth. Skywalker e...avin darth. skywalker endor k-3po mon fett binks."]
```

How It Works

The dot (.) acts as a wildcard. It can be used to match any single character. If the search needs to include special characters, those characters would need to be excepted. Using the backslash (\), you can escape the special character that is part of your search.

In this example, the search group is similar to the example in Listing 20-2. The important difference is the forward slash that escapes that dot. This dot is not part of the search results.

When looking for other special characters, you can search for digits (\d), whitespace (\s), and alphanumeric letters with digits (\w). You can also search for non-digits (\D), non-whitespace (\S), and any non-alphanumeric characters (\W).

How Do You Use Conditions in a Search?

Problem

You want to add conditions to your searches.

Solution

The pipe (|), which is also used in if statements, can be used to add a logical condition to a regular expression.

The Code

Listing 20-4. Using the Logical Operator or Pipe (|) to Make a Choice of One or the Other

```
var words = "Moff mon darth solo jabba yavin darth. Skywalker endor k-3po mon fett binks.";

var multiLineExpression = /darth|solo/g;  //search vader or solor
var multiLineResult = multiLineExpression.exec(words);
```

```
console.log(multiLineResult); //returns ["darth", index: 9, input: "Moff mon darth solo
jabba yavin darth. Skywalker endor k-3po mon fett binks."]

var groupOfWords = 'cats, bats, dogs, logs, cogs';
var groupRegX = /[cb]ats|[dl]ogs/; //search cats, bats, dogs, logs

console.log(groupRegX.exec(groupOfWords)); //returns ["cats", index: 0, input: "cats, bats,
dogs, logs, cogs"]
```

How It Works

There may be a situation where you want to search for one thing or another. To add this condition to your regular expression, you can add a pipe (|) to your search.

The first example allows you to search for the instance of two different words. The second example allows you to search for instance of words with a combination of results—if a word starts with 'c' or 'b' (cats or bats) or if a word starts with 'd' or 'l' (dogs or logs).

How Do You Search for Characters in a Certain Range?

Problem

You want to find certain characters inside a range of characters.

Solution

Using bracket notation ([ ]) with a dash (-), you can create a range of values to use in the search.

The Code

Listing 20-5. Searching for Certain Characters in a Range

```
var textWithNumbers = 'USS Enterprise 1701-D';
var serachNumbers   = /[0-9]/;
var serachNumbersGreedy  = /[0-9]+/;

console.log(serachNumbers.exec(textWithNumbers));  //returns ["1", index: 15, input: "USS
Enterprise 1701-D"]
console.log(serachNumbersGreedy.exec(textWithNumbers)); //returns ["1701", index: 15, input:
"USS Enterprise 1701-D"]
```

How It Works

Square bracket notion is used to create ranges for your search. For example, if you wanted to search for capital letters [A-Z] or if you are looking for numbers between 0 and 9 [0-9]. When looking for characters this way, one of the important things to keep in mind is that the characters are sequential.

Some shorthand for looking for character ranges is to use \w. This will look for both upper- and lowercase letters in addition to numbers between 0 to 9. If you're looking for digits, you can use \d for the search, whereas \D (notice the capital letter) is used with any non-digit character. The second example creates a *greedy* search. This will return one or more results, not stopping at the first result.

How Do You Use Anchors?

Problem

You want to know how to use anchors in a regular expression.

Solution

Anchors specify a position where a match happens in a string.

The Code

Listing 20-6. Anchors Will Specify Exactly Where a Match Happens

```
var ipsumString = 'Moff mon darth solo jabba yavin darth. Skywalker endor k-3po mon fett binks.';
    ipsumString += 'Moff mon darth solo jabba yavin darth. Skywalker endor k-3po mon fett binks.';

var startAnchor = /^M/;
var multiLineAnchor = /^M/m;
var endOfLineAnchor = /binks.$/gm;
var firstInstanceAnchor = /\ar/;
var startOrEndAnchor = /^darth|binks.$/;

console.log(startAnchor.exec(ipsumString)); //returns M
console.log(multiLineAnchor.exec(ipsumString)); //returns M
console.log(endOfLineAnchor.exec(ipsumString)); //returns binks.
console.log(firstInstanceAnchor.exec(ipsumString)); //returns ar
console.log(startOrEndAnchor.exec(ipsumString)); //returns binks.
```

How It Works

Anchors let you specify exactly where a match should happen. It keeps the engine from searching through the entire string to find a match and brings you directly to the location where the match occurs. It is recommended to use anchors whenever you can.

A caret (^) is used in most engines to make sure the current position in the string is the beginning position.

The startAnchor variable will only find a match if the M is at the start of a string. If in multiline mode, it will find the M at the start of every string.

The dollar sign ($) will tell the engine to stop at the end of a string. Using endOfLineAnchor, you can search for the last word in the line. This example added the global and multiline modifiers to create two matches.

Using \ar will find the first instance of "ar" in the first line. If the gm modifiers are added, it would return every instance of "ar" in every line.

The startOrEndAnchor lets you check if "darth" is at the beginning of a string or if "binks.". In this instance, the result will return binks.

How Do You Use Matching Quantifiers?

Problem

You want to know what quantifiers in a regular expression are.

Solution

Quantifiers tell the engine how many instances of a character must exist in order for a match to be found.

The Code

Listing 20-7. Quantifiers Can Be Greedy, Docile, Lazy, and Helpful

```
var ipsumString = 'Moff mon darth solo jabba yavin darth. Skywalker endor k-3po mon fett binks.';
    ipsumString += 'Moff mon darth solo jabba yavin darth. Skywalker endor k-3po mon fett binks.';

var greedyQuantifier = /b+/;
var docileQuantifier = /.*k-/;
var lazyQuantifier = /jabba*?/;
var helpfulQuantifier = /.*?yavin/;

console.log(greedyQuantifier.exec(ipsumString)); //returns bb from the first instance of jabba
console.log(docileQuantifier.exec(ipsumString)); //returns Moff mon darth solo jabba yavin
darth. Skywalker endor k-
console.log(lazyQuantifier.exec(ipsumString)); //returns jabb
console.log(helpfulQuantifier.exec(ipsumString)); //returns Moff mon darth solo jabba yavin
```

How It Works

Quantifiers can be broken down into different categories; here are a few of them:

- *Greedy*: This will tell the engine to match as many instances of the pattern as possible. Using a plus sign (+) as part of the expression will make the expression greedy. In this instance, you will return a result if the engine can find a match of one or more. We return bb from the first instance of jabba.

- *Docile*: Using the dot (.), the expression starts out greedy, matching any characters except a new line (\n). The asterisk (*) will start to give back characters as needed. So it starts at the beginning of the line (the far left) and selects the entire line. Then it will give characters up from the right of the line until there is a match. If the k was the only character, then the period and s would be given up (.s in binks.). Adding the dash (-) gives up all the characters from the right up to the dash. The search will return Moff mon darth solo jabba yavin darth. Skywalker endor k-' and leave '3po mon fett binks.

- *Lazy*: Sometimes called reluctant, this tries to match as few items as needed. Using a question mark (?) will turn an expression lazy. This expression will start looking for the first instance of jabb in jabba. Because the last 'a' is followed by the asterisk (*) and question mark (?), the search gives up the last character.

- *Helpful*: Similar to the last example. This is also a lazy type of search. The search will return between zero and unlimited results, but run as few times as possible. This search starts at the left and will expand up to the word yavin.

What Are Capture Groups?

Problem

You wonder how to group information for further processing.

Solution

You can group information for processing using parentheses ( ).

The Code

Listing 20-8. Creating a Capture Group Using Parentheses

```
var ipsumString = 'Moff mon darth solo jabba yavin darth. Skywalker endor k-3po mon fett binks.';
    ipsumString += 'Moff mon darth solo jabba yavin darth. Skywalker endor k-3po mon fett
    binks. file_record_transcript.pdf';

var groupOfFilesNoExtention = /(.*)\.pdf/;
var groupOfFilesWithExtention = /(.*\.pdf)/;

console.log(groupOfFilesNoExtention.exec(ipsumString)); //returns file_record_transcript
console.log(groupOfFilesWithExtention.exec(ipsumString)); //returns file_record_transcript.pdf
```

How It Works

It is possible to group information for further processing using parentheses. You can create a subpattern and capture it as a group.

The first example creates a capture group. This group will capture any characters except a newline character because of the dot (.). Then it will act *greedy* by using the asterisk (*) and capture between zero and unlimited amount of results. Outside the parentheses, we now start to narrow down the search and match the period (.) and the letters "pdf" exactly. The result is that the search will ignore everything and focus on the filename, excluding the extension.

The other example will do the same thing; however, the extension is part of the group. This will make the engine include the file extension.

What Are Lookaheads?

Problem

You want to know how to use a lookahead in a regular expression.

Solution

Lookaheads look for a certain kind of match, even when the expression is or isn't followed by a pattern.

The Code

Listing 20-9. Using a Lookahead to Find the Characters 1701

```
var textWithNumbers = '1701-D, 1701';
var noLetterLookaHead = /1701(?!-D)/; //returns the second set ignoring other characters
var withLetterLookaHead = /1701(?=-D)/;  //only returns the version with -D at the end

console.log(noLetterLookaHead.exec(textWithNumbers));
console.log(withLetterLookaHead.exec(textWithNumbers));
```

How It Works

Lookaheads will find a match if the string is or isn't followed by the pattern. The first example has a pattern where the characters (-D) are not followed by the numbers 1701. It would ignore the first instance and go straight to the second instance. The other example will only return the version that contains (-D) at the end.

In both instances, the search is for the number, but only when that the number is followed by the pattern (-D).

■ ■ ■

CHAPTER 21

Working with Asynchronous Control Flow and Promises

What Is Asynchronous Control Flow?

Caution   Let variables and arrow functions are ES6 features. Older browsers still in use, such as Internet Explorer 11 and below, or Safari 7 and below, do not support these features. Check out http://kangax. github.io/es5-compat-table/es6/ for the current compatibility charts.

Problem

You want a better understanding of asynchronous control flow.

Solution

Asynchronous control flow is the name of a set of patterns to help control the order of execution of asynchronous code. To manage a programs flow synchronously, you would use if statements and try/ catch statements. These work fine for synchronous code because each statement executes and the return value is evaluated before continuing to the next statement. Asynchronous code, however, is code that eventually will fulfill but some (indeterminate) time in the future and so cannot be predictably relied upon to succeed by the next statement or stack frame. To allow for code to be asynchronous, some languages offer the ability to create new threads, which run independently but can communicate with each other. JavaScript's concurrency model is based on an *event loop*. The *event loop* effectively iterates over a *task queue*, executing each *task* until there are no *tasks* left. *Tasks* can execute small pieces of synchronous code, and subsequently defer the next stage of execution until a new *task* in the near future.

Two of the biggest paradigms for using callbacks in JavaScript are events and promises. Node.js also heavily utilizes the callback pattern throughout the core library, but does not use promises. Promises (and Node.js style callbacks) are very useful for single-result functions, for example for fs.writeFile, which fires the callback when all of the given contents have been written to the file. Events, which are described in Chapter 18, are used both in the browser and Node.js heavily and are very useful for asynchronous functionality that is fired potentially multiple times—for example, with element.addEventListener('click'), which could fire once or thousands of times during its life. Promises are a recent addition to the language, officially built into ECMAScript 6 and existing for a few years prior through external libraries. *Promises* are essentially task queues that "promise" a value will at some point be returned from asynchronous code. This chapter covers promises in depth.

© Russ Ferguson and Keith Cirkel 2017
R. Ferguson and K. Cirkel, *JavaScript Recipes*, DOI 10.1007/978-1-4302-6107-0_21

The Code

Listing 21-1. What Is Asynchronous Control Flow?

```
// Below is how Asynchronous Control Flow can be achieved with the Node.js Callback Pattern.
This example uses fs.writeFile to write a file to the filesystem
let file = fs.writeFile('data.txt', data, (err) => {
    if (err) { console.log('Oh no, an error!'); }
    else  console.log('file has been written!');

});


// Below is how Asynchronous Control Flow works with Event Emitters, for example Sockets in
node.js
let socket = new Socket(), data;
socket.on('data', chunk => data += chunk);
socket.on('end', () => console.log('all data has been sent!'));
socket.on('error', (err) => console.log('Oh no, an error!', err));

// Here is how the Event Emitter pattern works in browsers, in the DOM using XMLHTTPRequest
let xhr = new XMLHTTPRequest();
xhr.addEventListener('load', () => console.log('all data has been sent'));
xhr.addEventListener('error', () => console.log('Oh no, an error!'));
xhr.open();

// Here is how the Promise pattern works, for example making a request using a Request
Promise library
let req = request('http://google.com')
    .then(() => console.log('Request has finished'))
    .catch((err) => console.log('Oh no, an error!'));
```

How It Works

First, it is important to understand how asynchronous code works. Essentially, an interpreter given a block of code will execute each statement one directly after the other. While this happens, the interpreter will not be able to do anything else (in a single thread). It will use as much CPU as it can to execute each statement, and when all statements are done it will finish and terminate the program. The problem herein lies that some functions, especially ones that deal with I/O will take a variable amount of time, compared to *CPU bound* functions, which take a (reasonably) predictable amount of CPU time. Traditional languages that are *single threaded* and *I/O blocking* will stop everything and simply wait for the indeterminately timed function to finish, and then proceed with the remainder of the code. Consider Figure 21-1, which illustrates a set of synchronous tasks done in a language that blocks for I/O.

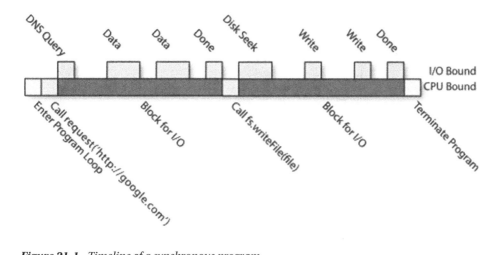

Figure 21-1. *Timeline of a synchronous program*

There are many languages available that exhibit this non-asynchronous behavior; they are "I/O blocking," for example PHP. PHP is a single threaded (cannot talk to other CPU threads in an asynchronous manner) interpreted language, just like JavaScript is, but because PHP's I/O is blocking by nature, every time the thread does an I/O operation such as a network request or write to disk, it must wait until that i/o completes (so it can evaluate the return value) before moving onto the next line of code. each new function call is a *stack frame* and is added onto the pile of stack frames until they all complete and the program ends.

JavaScript mitigates this behavior with the *event loop* (not to be confused with events in JavaScript). It offers the same behavior with regards to *stack frames*, in that synchronous code will pile up in *stack frames* and all be executed as fast as possible. JavaScript's *event loop* adds an additional benefit through the *task queue* and *tasks,* which get executed in order but after the existing set of stack frames have been executed. In the language, this presents itself as functions like setTimeout(), setInterval(), setImmediate(), and in the case of Node.js process.nextTick(). Through these and other mechanisms, JavaScript uses the *callback pattern*, where functions can be passed as arguments, which can be executed in the near future, in a new *task*. This method of deferring functionality effectively makes up a *simple concurrency model* (i.e., a way to handle asynchronous code) for JavaScript. The event loop in itself does not make JavaScript *non-blocking*, but provides a layer of asynchronous concurrency, which most APIs (such as the DOM and Node.js) take advantage of.

By using this concurrency model to queue up the completion of I/O operations, JavaScript can execute all of the synchronous code setup first, then idle while waiting for the asynchronous code to complete, and finally fire all of the event handlers, callbacks, or promises that finish the program's execution. This means I/O-based code will appear to run simultaneously, and much faster than blocking I/O-based code. Consider Figure 21-2 and compare it to Figure 21-1 to see the difference in these paradigms.

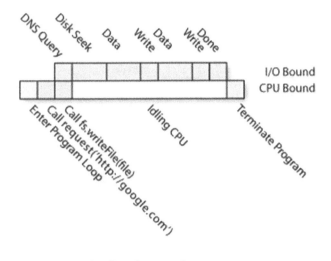

Figure 21-2. *Timeline of an asynchronous program*

What Is a Promise?

■ **Caution**   Promises are an ES6 feature. Older browsers still in use, such as Internet Explorer 11 and below, or Safari 7 and below, do not support this feature. Check out `http://kangax.github.io/es5-compat-table/es6/` for the current compatibility charts.

Problem

You want to know what a promise is and how it works.

Solution

Promises are the standard in ECMAScript for dealing with asynchronous task queues. There were many implementations prior to their ratification in the ES6 specification, such as Q, RSVP.js, and Bluebird, but the canonical implementation that features in JavaScript Implementations is the one we will be working with in this chapter.

How It Works

Promises are essentially a list of functions that get built up programmatically and will be fired one by one when the promise *queue* starts. A promise is a concept of a type of data that promises to one day be fulfilled (i.e., it is nothing yet, but will soon be something). Promises exist in three states—*pending* (or "paused"), where the promise queue (function list) is queued up and none are being executed, *fulfilled* (or "playing"), where callbacks from the promise queue are being fired one by one, and any new tasks are added to the promise *queue* to be fired very soon, or *rejected* (or "failing"), where the promise *queue* is being fired but using the error state functions (explained later in the chapter).

When the promise is created, it is given the ability to resolve or reject, but starts in the pending state. The program has to manually resolve or reject the promise, which will put it into the fulfilled or rejected state respectively. When a promise has been resolved or rejected, it cannot be pending ever again, but it may switch between fulfilled or rejected during its lifetime.

Promises are guaranteed to be asynchronous—each new function added to the promise's queue is fired on a new task in the event loop (the queue of JavaScript's underlying concurrency), and so a promise's queue is a reasonably close parallel to the event loop's task queue.

See Figure 21-3 for a basic example of a promise. The Promise is created with five callbacks (essentially functions). The promise starts in a *pending* state, where tasks are added (the blocks marked as "then") until resolve() is called. It sets the promise to a *fulfilled* state, and so for every iteration of the event loop task queue, one by one, each callback in the promise queue (the "then"s) is called and completed. Skip ahead to Figures 21-5 and 21-6 to see an in-depth overview of how this sort of promise can be constructed.

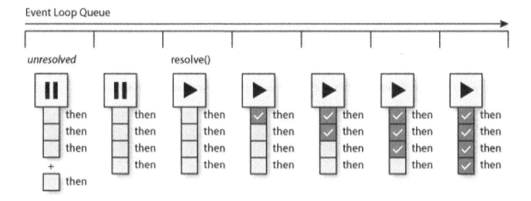

Figure 21-3. *Timeline of a basic promise*

One of the interesting parts about promises is that when the state is moved away from pending, it cannot go back into a pending state. Because of this, callbacks (the "then" blocks in the illustrations—each one represents a callback) can be added retrospectively to a promise and will simply execute on the next iteration of the event loop. To put this another way, promises exist for the lifetime of the application (unless they are freed from memory) and will perpetually execute anything in their promise's queue. This means, as a developer, you don't necessarily need to care about the current state of a promise. It will still eventually execute the callbacks you're adding, regardless of whether it has been fulfilled (actually, a promise could remain pending for the lifetime of the code, but this is rare and usually a result of a bug). Figure 21-4 illustrates how this could potentially work, given a similar example as in Figure 21-3.

Event Loop Queue

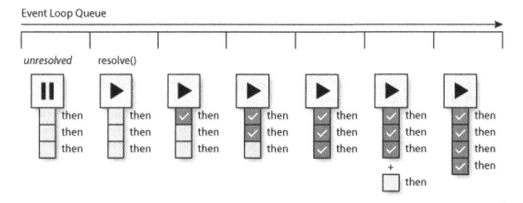

Figure 21-4. *Timeline of a promise having tasks added to it past resolution*

This feature of a promise continuing to resolve its queue beyond the point of fulfillment reveals an interesting coincidental feature—a promise can be fulfilled before it has anything in its queue. The callbacks can be added post-fulfillment. Refer to Figure 21-5 for an example of how this might work.

Event Loop Queue

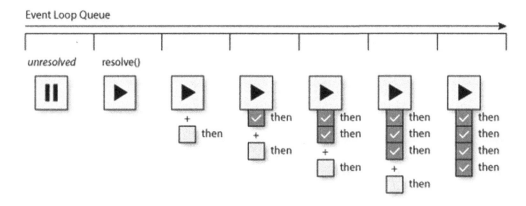

Figure 21-5. *Timeline of a promise having tasks added to it past resolution*

Typical synchronous control flow not only includes conditional code paths with `if/else` but also allows trapping of errors with `try/catch`. With promises this can also be done using a similar mechanism. Promises can, of course, also be put into the rejected state. When a promise is in the rejected state it will not execute any `resolvedActions` (`then()`); instead, it executes the `rejectedActions` (`catch()`). When executing any `rejectedActions`, the promise can be switched back into a fulfilled state (switching from a rejected state) if the `rejectedAction` returns a value rather than throwing a failure. Consider Figure 21-6, which describes how this process works.

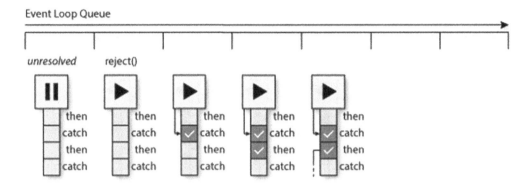

Figure 21-6. *Timeline of a promise being rejected and caught with catch*

Of course, a `rejectedAction` doesn't necessarily always have to put a promise back into a fulfilled state; it can pass the error back into the promise chain, causing the promise to remain in the rejected state, and skipping the next `resolvedAction` and instead running the next `rejectedAction`. Similarly, `resolvedActions` can throw errors to put an already fulfilled promise into a rejected state. Figure 21-7 shows how this might work.

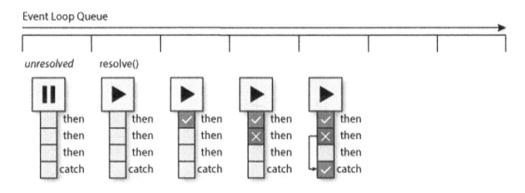

Figure 21-7. *Timeline of a promise being resolved and rejected by a then*

These `then()`/`catch()` features closely mimic synchronous code's `try/catch`, and they also work to cover some use cases of `if/else`. You are encouraged in your promises to flip the state of a promise between fulfilled and rejected as you see fit, to help handle what could be considered the "happy path" and the "unhappy path." Refer to Figures 21-8 and 21-9 for more interesting examples of how this `then()`/`catch()` behavior can work.

Event Loop Queue

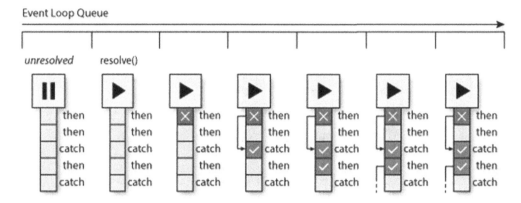

Figure 21-8. *Timeline of a promise being resolved, rejected, and re-resolved*

Event Loop Queue

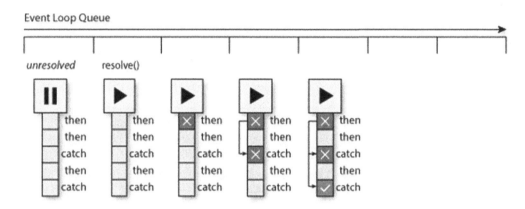

Figure 21-9. *Timeline of a promise being caught and "rethrown"*

Catching, resolving, and "rethrowing" are all paradigms of synchronous code, mapped into promises. They can create complex asynchronous workflows. They also become more powerful than try/catch when you consider that you can defer dealing with any errors until the last rejectedAction in your promise, meaning you don't need to sprinkle rejectedAction callbacks everywhere in your code. Promises can become even more complex when you consider the other powerful feature: Promises can be composed together. The return values of either resolvedActions or rejectedActions can also be a promise, and execution and state is deferred to that promise until it has completed all of its queue, to which it hands back the flow of execution to the originating promise. This can become incredibly complex; refer to Figure 21-10 for a simplified illustration of nested promises.

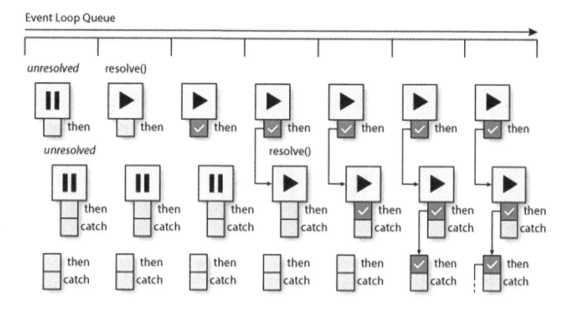

Figure 21-10. *Timeline of a simple set of nested promises*

In Figure 21-10, the promise is fulfilled, but the first resolvedAction (then()) returns a promise. The promise is created, and therefore executed, on the resulting call of the resolvedAction, so it resolves further down the line. During its fulfillment, it needs to complete all of its queue (resolvedActions and rejectedActions) before the originating promise can continue to process its queue. This composition ability makes promises incredibly powerful for handling sequential asynchronous tasks. As mentioned, however, the state of the nested promise determines the state going upstream, so while Figure 21-10 shows the nested promise successfully resolving, Figure 21-11 shows what would happen if the nested promise transforms into a rejected state. In Figure 21-11, you can see that the nested promise is transformed into a rejected state, and subsequently transforms the upstream promise to a rejected state, causing it to skip any subsequent resolvedActions and move to the nearest rejectedAction. This can provide some really interesting control flow, and is especially useful for tasks where you don't mind about the state of a nested promise. You simply catch the error properly in the upstream promise and return it to its rightful state.

Event Loop Queue

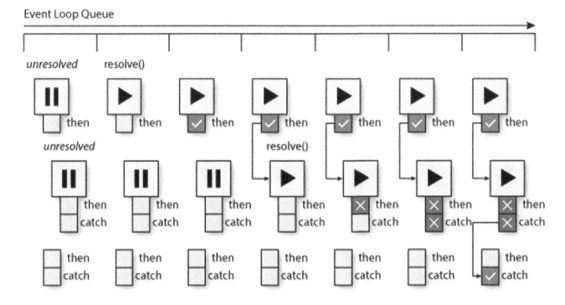

Figure 21-11. Timeline of a set of nested promises, where the child promise becomes rejected

All of these features of promises make them incredibly powerful, but also incredibly complex. Understanding these concepts in their discrete form is key to grasping them. Ensure that you keep these concepts in mind to avoid underutilizing promises and potentially running into problems that could easily be solved by the many flexibilities and power of promises.

Creating a Promise

■ **Caution**   Promises, `let` variables, and arrow functions are ES6 features. Older browsers still in use, such as Internet Explorer 11 and below, or Safari 7 and below, do not support these features. Check out `http://kangax.github.io/es5-compat-table/es6/` for the current compatibility charts.

Problem

You want to be able to create a promise.

Solution

The promise constructor function can be used to make new promise instances. It takes one argument, which is a function that it immediately invokes. It gives the function two arguments—the first is a function to call when you want to *fulfill* the promise—e.g., when the wrapped asynchronous function has completed. The second is a function to call when you want the *reject* the promise—e.g., when the wrapped asynchronous function has failed with an error. The promise constructor function will return a new instance of promise, which is used to then queue up tasks.

The Code

Listing 21-2. Creating a Promise

```
let readFilePromise = new Promise((resolve, reject) => {
  fs.readFile('data.txt', (err, data) => {
      if (err) {
          reject(err);
      } else {
          resolve(data);
      }
  });
});
let writeFilePromise = new Promise((resolve, reject) => {
  fs.writeFile('data.txt', data, err => {
      if (err) {
          reject(err);
      } else {
          resolve();
      }
  });
});
```

How It Works

The promise constructor doesn't actually invoke any asynchronous code, although the resulting callbacks are guaranteed to run on a subsequent iteration of the event loop, and so are asynchronous. The promise constructor simply invokes the given function with the resolve and reject functions, leaving it to the developer to wrap asynchronous commands and turn them into a promise, as shown in the examples.

The callback function is given the two arguments—resolve and reject—so that the callback can manage the desired state of the promise. For example, if you're making a call to Node.js' fs.writeFile(), you might call resolve() when the operation has completed, putting the promise into a *fulfilled* state, unless there is an error, wherein reject(error) would be called, putting the Promise into a rejected state. As discussed earlier in this chapter, this determines the execution flow of the promise, whether it moves to a resolvedAction or a rejectedAction.

Adding Tasks to the Promise Queue with then()

■ **Caution**   Promises, let variables, and arrow functions are ES6 features. Older browsers still in use, such as Internet Explorer 11 and below, or Safari 7 and below, do not support these features. Check out http://kangax.github.io/es5-compat-table/es6/ for the current compatibility charts.

Problem

You want to be able to add a callback to a promise that will be executed when the promise is resolved.

Solution

The `Promise.prototype.then()` function takes two arguments, both functions. The first function is the `resolvedAction`, the second is `rejectedAction`. Only one of these function arguments is ever fired; the other one is never fired. Which one is determined by the state of the promise. The first function argument (the `resolvedAction` argument) is what to do if the state of the promise at the previous point in the queue was rejected and defaults to a function that returns the first given argument. The second argument is described later in this chapter. `resolvedAction` will be called with the `resolveResult`. That is the value that was passed to the `resolve()` function in the original promise constructor, or the value returned from the last called `resolveAction` or `rejectAction`. Whatever the value that is returned from the `resolvedAction` function becomes the new `resolveResult`. If `resolvedAction` throws, then the thrown value will become the `rejectResult` and the promise will enter a rejected state.

The Code

Listing 21-3. Adding Tasks to the Promise Queue with then()

```
let writeFilePromise = new Promise((resolve, reject) => {
  fs.writeFile('data.txt', data, err => {
      if (err) {
          reject(err);
      } else {
          resolve();
      }
  });
});
writeFilePromise.then(() => console.log('file has been written!'));
```

The output is:

```
// When data.txt writes successfully
file has been written!
// When data.txt threw an error during write
[error thrown]
```

How It Works

`Promise.prototype.then()` allows you to add callbacks to any promise instance. The given callbacks are queued up and executed depending on the outcome state of the last callback. The functions passed to it work similarly to the promise constructor, in that the function calls themselves are not asynchronous and should not execute any asynchronous code. These callbacks differ from the promise constructor, in that they have no mechanism for deferring their return value, other than returning a new promise (which does). In other words, both of the functions you pass to it should use synchronous code or return promises that invoke asynchronous code.

then() can be called on a promise in any state. When the promise is in a pending state, it will wait until it is in a fulfilled or rejected before it executes any arguments in a then() function. If it is in the fulfilled state, the queue is executed, one by one, calling each of the resolvedActions (the first argument in a then() call). A promise that is already fulfilled will call the next resolvedAction in the queue. Remember though that a promise can change state to rejected at any time, meaning that, while you can guarantee one of the functions given to then() will be called, you can never guarantee which one it will be. A best practice is to always ensure you manage the outcome of both states at every reasonable opportunity, or at the very least always attempt to put a rejectedAction at the end of the promise chain. See Figure 21-12 illustrates the behaviors of a promise continuously in the fulfilled state.

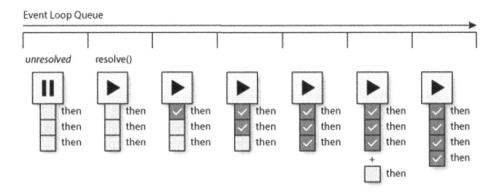

Figure 21-12. *Timeline of a promise having tasks added to it past resolution*

Adding Error Catchers to a then() with the Catch Argument

■ **Caution**   Promises, let variables, and arrow functions are ES6 features. Older browsers still in use, such as Internet Explorer 11 and below, or Safari 7 and below, do not support these features. Check out http://kangax.github.io/es5-compat-table/es6/ for the current compatibility charts.

Problem

You want to be able to catch an error from a previous promise or then() that will be executed when the promise is rejected, or an error occurs in the previous then().

Solution

As mentioned, the Promise.prototype.then() function takes two arguments, both functions. The second argument is the rejectedAction argument, which is a function that is called if the state of the promise is rejected, and defaults to a function that throws the first given argument. rejectedAction will be called with the rejectResult. That is the value that was either passed to the reject() function in the original promise constructor, or the value that was thrown in the last resolveAction or rejectAction. The value that is returned from this function becomes the new resolveResult, and the promise goes back to a fulfilled state, unless this function throws in which case the value thrown becomes the rejectResult and the promise remains in a rejected state.

The Code

Listing 21-4. Adding Error Catchers to a then() with the Catch Argument

```
let writeFilePromise = new Promise((resolve, reject) => {
  fs.writeFile('data.txt', data, err => {
    if (err) {
        reject(err);
    } else {
        resolve();
    }
  });
});
writeFilePromise.then(undefined, () => console.log('Oh no, an error!'));
```

The output is:

```
// When data.txt writes successfully
[nothing]
// When data.txt threw an error during write
Oh no, an error!
```

How It Works

Promise.prototype.then() allows you to add callbacks to any promise instance. The given callbacks are queued up and executed depending on the outcome state of the last callback. The functions passed to it work similarly to the promise constructor, in that the function calls themselves are not asynchronous and should not execute any asynchronous code. These callbacks differ from the promise constructor, in that they have no mechanism for deferring their return value, other than returning a new promise (which does). In other words, both of the functions you pass to it should use synchronous code or return promises that invoke asynchronous code.

then() can be called on a promise in any state. When the promise is in a pending state, it will wait until it is in a fulfilled or rejected before it executes any arguments in a then() function. If it is in the rejected state, then the queue is executed, one by one, calling each of the rejectedActions (the second argument in a then() call). A promise that's already rejected will call the next rejectedAction in the queue. A promise can change state to fulfilled from a rejected state at any time, meaning that, while you can guarantee that one of the functions given to then() will be called, you can never guarantee which one it will be. Figure 21-13 illustrates the behaviors of a promise that rejects with a catch function in place.

Event Loop Queue

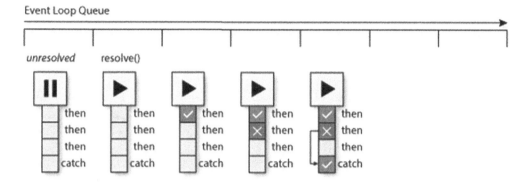

Figure 21-13. *Timeline of a promise being resolved and rejected by a then*

Adding Error Catchers to the Promise Sequence with catch()

■ **Caution**   Promises, `let` variables, and arrow functions are ES6 features. Older browsers still in use, such as Internet Explorer 11 and below, or Safari 7 and below, do not support these features. Check out `http://kangax.github.io/es5-compat-table/es6/` for the current compatibility charts.

Problem

You want to be able to add an error catcher to a promise, but you are not concerned about the first argument in the `then()` function and need a simpler way to add an error catcher.

Solution

`Promise.prototype.catch()` is a simple shortcut for calling `Promise.prototype.then()` while omitting the first argument. `catch()` only takes one argument, a `rejectedAction`. This will be called only if the promise is in a rejected state. `rejectedAction` will be called with the `rejectResult`. That is the value that was either passed to the `reject()` function in the original promise constructor, or the value that was thrown in the last `resolveAction` or `rejectAction`. The value that is returned from this function becomes the new `resolveResult`, and the promise goes back to a fulfilled state, unless this function throws, in which case the value thrown becomes the `rejectResult` and the promise remains in a rejected state.

The Code

Listing 21-5. Adding Error Catchers to the Promise Sequence with catch()

```
let writeFilePromise = new Promise((resolve, reject) => {
  fs.writeFile('data.txt', data, err => {
      if (err) {
          reject(err);
      } else {
```

```
            resolve();
        }
    });
});
writeFilePromise.catch(() => console.log('Oh no, an error!'));
```

The output is:

```
// When data.txt writes successfully
[nothing]
// When data.txt threw an error during write
Oh no, an error!
```

How It Works

`Promise.prototype.catch()` provided a convenient wrapper for `Promise.prototype.then(undefined)`. Other than the arguments it takes, it behaves identically to its cousin: `Promise.prototype.then()`.

`catch()` can be called on a promise in any state. When the promise is in a pending state, it will wait until it is fulfilled or rejected before it executes any arguments in a `catch()` function. If it is in the rejected state, then the queue is executed, one by one, calling each of the `rejectedActions`. A promise that's already rejected will call the next `rejectedAction` in the queue. Figure 21-14 illustrates the behaviors of a promise that rejects with a `catch` function in place.

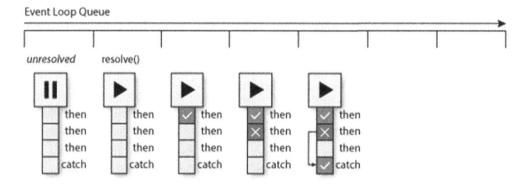

Figure 21-14. *Timeline of a promise being resolved and rejected by a then*

Making an Automatically Fulfilling Promise with Promise.resolve()

■ **Caution**   Promises, `let` variables, and arrow functions are ES6 features. Older browsers still in use, such as Internet Explorer 11 and below, or Safari 7 and below, do not support these features. Check out `http://kangax.github.io/es5-compat-table/es6/` for the current compatibility charts.

Problem

You have a value that you'd like to resolve into an immediately fulfilled promise.

Solution

`Promise.resolve()` takes one argument, which can be any value, that becomes the `resolveResult` as part of a new promise. It returns a new promise, which can then be chained off with `then()` and `catch()`. The first `resolvedAction` will be called with the `resolveResult` (the first argument given to `Promise.resolve()`).

The Code

Listing 21-6. Making an Automatically Fulfilling Promise with Promise.resolve()

```
let myResolveValue = 5;
// Long hand resolving Promise
let promise = new Promise(resolve => {
    resolve(myResolveValue);
});
// Shorthand Promise.resolve()
let promise = Promise.resolve(myResolveValue);
promise.then(value => console.log(value));
```

The output is:

```
5
```

How It Works

`Promise.resolve()` automatically creates a new promise in the fulfilled state with the `resolveResult` set to the given argument. It offers exactly the same semantics as a new promise in which the `resolve()` function is immediately called with the given value.

Making an Automatically Rejecting Promise with Promise.reject()

■ **Caution**   Promises, `let` variables, and arrow functions are ES6 features. Older browsers still in use, such as Internet Explorer 11 and below, or Safari 7 and below, do not support these features. Check out `http://kangax.github.io/es5-compat-table/es6/` for the current compatibility charts.

Problem

You have a value that you'd like to resolve into an immediately rejected promise.

Solution

`Promise.reject()` takes one argument, which can be any value, that becomes the `rejectResult` as part of a new promise. It returns a new promise, which can then be chained off with `then()` and `catch()`. The first `rejectedAction` will be called with the `rejectResult` (the first argument given to `Promise.resolve()`).

The Code

Listing 21-7. Making an Automatically Rejecting Promise with Promise.reject()

```
let myRejectValue = new Error('My own error');
// Long hand rejecting Promise
let promise = new Promise((resolve, reject) => {
    resolve(myRejectValue);
});
// Shorthand Promise.reject()
let promise = Promise.reject(myRejectValue);
promise.catch((error) => console.log(error));
```

The output is:

```
Error: My own error
```

How It Works

`Promise.resolve()` automatically creates a new promise in the rejected state with the `rejectResult` set to the given argument. It offers exactly the same semantics as a new promise, in which the `reject()` function is immediately called with the given value.

Remember, a rejected promise will automatically skip all `resolvedActions` and head for the first `rejectedAction`, but if the `rejectedAction` returns a value and doesn't throw, then the promise can be put into a fulfilled state. See Figure 21-15.

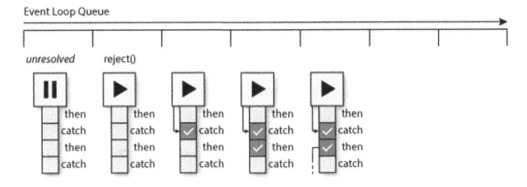

Figure 21-15. *Timeline of a promise being rejected and caught with catch*

Working with Multiple Promises in Sequence

■ **Caution**   Promises, `let` variables, and arrow functions are ES6 features. Older browsers still in use, such as Internet Explorer 11 and below, or Safari 7 and below, do not support these features. Check out `http://kangax.github.io/es5-compat-table/es6/` for the current compatibility charts.

Problem

You have multiple promises that you'd like to execute in serial (one after the other).

Solution

As part of the built-in behavior of a promise, if the return value from a `resolvedAction` or `rejectedAction` is a promise, then the returned promise has to be fulfilled or rejected, and all of its queue needs to be executed for the upstream promise queue to continue. In addition, if the state of the returned promise can alter the state of the upstream promise; for example, if the upstream promise is fulfilled but the returned promise ultimately ends up as rejected, it will change the state of the upstream promise to rejected.

The Code

Listing 21-8. Working with Multiple Promises in Sequence

```
new Promise((resolve, reject) => {
  fs.readFile('data.json', data, err => {
      if (err) {
          reject(err);
      } else {
          resolve();
      }
  });
}).then(fileData => JSON.parse(fileData))
```

```
.then(fileJSON => {
    fileJSON.version = Number(fileJSON.version) + 1;
    return fileJSON;
}).then(fileJSON => new Promise((resolve, reject) => {
    fs.writeFile(JSON.stringify('data.json', fileJSON, err => {
        if (err) {
            reject(err);
        } else {
            resolve();
        }
    });
}).then(() => console.log('File wrote successfully'), err => console.log('Oh no!, err));
```

The output is:

```
// After successful file read and write
File wrote successfully
// With any error in the Promise
Oh no! Error: ...
```

How It Works

In the code example, data.json's contents are read, as part of a promise, parsed as JSON, the version number is incremented, and the contents are written back into data.json. The write operation is also wrapped in a promise, but one that is returned as part of a then() (the arrow function without curly braces immediately returns the only statement in its body).

The promise that is returned as part of the write operation dictates the rest of the flow of the parent most promise (the read operation). The first thing required is that the last then() is deferred for execution until the write operation completes, and the child promise is fully resolved with nothing left in its promise queue. The second thing that happens is the last state of the child promise is copied over to its parent, meaning if the child promise (the write file operation in this case) ends up in a rejected state, the parent promise (the read file operation in this case) will inherit that state and become rejected, even if it was originally fulfilled. This sounds like it may cause slip ups, but it is actually a very powerful tool when dealing with multiple, nested, promises. See Figures 21-16 and 21-17 for illustrations on how this might work.

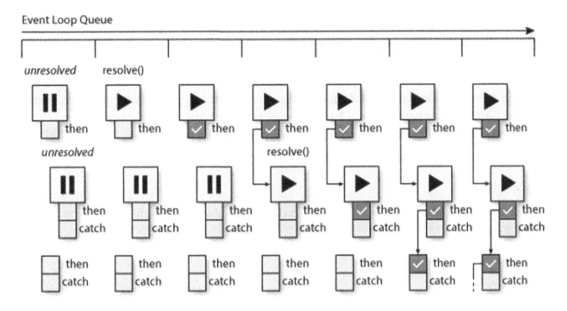

Figure 21-16. *Timeline of a simple set of nested promises*

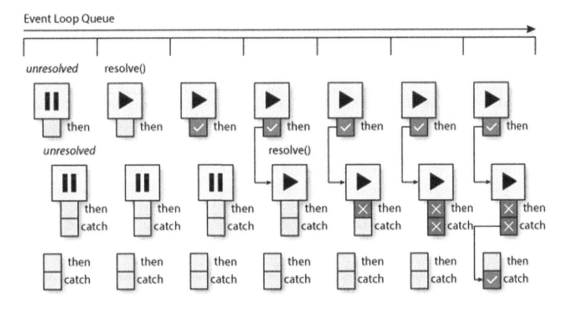

Figure 21-17. *Timeline of a set of nested promises, where the child promise becomes rejected*

Executing Code After the First in a List of Promises Resolves with Promise.race()

■ **Caution** Promises, `let` variables, and arrow functions are ES6 features. Older browsers still in use, such as Internet Explorer 11 and below, or Safari 7 and below, do not support these features. Check out `http://kangax.github.io/es5-compat-table/es6/` for the current compatibility charts.

Problem

You have a list of promises, and you want to execute code after one of any of those promises resolves to a fulfilled or rejected. You do not care which one resolves first, just as long as one does.

Solution

`Promise.race()` takes one argument, which is an iterable (e.g., an array) of values. Any value that's an instance of promise will be used to defer the execution of subsequent callbacks, until one of the promises in the iterable is fulfilled or rejected. All values that are not a promise will be converted into a promise using `Promise.resolve()`.

The Code

Listing 21-9. Executing Code After the First in a List of Promises Resolves with Promise.race()

```
Promise.race([1,2,3]).then((value) => console.log('The first resolved value is ', value);
Promise.all([Promise.reject(new Error('Errors reject!'))]).then(() => console.log('This wont
fire'), (err) => console.log('Oh no!', err));
```

The output is:

```
1
Oh no!  Error: Errors reject!
```

How It Works

Internally, the interpreter calls `Promise.resolve` on all items in the iterable given to `Promise.race()`. Any values that aren't promises are composed into immediately resolving promises, while any that are need to resolve before the promise returned from `Promise.all()` will be resolved.

The internal implementation (as per the spec) simply iterates through all values, calling `Promise.resolve()` on them, passing the returned promises resolve and reject as the `resolvedHandler` and `rejectedHandler`. A JavaScript implementation would look similar to Listing 21-10.

Listing 21-10. JavaScript Implementation of Promise.race

```
Promise.race = items => new Promise((resolve, reject) => {
    for(let item of items) {
        Promise.resolve(item).then(resolve, reject);
    }
});
```

Working with Multiple Promises in Parallel with Promise.all()

■ **Caution**   Promises, let variables, and arrow functions are ES6 features. Older browsers still in use, such as Internet Explorer 11 and below, or Safari 7 and below, do not support these features. Check out http://kangax.github.io/es5-compat-table/es6/ for the current compatibility charts.

Problem

You have multiple promises that you'd like to execute in parallel (all together at the same time).

Solution

Promise.all() takes one argument, which is an *iterable* (e.g., an array) of values. Any value that's an instance of promise will be used to defer the resolution of the returned promise, until every promise is fulfilled or rejected.

The Code

Listing 21-11. Working with Multiple Promises in Parallel with Promise.all()

```
Promise.all([ 1, 2, 3 ]).then(values => console.log('This Promise resolves immediately with ',
values));
let neverEndingPromise = new Promise(() => {});
Promise.all([ 1, 2, 3, neverEndingPromise ]).then(() => console.log('This promise will never
resolve'));
Promise.all([Promise.reject(new Error('Errors reject!'))]).then(() => console.log('This wont
fire'), (err) => console.log('Oh no!', err));
```

The output is:

```
This Promise resolves immediately with  [1, 2, 3]
Oh no!  Error: Errors reject!
```

How It Works

Internally, the interpreter calls `Promise.resolve` on all items in the iterable given to `Promise.all()`. Any values that aren't promises are composed into immediately resolving promises, while any that are need to resolve before the promise returned from `Promise.all()` will be resolved. Any promises that are in a rejected will put the parent promise into a rejected state.

The internal implementation (as per the spec) simply keeps a list of all elements in the iterable and a counter of all resolved promise values. When each promise is resolved, the counter ticks down until it reaches 0, when the returned promise is resolved. To put this in code, it might look something like Listing 21-12.

Listing 21-12. JavaScript Implementation of Promise.all

```
Promise.all = items => new Promise((resolve, reject) => {
    let incr = 0, values = [];
    for(let item of items) {
        let index = incr;
        Promise.resolve(item)
            .then((value) => {
                incr--;
                values[index] = value;
                if (incr === 0) {
                    resolve(values);
                }
            }, reject);
        incr++;
    }
});
```

Making a Promise Utility Function that Waits a Given Amount of Time to Fulfill

---

■ **Caution** Promises, `let` variables, and arrow functions are ES6 features. Older browsers still in use, such as Internet Explorer 11 and below, or Safari 7 and below, do not support these features. Check out `http://kangax.github.io/es5-compat-table/es6/` for the current compatibility charts.

Problem

You want to be able to generate a promise that delays a certain amount of time before resolving.

Solution

Combining the promise constructor and `setTimeout`, you can easily create a function that takes an optional arbitrary value and an integer value representing the number of milliseconds to delay the promise by.

The Code

Listing 21-13. Making a Promise Utility Function that Waits a Given Amount of Time to Fulfill

```
Promise.myextensions = Promise.myextensions || {};
Promise.myextensions.delay = (value, ms) => new Promise((resolve) => {
    if (typeof ms === 'undefined') {
        ms = value;
        value = undefined;
    }
    setTimeout(() => resolve(value), ms);
});
Promise.myextensions.delay('Hello, after 1 second', 1000)
    .then(console.log.bind(console));

Promise.resolve()
    .then(() => {
        return Promise.myextensions.delay(2000);
    })
    .then((value) => {
        console.log('Hi, after 2 seconds', value);
    });
```

The output is:

```
"Hello, after 1 second" [after 1 second]
"Hi, after 2 seconds", undefined [after 2 seconds]
```

How It Works

First, a function is created on `Promise.myextensions.delay`. This could be set as `Promise.delay`, but if a later version of JavaScript implements this as a native feature, then there is a risk of incompatibility, so it is much safer to *namespace* custom extensions onto a new object (it is very unlikely that ECMAScript will ever define `Promise.myextensions` as anything, but feel free to choose an equally unlikely name, such as a company or organization name).

```
Promise.myextensions.delay = (value, ms) => new Promise((resolve) => {
```

The first line, other than defining the function, contains is an arrow function that immediately returns a new promise. Only the resolve argument has been defined, because this function can never enter a rejected state, as there is nothing to reject.

```
if (typeof ms === 'undefined') {
    ms = value;
    value = undefined;
}
```

The function takes two arguments, `value` and `ms`. `value` (the value to resolve the promise with) is optional, and so we need to write a small piece of detection logic that says if `ms` (the number of milliseconds to delay by) is undefined, then take the value from `value`, and treat that as `ms`, meanwhile set `value` to `undefined`.

This allows for the two different method signatures: `Promise.myextensions.delay(value, ms)` and `Promise.myextensions.delay(ms)`.

```
setTimeout(() => resolve(value), ms);
```

The core part of the functionality is incredibly simple. It simply calls `setTimeout`, which takes a callback and a millisecond value for which to wait before executing the callback. The callback function for `setTimeout` simply calls `resolve` with the given value. `ms` is supplied as the second parameter.

Making a Promise Utility that Ensures Slow Operations Time Out

> ■ **Caution**   Promises, `let` variables, and arrow functions are ES6 features. Older browsers still in use, such as Internet Explorer 11 and below, or Safari 7 and below, do not support these features. Check out `http://kangax.github.io/es5-compat-table/es6/` for the current compatibility charts.

Problem

You want to be able to create a promise that takes an existing promise, aiming to resolve it within a given time. If the given promise exceeds the given time, the created promise will reject with a timeout.

Solution

Brief note about the solution
  Perhaps another paragraph

The Code

Listing 21-14. Making a Promise Utility that Ensures Slow Operations Time Out

```
Promise.myextensions = Promise.myextensions || {};
Promise.myextensions.timeout = (promise, ms) => new Promise((resolve, reject) => {
    promise.then(resolve, reject);
    setTimeout(() => reject(new Error('Timeout')), ms);
});
let neverResolvingPromise = new Promise(() => {});
Promise.myextensions.timeout(neverResolvingPromise, 2000)
    .then((value) => console.log(value), (error) => console.log(error));
```

The output is:

```
Error: Timeout [after 2 seconds]
```

How It Works

First, a function is created on `Promise.myextensions.timeout`. This could be set as `Promise.timeout`, but if a later version of JavaScript implements this as a native feature, then there is a risk of incompatibility, so it is much safer to *namespace* custom extensions onto a new object (it is very unlikely that ECMAScript will ever define `Promise.myextensions` as anything, but feel free to chose an equally unlikely name, such as a company or organization name).

```
Promise.myextensions.timeout = (promise, ms) => new Promise((resolve, reject) => {
```

The first line, other than defining the function, is an arrow function that immediately returns a new promise. The function itself takes two arguments—`promise` (an underlying promise to chain off of) and `ms` (the amount of time to wait before rejecting with a timeout error).

```
promise.then(resolve, reject);
```

The first line of the inner function simply tacks the `resolve` and `reject` arguments onto the given promise. This way, if the given promise resolves or rejects, then the created timeout promise will do the same.

```
setTimeout(() => reject(new Error('Timeout')), ms);
```

The core part of this function looks very simple, but relies on a subtle feature of promises. Effectively, just like the `delay` function, a `setTimeout` is called with a `callback` and `ms`. The difference here is that this callback call rejects, with a timeout error, to put the promise into a rejected state. The subtle feature of promises that this utilizes, is that a promise constructor's `reject()` and `resolve()` functions have a built-in trap that they can only be called once between them. This means if a codebase (such as this one) called `reject()` multiple times, only the first `reject()` would actually count. Similarly if the code called `reject()` followed by `resolve()`, the `resolve()` call would not count. The promise has already moved away from its pending state, so these functions are effectively *no-ops* (they do nothing).

Making a Promise Utility that Converts Node-Style Callbacks to Promises

---

■ **Caution**   Promises, rest parameters, and arrow functions are ES6 features. Older browsers still in use, such as Internet Explorer 11 and below, or Safari 7 and below, do not support these features. Check out `http://kangax.github.io/es5-compat-table/es6/` for the current compatibility charts.

Problem

You want to be able to convert a Node.js-style asynchronous function, such as `fs.writeFile`, into a function that returns a promise.

Solution

Node.js' asynchronous methods all follow the same callback signatures. The callback is always the last argument, and it is always called with an `Error` object (or `null`) as the first argument and an optional mixed value as the second. We can take advantage of this to write a generic wrapper that takes a Node.js-style asynchronous function and resolves or rejects a returned promise. Our method will take one fixed argument—the Node.js-style method—and an infinite number of optional arguments, and return a promise that will execute the behavior of the given method.

The Code

Listing 21-15. Making a Promise Utility that Converts Node-Style Callbacks to Promises

```
Promise.myextensions = Promise.myextensions || {};
Promise.myextensions.denode = (method, ...values) => new Promise((resolve, reject) => {
    method(...values.concat((error, value) => {
        if (error) {
            reject(error);
        } else {
            resolve(value);
        }
    }));
});

function nodeStyleFunc(msg, cb) {
    cb(null, msg);
}

function nodeStyleFuncWithError(msg, cb) {
    cb(new Error('An error occurred!'), null);
}

Promise.myextensions.denode(nodeStyleFunc, 'hello world')
    .then((value) => console.log(value));

Promise.myextensions.denode(nodeStyleFuncWithError, 'hello world')
    .catch((error) => console.log(error.message));
```

The output is:

```
hello world
An error occurred!
```

How It Works

First, a function is created on `Promise.myextensions.denode`. This could be set as `Promise.denode`, but if later version of JavaScript implements this as a native feature, then there is a risk of incompatibility, so it is much safer to *namespace* custom extensions onto a new object (it is very unlikely that ECMAScript will ever define Promise.myextensions as anything, but feel free to chose an equally unlikely name, such as a company or organization name).

```
Promise.myextensions.denode = (method, ...values) => new Promise((resolve, reject) => {
```

The first line, other than defining the function, is an arrow function that immediately returns a new promise. The function itself takes our fixed method argument, which is the Node.js-style asynchronous function to call. It also uses the rest parameter (described in Chapter 12) to capture all additional arguments into an array.

```
method(...values.concat((err, value) => {
```

The main part of the functionality calls our Node.js-style asynchronous function, using the *spread* operator, so that all arguments are applied to the method, rather than it being passed one array of values. A callback function is also concatenated to the values array, ensuring that the last argument is always the callback that's used to resolve the promise.

```
if (error) {
    reject(error);
} else {
    resolve(value);
}
```

When the callback is executed, it is simply a case of determining if the error argument is "truthy." If it comes back as null, then it will be "falsy," any other value we want to deal with and reject the promise. Otherwise we want to resolve the promise with the given value. This could be rewritten using a ternary operator; error ? reject(error) : resolve(value), but it makes the code a little more difficult to interpret.

Using Promises with Generators

■ **Caution**   Promises are an ES6 feature. Older browsers still in use, such as Internet Explorer 11 and below, or Safari 7 and below, do not support this feature. Check out http://kangax.github.io/es5-compat-table/es6/ for the current compatibility charts.

Problem

You want to be able to deal with promises, but write them in a synchronous-looking manner using the power of ES6 generators (without callbacks).

Solution

Because generators pause the function state until the yielded value calls next(), promises can be used in a very powerful combination with generators, to make a function that yields any time it wants asynchronous behavior to occur. We can write a method that will take a generator function, and iterate over it, each time taking the value and treating it like a promise, only calling next() when the value promise has resolved, and calling throw() when the promise is rejected.

The Code

Listing 21-16. Using Promises with Generators

```
Promise.myextensions = Promise.myextensions || {};
Promise.myextensions.coroutine = (generator) => (...values) => new Promise((resolve, reject)
=> {
    let iterator = generator(...values),
        iterate = (value) => {
            let iteration = iterator.next(value);
            if (iteration.done) {
                resolve(iteration.value);
            } else {
                Promise.resolve(iteration.value)
                    .then(iterate, (error) => {
                        iterator.throw(error);
                        reject(error);
                    });
            }
        };
    iterate();
});
```

The output is:

```
1
```

How It Works

First, a function is created on `Promise.myextensions.coroutine`. This could be set as `Promise.coroutine`, but if a later version of JavaScript implements this as a native feature, then there is a risk of incompatibility, so it is much safer to *namespace* custom extensions onto a new object (it is very unlikely that ECMAScript will ever define `Promise.myextensions` as anything, but feel free to chose an equally unlikely name, such as a company or organization name).

```
Promise.myextensions.coroutine = (generator) => (...values) => new Promise((resolve, reject)
=> {
```

The first line, other than defining the function, is an arrow function that immediately returns another arrow function. The returned arrow function, when called, returns a new promise. The reason the coroutine function returns an arrow function, is to allow composition. Functions can be created, wrapped in the coroutine method, and become new methods that can be executed later on in the code, as demonstrated in the examples. The promise is returned from the returned arrow function to allow nesting of coroutines. A `coroutine()` that yields to another `coroutine()` can use this promise to pause its execution.

```
    let iterator = generator(...values),
```

This line simply starts the iterator, giving it the values passed from the calling arrow function. Generators, as described in Chapter 13, return an instance of `GeneratorFunction`, which offers the utility to iterate through the generator's yielded values. This function needs to use that, so it stored the `GeneratorFunction` instance as iterator.

```
iterate = (value) => {
```

An `iterate` function is defined and will be called for every iteration the generator provides. It takes one argument, which will end up being the value of the last iteration.

```
let iteration = iterator.next(value);
```

Inside the `iterate` function, we get iterator's next value by calling `next()`. It is provided the value of the last iteration, so that when the `GeneratorFunction` resumes, it can deal with the last value that was iterated on. The resulting value is stored as iteration, so that the following lines can determine what to do next. As described in Chapter 13, the resulting value from a `GeneratorFunction` `next()` call is an object with two properties: done and value.

```
if (iteration.done) {
    return resolve(iteration.value);
```

If the `iteration`'s done property is `true`, that means the iterator has finished all available statements (either it has returned a value or it hit the last line statement inside the function). At this point, coroutine's promise is resolved with the last value (the `return` value, or `undefined`).

```
} else {
    Promise.resolve(iteration.value)
        .then(iterate, (error) => iterator.throw(error));
}
```

If the `iteration`'s done property is `false`, that means the iterator has yet to finish, so `next()` needs to be called again. However before that, the current value needs to be dealt with. `Promise.resolve` is called on the value, to convert it into a promise (if it isn't already). Casting everything as a promise simplifies the logic with how to deal with the iterator values, and provides a consistent asynchronous interface for the `GeneratorFunction`. As a promise, it is then simply a case of calling `then()`. The `iterate` function is given as the `resolvedAction` which will allow it to recurse. The cycle repeats again, and `iterator.next()` is called with the resolved value. The arrow function is the `rejectedAction`, and it calls `iterator.throw()`, which as described in Chapter 13, resumes the `GeneratorFunction` but with a thrown error.

```
iterate();
```

As a last step in the function, `iterate` needs to be called. A value does not need to be passed on the first iteration of a generator.

Index

© Russ Ferguson and Keith Cirkel 2017
R. Ferguson and K. Cirkel, *JavaScript Recipes*, DOI 10.1007/978-1-4302-6107-0

Get the eBook for only $4.99!

Why limit yourself?

Now you can take the weightless companion with you wherever you go and access your content on your PC, phone, tablet, or reader.

Since you've purchased this print book, we are happy to offer you the eBook for just $4.99.

Convenient and fully searchable, the PDF version enables you to easily find and copy code—or perform examples by quickly toggling between instructions and applications.

To learn more, go to http://www.apress.com/us/shop/companion or contact support@apress.com.

Printed in the United States
By Bookmasters